Who Speaks for the Poor?

Who Speaks for the Poor? explains why parties represent some groups and not others. This book focuses attention on the electoral geography of income, and how it has changed over time, to account for cross-national differences in the political and partisan representation of low-income voters. Jusko develops a general theory of new party formation that shows how changes in the geographic distribution of groups across electoral districts create opportunities for new parties to enter elections, especially where changes favor groups previously excluded from local partisan networks. Empirical evidence is drawn first from a broadly comparative analysis of all new party entries and then from a series of historical case studies, each focusing on the strategic entry incentives of new low-income peoples' parties. Jusko offers a new explanation for the absence of a low-income people's party in the USA and a more general account of political inequality in contemporary democratic societies.

Karen Long Jusko is Assistant Professor of Political Science at Stanford University and an affiliate of the Europe Center and the Center for the Study of Poverty and Inequality. She received her Ph.D. from the University of Michigan and was a fellow at the Center for the Study of Democratic Politics at Princeton University and a National Hoover fellow. Jusko has received research support from the National Science Foundation, as part of a European Science Foundation Collaborative Research Program. *Who Speaks for the Poor?* builds on graduate research that received the Harold D. Laswell Prize for the best dissertation in the field of public policy from the Policy Studies Organization and the APSA Public Policy Organized Section.

T0381770

Cambridge Studies in Comparative Politics

General Editors

Kathleen Thelen *Massachusetts Institute of Technology*
Erik Wibbels *Duke University*

Associate Editors

Catherine Boone *London School of Economics*
Thad Dunning *University of California, Berkeley*
Anna Grzymala-Busse *Stanford University*
Torben Iversen *Harvard University*
Stathis Kalyvas *Yale University*
Margaret Levi *Stanford University*
Helen Milner *Princeton University*
Frances Rosenbluth *Yale University*
Susan Stokes *Yale University*
Tariq Thachil *Vanderbilt University*

Series Founder

Peter Lange *Duke University*

Other Books in the Series

Christopher Adolph, *Bankers, Bureaucrats, and Central Bank Politics: The Myth of Neutrality*

Michael Albertus, *Autocracy and Redistribution: The Politics of Land Reform*

Ben W. Ansell, *From the Ballot to the Blackboard: The Redistributive Political Economy of Education*

Ben W. Ansell, David J. Samuels, *Inequality and Democratization: An Elite-Competition Approach*

Leonardo R. Arriola, *Multi-Ethnic Coalitions in Africa: Business Financing of Opposition Election Campaigns*

David Austen-Smith, Jeffry A. Frieden, Miriam A. Golden, Karl Ove Moene, and Adam Przeworski, eds., *Selected Works of Michael Wallerstein: The Political Economy of Inequality, Unions, and Social Democracy*

Andy Baker, *The Market and the Masses in Latin America: Policy Reform and Consumption in Liberalizing Economies*

[Continued after the index]

Who Speaks for the Poor?

Electoral Geography, Party Entry, and Representation

KAREN LONG JUSKO

Stanford University

CAMBRIDGE
UNIVERSITY PRESS

CAMBRIDGE
UNIVERSITY PRESS

University Printing House, Cambridge CB2 8BS, United Kingdom

One Liberty Plaza, 20th Floor, New York, NY 10006, USA

477 Williamstown Road, Port Melbourne, VIC 3207, Australia

314-321, 3rd Floor, Plot 3, Splendor Forum, Jasola District Centre, New Delhi - 110025, India

79 Anson Road, #06-04/06, Singapore 079906

Cambridge University Press is part of the University of Cambridge.

It furthers the University's mission by disseminating knowledge in the pursuit of
education, learning and research at the highest international levels of excellence.

www.cambridge.org
Information on this title: www.cambridge.org/9781108412315
DOI: 10.1017/9781108304382

First published 2017

A catalogue record for this publication is available from the British Library

ISBN 978-1-108-41988-8 Hardback
ISBN 978-1-108-41231-5 Paperback

Cambridge University Press has no responsibility for the persistence or
accuracy of URLs for external or third-party internet websites referred to in
this publication, and does not guarantee that any content on such websites is,
or will remain, accurate or appropriate.

For Ryan, Anna, Jack, and Joanie.

I see one-third of a nation ill-housed, ill-clad, ill-nourished.

But it is not in despair that I paint you that picture. I paint it for you in hope—because the nation, seeing and understanding the injustice in it, proposes to paint it out. We are determined to make every American citizen the subject of his country's interest and concern; and we will never regard any faithful law-abiding group within our borders as superfluous. The test of our progress is not whether we add more to the abundance of those who have much; it is whether we provide enough for those who have too little.

President Franklin D. Roosevelt, Second Inaugural Address (1937)

Contents

Figures

Tables

Preface and Acknowledgments

This book is the result of a decade-long effort to understand how electoral rules affect the political representation of low-income citizens. In practice, individuals' votes are (almost) never weighted equally in the tallying of election results: legislatures are limited in size, and seats are almost always contested in districts. When the relationship between votes and seats for groups (rather than individuals) is examined, differences between national vote shares and seat shares can be profound. Groups vary in their electoral power because of the way their members are distributed across districts, and because of the way seats are allocated. What are the consequences of inequality in electoral power, particularly differences in the electoral power of income groups, for public policy and, ultimately, the common good?

My dissertation, completed while I was a visiting graduate student in the Center for the Study of Democratic Politics (CSDP) at Princeton University, provides the motivation for this larger project. A key finding in my dissertation shows that the electoral power of a low-income voting bloc varies across countries. That is, if all low-income citizens (defined as the poorest third in each country) turned out to vote, and they all cast ballots for the same parties, they would elect dramatically different proportions of their legislatures, despite their equivalent shares of each population. This variation transcends the usual distinction between majoritarian and proportional representation: there are consequential differences in the electoral power of the poor, even among countries with similar electoral systems. Importantly, low-income Americans were most under-represented in the mapping of votes to seats, and were pivotal in only about 5 percent of contests for the House of Representatives. (Chapter 8 replicates this analysis with new data, and a new measurement strategy.)

When viewed from the perspective of electoral power, it is not surprising that American legislators appear more responsive to their wealthier constituents (see Gilens 2012, Bartels 2008). American legislators rarely rely on the electoral support of low-income voters, and few have incentives to be responsive to their interests. Further, because there is a positive relationship between the electoral power of low-income voting blocs and levels of social spending (this finding is also replicated in Chapter 8 in a small cross-national set of countries, but also for the American states), the electoral geography of income offers a new perspective on the relatively limited effectiveness of American social programs.

This earlier comparative analysis of electoral power and social policy drew attention to the importance of parties, and led to a broader question about why parties represent the interests of some groups, and not others. This book develops a general theoretical argument about how changes in electoral geography, or the way in which groups are distributed across electoral districts, create incentives for political entrepreneurs to form new parties. Especially when newly pivotal groups have been excluded from local partisan networks, political entrepreneurs will craft new party platforms that represent the interests of these groups. What matters, then, for the political representation of a particular group in a society is whether it has been favored by changes in electoral geography.

Here, I test this argument by focusing on low-income citizens, and present broadly comparative and detailed historical analysis as supportive evidence. This book includes a chapter that focuses on new parties of all types, as well as several analytic case studies of the formation and entry of low-income peoples' parties in the US, Canada, Great Britain, and Sweden. Original datasets that describe the electoral geography of income in each country during the late nineteenth or early twentieth centuries provide the empirical foundation of this work, and tie new party entry decisions to changes in the local distribution of electoral power.

Who Speaks for the Poor?, therefore, accounts for both the timing of entry, and presence of low-income peoples' parties. Importantly, this book also provides a new explanation for the current absence of a low-income people's party in the US. When the implications of electoral geography are understood, as this book shows, the absence of a third party is no longer a puzzling feature of contemporary American politics. Instead, the limited responsiveness of American legislators to the interests of low-income voters clearly results from the political economic incentive structures created by American electoral geography.

I am especially grateful to the faculty, who were so generous with their time and support while I was a graduate student. Chris Achen focused my attention on the uneasy relationship between contemporary democratic politics and the common good, and insisted that my question, about democratic responsiveness to poverty, be addressed with clear thinking and straightforward empirical analysis. I hope Chris finds both here, and that this book reflects the best of his teaching.

Larry Bartels made space and provided support for me in the Center for the Study of Democratic Politics at Princeton University. The work done by Chris,

Larry, and others at Princeton, including Carles Boix, Martin Gilens, David Lewis, Nolan McCarty, Jonas Pontusson, and Thomas Romer, provided the starting point and motivation for my own research agenda. Michele Epstein created a terrific community among faculty, students, and fellows, and I was so glad to be a part of it. CSDP was, at least for me, revolutionary.

In the Department of Political Science at the University of Michigan, and in the Center for Political Studies in the Institute for Social Research, John Jackson (my dissertation co-chair), Jenna Bednar, Bill Clark, Robert Franzese, Vincent Hutchings, Ken Kollman, Burt Monroe, and Scott Page offered important guidance and training. Nancy Burns, Don Kinder, and David Howell provided early support while I worked as a research associate with the Comparative Study of Electoral Systems (CSES) and the National Election Study. I am also grateful to Phil Shively, who was then the Chair of the CSES Planning Committee. Phil provided indispensable professional advice, and encouraged my participation in CSES plenary and planning committee meetings. These meetings were some of the best seminars on democratic politics that I have attended.

I feel very fortunate to have held my first position in the Department of Political Science at Stanford University. Those who have served as Chair of the Department during my time here, principally Judith Goldstein, but also Josiah Ober, James Fearon, and Terry Moe, have been extremely generous in their financial support, and have provided the important releases from teaching and service that facilitated the completion of this long-term project. I also appreciate the insightful comments offered by my colleagues who read and reacted to this project, especially Josh Cohen, Gary Cox, David Grusky, Stephen Haber, Jens Hainmueller, Saumitra Jha, Simon Jackman, David Laitin, Margaret Levi, Neil Malhotra, Clayton Nall, Ken Scheve, Gary Segura, Paul Sniderman, Michael Tomz, and Barry Weingast. David Brady and Stephen Haber also provided valuable support in the form of a Hoover National Fellowship. Karen Cook, through the Institute for Research in the Social Sciences, also provided for focused research time. Jackie Sargent supported me and my research in so many, many ways; my debt to her is enormous.

I am especially grateful to my colleague and very good friend Jonathan Rodden, who read, re-read, and commented, who was constantly engaged, and from whom I learned an enormous amount. Jonathan has also been an extremely effective advocate for me, and I appreciate his efforts on my behalf.

While at Stanford, I have often taught the graduate-level course on research design with David Laitin. (In 2016, Mike Tomz, and then in 2017, Judy Goldstein, joined our teaching team.) This is one of my favorite courses to teach, and many discussions held in our class sessions have structured my research program in important ways. I appreciate David's frank comments and straightforward advice on my own work, am grateful our time together, and for the opportunity to work with really terrific students.

Richard Sinnott recruited me to participate in the proposal and development of the European Collaborative Research (EUROCORES) Cross-National and Multi-level Analysis of Human Values, Institutions and Behaviour (HumVIB) Scheme. With National Science Foundation support, this collaboration provided important financial resources for this project, as well as access to a European community of scholars who were motivated by similar questions. Richard also provided valuable time and space at University College Dublin, and careful, helpful comments on this project in its early stages.

Patrick Egan, who was a member of my CSDP cohort, has read and offered comments on several versions of this manuscript, always with generosity and a sense of humor. Patrick also facilitated valuable research time at NYU.

This project benefited enormously from participants in a manuscript conference, held at Stanford. Pablo Beramendi, Miriam Golden, Erik Wibbels, John Zaller, and Daniel Ziblatt provided fresh perspectives on the project, and it is much better as a consequence. Others, including Nick Carnes, Richard Johnston, Torben Iversen, Ira Katznelson, Gabriel Lenz, Johannes Lindvall, Keena Lipsitz, Julia Lynch, Eleonora Pasotti, Grigore Pop-Eleches, Dawn Teele, and Jessica Trounstine, have also been generous with their time and comments. I also appreciate the opportunity to present research that contributed to this project at the Political Development Workshop, held at the University of Toronto, the Harvard Meeting on Political Geography, the Inequality Workshop at UBC, and many other seminars and conferences.

Several Stanford graduate students made significant contributions to this project, including Molly Jackman, Simon Ejdemyr, Nick Eubank, and Alex Kuo. Dylan Marando, at the University of Toronto, also provided valuable research assistance. Undergraduate research assistants, including Kevin Allen, Katie Brigham, Nkechi Erondu, Dina Hassan, Justin Lin, Paton Moody, Sara Ramsey, Santana Shorty, Carlie Tenenbaum, and other participants in the Department of Political Science Summer Research College, assisted in the construction of several of the digital shape files used in this book.

Finally, my husband Ryan was steadfast in his commitment to this project, and to my larger research agenda. Ryan's enthusiasm for this book was unbounded, and I appreciate his keen willingness to read and comment. I am so very grateful for our life together, for our families, and for our children, Anna, Jack, and Joanie.

1

Who Speaks for the Poor?

Who speaks for the poor? More generally, why do parties and legislators represent the interests of some groups, and not others? In the United States, advocates for low-income citizens are hard to identify: Recent political science research demonstrates, for example, that elected officials often ignore low-income Americans' preferences and interests (e.g., Gilens 2012, Bartels 2008). Further, the absence of social democratic or workers' parties – parties that usually represent the interests of low-income citizens – distinguishes the US from all other post-industrial democracies. Why have social democratic or workers' parties formed and persisted in other countries? Why are legislators in other democratic societies more responsive to the preferences of low-income citizens, compared to their American counterparts?

By focusing on the political and partisan representation of low-income citizens, this book will offer an innovative explanation for a long-standing puzzle of comparative politics – why do parties represent the interests of some groups, while others are never mobilized as a partisan constituency? Specifically, this book will show that parties represent the interests of those groups who are favored by changes in electoral geography. In the case of low-income voters, political entrepreneurs saw electoral opportunities in the changing electoral geographies of the late nineteenth and early twentieth centuries, and responded by forming new parties and mobilizing low-income communities. Whether these "third-party men" developed populist or social democratic platforms reflects the location and interests of newly pivotal voters. That is, when the newly pivotal low-income voters were predominantly agricultural, new parties developed populist platforms; alternatively, social democratic platforms reflected the interests of newly pivotal industrial workers. Policy (i.e., poverty) responsiveness varied with the structure of local needs, and had lasting, cumulative effects on social policy in each country. Importantly, therefore, elections do not simply aggregate preferences (or grievances) around which parties and candidates mobilize. Rather, which preferences – whose interests – are expressed by parties and candidates is a direct consequence of which groups are favored by changing electoral geographies.

This explanation is quite different from existing accounts of cross-national variation in social policy, which typically emphasize tastes (or demand) for redistribution and beliefs about the origins of poverty, the historical role of unions and class-based organizations in Europe, the disenfranchising effects of increasing income inequality in the United States, or electoral rules and their effects on government formation. But, in addition to explaining important differences in the politics of contemporary democracies, this research also offers a reason for the muted political voice of American workers and their families, the limited efforts of American political parties to mobilize a low-income constituency, and the comparatively limited social spending and anti-poverty policy in the US. When the effects of electoral geography are understood, especially from the comparative perspective this manuscript will offer, the limited responsiveness of American legislators to low-income voters, and indeed, the absence of partisan representation for low-income and working-class voters, are no longer puzzling features of contemporary American politics. Instead, these are the clear consequences of the political economic incentive structures created by current and historical geographic distributions of income.

To provide theoretical justification for my emphasis on electoral geography, and to connect to the existing explanations of cross-national differences in the political representation of low-income citizens, this chapter uses a stylized account of democratic policy-making to show how electoral geography matters. Then, this chapter focuses on two features of this book that set it apart from earlier research on the political economics of social policy: the analytic advantages of using income groups, rather than class or occupational groups, as the unit of analysis, and the uncoupling of income and ideological preference.

Chapter 2 then offers a theory of strategic party formation and entry, and outlines the conditions under which we might expect a new party to enter electoral competition and mobilize a low-income constituency. This theoretical framework sets the stage for the broadly comparative analysis presented in Chapter 3, which accounts for the *timing* of new party entry into electoral competition by examining the timing of important changes in electoral geography, and for later analytic case studies (Chapters 4–7). If political entrepreneurs respond to changes in the distribution of electoral power in their decision to form new parties, then it ought to be the case that new parties *generally* form when there are important, concentrated changes in the local populations.

Changing electoral geography has implications, too, for *where* new parties recruit candidates and enter electoral contests. As we shall see, new low-income peoples' parties enter those electoral contests where the composition of the district has changed most dramatically, in ways that favor low-income voters. Chapters 4 through 7 examine the strategic recruitment of candidates and allocation of campaign resources in four analytic case studies, from the United States, Canada, Great Britain, and Sweden. In each of these cases, substantial changes in the composition of electoral districts created new incentives for political entrepreneurs to mobilize a low-income constituency, form new parties, and challenge two established parties in single-member districts (SMDs).[1] The new parties often recruited members of groups who were excluded from existing partisan networks, including recent migrants and immigrants. In several cases, the best electoral opportunities were in rural districts, and the political entrepreneurs developed platforms that incorporated the interests of a low-income, agrarian constituency. Elsewhere, it was the new concentration of low-income citizens in industrial districts that created the opportunities for party entry, and the "third-party men" crafted party platforms that reflected the preferences of an industrial working class. Finally, in the case of Sweden, we will also examine the impact of electoral reform on the long-term distribution of electoral power across income groups.

Together, the broadly comparative analysis and the analytic case studies support a new and important explanation for the origins of cross-national differences in the quality of the political and partisan representation of the poor, and for variation in the representation of different groups, more generally. As we shall see, what matters for the representation of a particular group is whether they have been favored by changes in electoral geography that alter the distribution of electoral power. By focusing on electoral power, this research draws attention to a fundamental inequality that characterizes contemporary democracies: only rarely are votes counted equally. As the next section suggests, the nature of this inequality – differences in how groups' votes map into seats – creates policy-making incentives that undermine the equal consideration of interests. Instead, the incentives created by electoral geography and the distribution of electoral power within a society determine, to an important extent, the quality of political representation, with profound implications for the relationship between the democratic value of equality and contemporary democratic practice.

---

[1] While the implications of electoral geography are most dramatic when elections are contested under SMD electoral rules, the argument here applies to multi-member district systems as well, although the effect of changes in the distribution of groups across districts is moderated by proportional representation (PR) rules for seat allocation. That is, particularly when districts elect large numbers of legislators, when seats are allocated proportionately, the change in the composition of the electorate necessary to create new opportunities for party entry is related to the number of legislators elected. Opportunities for entry resulting from changes in the composition of each district are also mitigated by compensatory tiers and national vote share requirements – other features more common in PR systems.

1.1 ELECTORAL GEOGRAPHY AND DEMOCRATIC REPRESENTATION

How does electoral geography affect democratic politics, and the quality of representation? This section uses a stylized model of democratic policy-making, like Achen and Bartels's (2016) "folk theorem" of democracy and builds on Cox's (2004) representational loop to show how electoral geography shapes the incentives of legislators and parties to be responsive to different groups in society. Specifically, suppose that democratic policy-making proceeds in the following way:

Stage 0. Group Membership. A society is composed of groups that are associated with more or less coherent identities, and whose memberships may be overlapping. These groups may be defined according to ethnic or racial identities, occupations or status, income, wealth or resources, shared geographic locations, or other individual-level attributes that provide a sense of common interest.

Stage 1. Preference Formation. Individuals develop preferences over one or more policy dimensions, usually including social or tax and transfer policy. Certain preferences or policy positions often come to be associated with particular groups and their members.

Stage 2. Mobilization. This stage includes both the mobilization of parties and candidates – their "strategic entry" – and the engagement of voters in the electorate.

Stage 3. Elections. This is the crucial step in which the effects of electoral geography enter, but note that it is a purely mechanical step: votes are tallied and seats are allocated according to the current electoral rules.

Stage 4. Government Formation. Usually, governments are formed by the party that wins the plurality of seats in the legislature, sometimes in coalition with other parties.

Stage 5. Legislation. Once formed, governments will implement policy more or less in accordance with the preferences of the constituencies they (and their coalition partners) represent.

In this stylized framework, group identities (Stage 0) and preferences (Stage 1) are often treated as given and/or fixed, and mobilization results mainly from individual-level facilitative and motivational factors (Stage 2). Importantly, elections (Stage 3) represent the aggregation of preferences, and in this stylized model, provide the crucial mechanism that ensures accountability in government formation (Stage 4) and (usually) equal consideration in policy-making (Stage 5).

This book suggests that the ways in which votes are tallied and seats are allocated in Stage 3 directly contribute to political inequality, as suggested above, with important implications for which parties and voters – which groups – are mobilized, and indeed, which groups' preferences are articulated and ultimately given consideration. Put simply, this book suggests that the democratic folk theorem has the ordering of Stages 1–3 reversed: What happens at Stage 3 certainly affects what happens at Stage 2, and likely affects Stage 1, as well. (While group identities are also likely to be mobilized by political actors, Stage 0 may also represent a society's historical endowments; see, e.g., Bartolini 2000).

The stages represented in this stylized framework, nevertheless, provide a useful way to characterize the existing literature on the origins of differences in the quality of representation. When organized in this way, limitations of the existing literature also become clear. The rest of this section offers a review of current thinking about what contributes to effective and equitable political representation and social policy, and focuses on the mechanisms that link each stage of this framework to these outcomes.

Classic political economic accounts of the generosity of social policy often begin with fixed distributions of types (Stage 0) and preferences (Stage 1). In Romer's (1975) and Meltzer and Richard's (1981) accounts, for example, the preferences of the median voter matter most for redistributive politics. To the extent that the median voter stands to gain from a lump-sum tax-and-transfer policy (i.e., when levels of income inequality are high), she will prefer higher tax rates and more redistribution. While comparative political economists have been able to provide only limited empirical support for the main implication of the Romer–Meltzer and Richard account – that income inequality contributes to demand for redistribution – many analysts have built on the key intuition of these models to show that the structure of national income distributions contribute to redistributive policy preferences (e.g., Lupu & Pontusson 2011), and that these preferences are correlated with actual levels of social spending (Brooks & Manza 2006, Soroka & Wlezien 2005, although see Bartels 2015).[2] Of course, what is obvious in the stylized framework proposed above is that the path from preferences to legislation is mediated by representative institutions. For example, the national median voter may hold preferences that are different from the median voter in the median SMD, or from the median supporter of the governing party or coalition, and so on. The question of *whose* preferences, therefore, are (or ought to be) reflected in policy immediately arises.

A second tradition (corresponding to Stage 2) in the study of comparative politics emphasizes the historical balance of power among class-based organizations – "Power Resource Theory" – and attributes cross-national differences

---

[2] Other accounts that emphasize preferences attribute cross-national differences in social policy to, for example, levels of income inequality (Anderson & Beramendi 2012, Lupu & Pontusson 2011), employment risk (Cusack, Iversen, & Rhem 2007, Iversen 2005, Iversen & Soskice 2001, Moene & Wallerstein 2001), differences in earnings and expectations of benefits across racial and ethnic groups (Shayo 2009, Alesina & Glaeser 2004, Gilens 1999), and the role of religion (Scheve & Stasavage 2006).

in the political representation of low-income and especially working-class citizens to the strength of unions and social democratic parties (e.g., Huber & Stephens 2001, Bartolini 2000, Hicks 1999, Esping-Andersen 1990). Even when social democratic parties are excluded from government, Pierson's (1996) emphasis on path dependence suggests, their contributions to earlier governments increase the likelihood of current social policy that is generous and responsive. Related to this work are analyses that emphasize differences in rates of voter mobilization. For example, Pontusson and Rueda (2010) find that the success of left parties in responding to increases in income inequality is dependent on levels of rates at which low-income voters are mobilized (see also Anderson & Beramendi 2012). The sources of original power distributions, however, are unclear: Is there some other feature that systematically accounts for variation in the success of class-based organizations?

Political economists have focused, as I do in this book, on the election stage (Stage 3) of policy-making – that is, the mapping of votes to seats – and its implications for social and redistributive policy. Accounts that focus on preferences, or the distribution of power across class-based organizations, simply miss how electoral institutions moderate the translation of preferences to policy, and might contribute to the success of different parties. Persson and Tabellini (2003, 17), for example, outline the now-standard assessment of the relationship between electoral rules and social spending:

The winner-takes-all property of plurality rule reduces the minimal coalition of voters needed to win the election, as votes for a party not obtaining plurality are lost. With single-member districts and plurality, a party thus needs only 25% of the national vote to win: 50% in 50% of the districts. Under full proportional representation it needs 50% of the national vote. Politicians are thus induced to internalize the policy benefits for a larger proportion of the population, leading to the prediction of larger broad spending under proportional representation.

Persson, Roland, and Tabellini (2007), Iversen and Soskice (2006), and Bawn and Rosenbluth (2006) have further developed arguments that clarify the mechanism that links electoral rules to levels of social policy. In each of these later analyses, coalition governments are more likely to result from elections contested under proportional representation rules, and in fact, are more likely to invest in public spending in ways that reflect the preferences of low-income voters than are the single-party governments elected under plurality rules (Stages 4 and 5).[3]

Clearly, the distribution of electoral support (Stage 3) affects which party forms the government (Stage 4) and what legislation will pass (Stage 5). However, the ways in which the mechanical mapping of votes to seats affect incentives for candidate and party mobilization (and, probably, preference

---

[3]   In Iversen and Soskice (2006), this is because coalitions between low-income and middle-income parties are more likely, and more extensive redistributive policy will be implemented. In Bawn and Rosenbluth (2006) and Persson, Roland, and Tabellini (2007), coalition governments "log-roll" across a variety of policy dimensions.

formation) are often assumed or taken for granted. Usually, the political economic models that link electoral institutions to redistributive policy, for example, take the nature of party competition as exogenously determined: Iversen and Soskice (2006) and Austen-Smith (2000), for example, assume that while three parties compete under (single national district) PR rules, electoral competition is limited to two parties under SMD rules (Lizzeri & Persisco 2001, Persson & Tabellini 2000, for example, assume two-party competition, regardless of the electoral rules).

Here, I take a different approach, and suggest that behavior at Stage 2 – voter, candidate, and party mobilization – is structured by incentives created in Stage 3, when votes are mapped into seats. Vote-to-seat mappings vary across groups in a society; variation in the geographic distribution of groups across electoral districts will ensure that some groups are over-represented in the legislature while others are under-represented. Importantly, parties and candidates will represent those groups whose support is essential to their electoral success. And, new parties will form and contest elections when changes in electoral geography favor their constituency. This reversal – Stage 3 affects Stage 2 – implies that elections do not simply aggregate voters' preferences, which are then incorporated into party and candidate platforms. Rather, *which* preferences are expressed by parties and candidates is determined by of differences in the ways groups' votes map into seats.

The distorting effects of electoral rules on the ways votes map into seats, and thus on opportunities for fully equitable representation of partisan constituencies, are well known and well explored (recently, Chen & Rodden 2013, Rodden 2011). In some ways, an emphasis on electoral geography is old-fashioned. Political analysts, especially those in SMD systems, have long been concerned with how electoral rules interact with the social geographies of their societies to create or undermine support for specific parties (e.g., Tingsten 1975, Gosnell 1937, Krebheil 1916). What is often missing from these earlier "input/output" analyses of electoral geography is a recognition of how electoral geography shapes the strategic incentives of voters, candidates, and parties – specifically, which parties will form, which candidates will be recruited, and which voters will turn out.[4] This book is premised on two important departures from the existing literature:

First, this book focuses on low-income citizens, and *not* on a specific partisan constituency or occupational group. As the next section will argue, this focus offers important analytic advantages.

The second departure is closely related to the first. By focusing on low-income citizens, their geographic distribution and preferences, this book

---

4 Johnston *et al.* (2005), though, do include "local pressure" in their revised list of Miller's (1977) list of mechanisms by which neighborhood effects might operate, but do not consider how mobilization incentives vary across districts, or evaluate local pressure, relative to other mechanisms.

is able to explain the form that partisan representation of low-income citizens takes. Specifically, this book will show that the political entrepreneurs that formed and mobilized social democratic parties were responding to the same incentive structures as those who established the agrarian/populist parties. On both sides of the Atlantic, political entrepreneurs saw opportunities created by changes in the electoral power of low-income voters, and crafted policy platforms that were responsive to the needs of newly pivotal voters; that this responsiveness more often took a social democratic form, rather than populism, in Europe simply reflects the geographic location of these opportunities. Chapter 2 will develop this theoretical account more completely.

The next two sections of this chapter address these departures from the literature, and highlight the advantages of focusing on a (hypothetical) low-income voting bloc, first, before justifying the broad classification of low-income peoples' parties.

1.2 WHY FOCUS ON LOW-INCOME CITIZENS?

This book's attention to low-income citizens – here, defined as the lowest-earning third of the national market income distribution – as the basis for analysis offers both normative and analytic advantages.

Many analysts, for example, have documented the ways rates of political participation vary across income groups. In their now-classic study, Verba, Nie, and Kim (1978), for example, show that low-income citizens in seven countries are least likely to participate in electoral campaigns, contribute money, or participate in organizations and meetings. More recently, Gallego (2007) reaffirms this participation gap in 24 countries, and in an analysis that includes participation in demonstration and boycotts. In the US, differences in participation rates are especially stark: Leighley and Nagler (2014) find that citizens with very low incomes (i.e., in the first quintile) of the national income distribution turn out to vote about half of the time, while about 80 percent of the wealthy regularly cast ballots.

These persistent participation gaps suggest that, in the absence of the explicit mobilization of low-income citizens by parties and candidates, the preferences of low-income citizens are unlikely to be expressed in politics. As a consequence, attention to low-income citizens provides insight into the quality of democratic representation provided through *elections*, rather than through lobbying, campaign contributions, or other forms of political participation, and from the perspective of those who are unlikely to be well represented.

A focus on low-income citizens, rather than groups defined by ethnicity, race, occupation, or social class, for example, also offers analytic advantages: First, by defining low-income status in relative terms (i.e., location in the national income distribution), this book fixes the size of the group and provides a bench-mark for equitable electoral geographies. The *electoral power* of low-income voters – the share of seats in the legislature that a low-income voting bloc can elect, if all low-income voters turn out to vote, and all vote for the same party – is the key explanatory variable in this analysis. In a fair electoral system, low-income voters who comprise a third of the population should elect about a third of the seats in the legislature. As we shall see, however, the electoral power of low-income voters varies substantially across systems and over time. By fixing the size of the group studied to 33 percent of the electorate, this cross-national and temporal variance can be attributed to changes in electoral geography, rather than the group's size, subscription, or status.[5]

With an emphasis on low-income citizens, this book also offers a concreteness to political representation that cannot be accommodated by studies that analyze, instead, ideological congruence in the distributions of preferences of legislators and citizens. Put slightly differently, the mapping of preferences to party positions and policy is more straightforward when defined in terms of the interests of a specific group. This book can examine, for example, the extent to which new party platforms incorporated the preferences of newly pivotal low-income voters: Do new party platforms incorporate concerns specific to the constituencies they mobilized? Similarly, in the contemporary period, the quality of the political representation of low-income citizens can be evaluated through the generosity of anti-poverty programs.

There is a final, important, advantage in focusing on an "imagined" or hypothetical voting bloc. One might worry, for example, that defining "low-income" as the lowest third of the national income distribution might seem arbitrary, particularly in light of political science research on class consciousness (see Katznelson 1986). However, the identification strategy employed in this manuscript *requires* an arbitrary definition. In order to identify the strategic actions of political entrepreneurs in party formation and mobilization, the analysis must proceed in anticipation of their incentives, rather than their realization. Specifically, by focusing on a "hypothetical" group, instead of a group with an already-activated identity, this manuscript can investigate the conditions under which political entrepreneurs will mobilize that group *as a group* – a cohesive, partisan constituency. Further, if the definition of "low-income" is different from the way political entrepreneurs in each case thought about which groups were "ripe for mobilization," then the relationships between changing electoral geography and new party entry decisions are likely to be observed with more variance.

A related concern emphasizes the ways in which ethnic, racial, or religious group identities potentially work to undermine the existence of a low-income voting bloc. Particularly for the US case, some analysts have argued that the important political cleavages cut across class lines to sustain racial and ethnic cleavages, particularly between white and African Americans (see, e.g.,

---

5 As Stoll (2013) shows, group size is also important: By defining "low-income" as a third of the population, under an equitable electoral geography, the benefits of representing this group in the legislature would be substantial.

Shefter 1986). Further, race is an important part of the contemporary politics of social policy in the US (see Gilens 1999). Nevertheless, some of those who have built electoral coalitions have worked to overcome the resistance of white Americans to the incorporation of black voters, particularly when it furthered their office-seeking goals (e.g., the New Deal Coalition).

To the extent that this analysis measures changes in electoral geography in a way that incorporates low-income groups that are, in fact, divided by social cleavages, electoral opportunities will appear where they do not actually exist. That is, the empirical analysis presented in later chapters exaggerates incentives to enter particular electoral contests, if some proportion of (those who are identified here as) newly pivotal voters were unavailable to new parties' candidates because of their racial or ethnic identity. Their inclusion in measures of local electoral opportunities biases later analysis against the main hypothesis of this book, and introduces further variance into the relationship between changing electoral geography and strategic entry decisions.[6]

In sum, if voting blocs are endogenous to party entry – that is, to the extent that electoral geography favors a particular group, and candidates and parties have incentives to mobilize that group *as* a bloc – this analysis must proceed in anticipation of these incentives, rather than their realization. The presence of alternate salient group identities, or other policy dimensions, heightens the challenge both for political entrepreneurs and for this analysis. Therefore, by focusing on the electoral power of a hypothetical group, we gain analytical leverage on the conditions under which political entrepreneurs will mobilize *that* group, rather than another, as a partisan constituency.

The next section of this discussion focuses on that effort – the mobilization of low-income voters as a partisan constituency. It is not simply the case that low-income voters are represented by only social democratic, labor, or other left-leaning parties. Early in the twentieth century, particularly, low-income citizens' preferences were also incorporated into the platforms of new agrarian and populist parties. The next section provides some early evidence that political entrepreneurs carefully crafted their parties' platforms to be responsive to the newly pivotal low-income voters (more detailed evidence will follow in the analytic case studies presented in later chapters), and justifies attention to this broad class of parties.

1.3 IDENTIFYING LOW-INCOME PEOPLES' PARTIES

How did political entrepreneurs – those who bore the initial costs of forming a new party, often by organizing conventions, announcing platforms, and

---

[6] In other places, e.g., Jusko 2015b, I have examined how differences in the rates of turnout vary across income groups, and with their electoral power. Similar analysis could examine the extent to which low-income voters act as a voting bloc, as a function of electoral power.

recruiting candidates – think about the nature of electoral opportunities, at the turn of the twentieth century?

Here, the focus on low-income voters, instead of occupational or class-based groups, is justified (beyond the analytic advantages described above) because it is consistent with the way in which (at least some) political entrepreneurs thought about their potential constituencies: "We know that the interests of rural and urban labor are the same and that their enemies are the controllers of credit, commerce and land that others must use, those who by our present laws have the power to collect from workers, interest, and unjust freights and rents" (*Farmers' Alliance and Nebraska Independent* April 7, 1892, in Pollack 1962). In fact, as the analytic case studies developed in Chapters 4 through 7 will show, the US People's Party, Canada's Cooperative Commonwealth Federation (CCF, which would become the New Democratic Party), British Labour, and the Swedish Social Democrats were each hesitant to define their constituencies as exclusively rural or urban, or as tied to a particular industry or occupation.[7]

Each of these parties, instead, expressed the interests of those at the very lowest end of the *national* income distribution, explicitly advocating for the impoverished. The CCF founding document, the "Regina Manifesto" (1933), for example, expresses a frustration that is common to each of the parties considered, despite their different periods and national contexts:

The present order is marked by glaring inequalities of wealth and opportunity, by chaotic waste and instability; and in an age of plenty it condemns the great mass of the people to poverty and insecurity. Power has become more and more concentrated into the hands of a small irresponsible minority of financiers and industrialists and to their predatory interests the majority are habitually sacrificed.

The Populists similarly observed, in their "Omaha Platform" (1892), that "[t]he fruits of the toil of millions are badly stolen to build up colossal fortunes for a few, unprecedented in the history of mankind; and the possessors of these, in turn, despise the Republic and endanger liberty. From the same prolific

---

7 In a further example, Przeworski and Sprague (1986, 16) recount Palmiro Togliatti's characterization of the Partito Comunista d'Italia as a broad-based coalition: "The secret of our success rests in the fact that we have been faithful to the thought of Gramsci, who wanted the party of the working class and laboring classes to be a profoundly national party, which would not separate the causes of workers, of peasants, of the working people from the cause of classes which contribute to the life and prosperity of the nation, and which would know how to combine closely the struggle for the emancipation of the working people with the struggle for the renovation of the entire national life."

Note that the argument presented here is different from others that suggest the necessity of, for example, socialist parties incorporating other allies (e.g., Przeworski & Sprague 1986). The case of the Social Democratic Party of Germany (SPD), which famously debated the incorporation of agricultural workers – the "agrarian issue" – in the mid-1890s, may be an exception. Nevertheless, very early in the party's development, between 1890 and 1912, the SPD recruited candidates in highly agricultural districts, and allocated funds to their campaigns (see, e.g., Kuo & Jusko 2012).

womb of governmental injustice we breed the two great classes – tramps and millionaires." They advocated the election of the "plain people" to government, with the hope "that oppression, injustice, and poverty shall eventually cease in the land." The first planks of Labour's (1900) founding platform similarly expressed the needs of low-income people, calling for "Adequate maintenance from National Funds for the Aged Poor, Public Provision of Better Houses for the People, Useful Work for the Unemployed, [and] Adequate Maintenance for Children." Finally, in defining their constituency as "industrial workers, farm workers, seamen and servants," the Swedish Social Democrats (1897) were inclusive: they spoke for those at the lowest levels of the national income distribution, without discriminating by occupation or industry.

A careful read of social democratic/labor and agrarian/populist party platforms from the early twentieth century also suggests that low-income peoples' parties of both the left and the right sometimes shared policy preferences, as well. For example, the founding platforms of the US People's Party, the Canadian Cooperative Commonwealth Federation, British Labour, and the Swedish Social Democrats *all* call for the adoption of a graduated income tax and the nationalization of the railways. Certainly, the political entrepreneurs who established these parties disagreed on fundamental issues, particularly on the role of government in addressing the poverty they observed, and indeed, who is entitled to the remedy. As will be shown, however, even socialist party leaders were quick to revise the founding platforms of their parties in order to pursue their electoral goals.[8]

To be clear, then, *low-income peoples' parties* are those parties *founded* with the intention of mobilizing and representing the interests of a low-income constituency.[9] This idea, that agrarian/populist and social democratic/labor parties were formed by political entrepreneurs with the intention of representing a national low-income constituency, will be developed more completely in later chapters. In each case, we will see that "third-party men" were responding to similar opportunity structures; what varied across countries was the geographic *location* of the opportunities. In fact, the location of these early opportunities would have profound consequences for the later development of each party, and ultimately social policy.

---

[8] See, e.g., Przeworski and Sprague (1986), who also describe efforts of socialist parties to build cross-class coalitions.

[9] There is an important distinction made here, between the current basis of support, and the intentions of the political entrepreneurs who established the party: low-income Americans, for example, often support the Democrats, who would not qualify as a low-income people's party. As I suggest elsewhere, contemporary American electoral geography, specifically because of its heterogeneous electoral districts, creates incentives for low-income voters to vote strategically for the Democrats (Jusko 2015a). In contrast to the founding manifestos described in the text, the first reference to the "impoverishment of the people" appears in the 1896 Democratic platform, adopted only when the Populist-endorsed Bryan received the Democratic nomination. Commitments to a progressive income tax and labor protections are made in the 1908 platform, although with qualifications, and are only gradually strengthened over time.

1.4 EVALUATING THE IMPORTANCE OF ELECTORAL GEOGRAPHY TO STRATEGIC ENTRY DECISIONS (OVERVIEW OF THE RESEARCH STRATEGY)

To evaluate how (and where) changes in electoral geography created opportunities for new party entry, and especially the entry of low-income peoples' parties, the analysis presented in this book proceeds at two levels:

First, Chapter 3 presents a *broadly comparative analysis* that links changes in electoral geography to all new party entry. By examining local changes in population, for stable geographic units, and over the twentieth century, Chapter 3 provides evidence that political entrepreneurs are generally responsive to opportunities created by changes in the local distribution of power. Later, in Chapter 8, this broadly comparative analysis will be extended to link the nature and timing of changes in local electoral geography to contemporary distributions of electoral power, and ultimately, the generosity of social policy.

Chapter 3 will also suggest that, in fact, most low-income peoples' parties entered electoral competition under SMD electoral rules, when the effects of changing electoral geography are most pronounced.

After this broadly comparative analysis, Chapters 4–7 present a series of analytic case studies that identify the nature of the electoral opportunities facing political entrepreneurs in the US, Canada, the UK, and Sweden. These analyses focus on critical elections in which political entrepreneurs, who often formed new parties much earlier, entered electoral competition. If the opportunities created by changes in local distributions of electoral power were important to their entry decisions (rather than, for example, overwhelming discontent), we ought to see candidates more often recruited in those districts where these changes are most apparent.

In fact, despite the very different contexts of each analytic case study, we observe the same political processes at work: Political entrepreneurs form new parties, tailoring platforms to reflect the nature of electoral opportunities, and recruit candidates in those districts where demographic and economic changes have altered local distributions of electoral power, creating newly pivotal low-income constituencies that are ripe for mobilization.

Each of the cases also offers a unique perspective on the nature of these strategic entry decisions. In the US, for example, where we examine the strategic entry decisions of the most successful American third party, the People's Party, the stability of established partisan networks and the opportunities created by migration are especially apparent. In Canada, we see low-income peoples' parties form on both sides of the ideological spectrum, competing for the same, newly pivotal low-income voters. The case of British Labour, in its pre-electoral coordination with the established Liberal party, offers perhaps the clearest evidence of the strategic nature of entry decisions: the political entrepreneurs were explicit in their choice of districts, and undermined would-be Labour candidates who were not recruited by the party leaders. Finally, in Sweden, we see the (exogenous) expansion of suffrage operate similarly to migration, creating new opportunities through dramatic changes in the composition of local electorates, and the availability of new voters who were excluded from local partisan networks.

This book, therefore, presents two forms of empirical evidence that are consistent with a theoretical emphasis on the importance of changing electoral geography for new party entry, and the representation of low-income voters: (1) broadly comparative, cross-national evidence that establishes the general pattern of association, and (2) analysis of changing electoral geography, supported by historical and archival materials, that documents new parties' strategic entry decisions within each country. Together, these components offer compelling support for a new and innovative account of the origins of partisan representation.

1.5 CONTRIBUTIONS

The beginning of this chapter used a stylized model of democratic policy-making to focus attention on the incentives that are created by electoral geography for the mobilization of parties and voters, and especially on the ways electoral power varies across groups in a society. By emphasizing basic electoral power, and the ways in which electoral geography shapes the incentives of parties and legislators, this book provides a powerful explanation for differences in the quality of political representation across groups within a society, and across similar groups in different cities, states, or countries.

This emphasis on electoral power also focuses attention on a potential remedy to evidence of political inequality: Chapter 8 provides evidence that suggests that the profound lack of responsiveness to low-income voters in the US results, at least in part, from the fact that they have very little electoral power. As suggested above, low-income Americans are almost never pivotal in national legislative elections. While observers might be tempted to attribute this to gerrymandering, or the strategic manipulation of district boundaries, the evidence suggests that district *size* is important. American House of Representative districts, for example, are significantly larger and more heterogeneous than other electoral districts, even in SMD systems. If US electoral rules could be reformed to enhance the electoral power of low-income voters – perhaps simply by increasing the number of districts – the evidence presented here suggests that the political representation of low-income Americans would undoubtedly improve, even in the absence of partisan representation.[10]

---

[10] When the importance of electoral geography, is taken into account, Przeworski and Sprague's (1986) motivating insight – that social democratic parties almost never won a majority of votes, despite the potentially large constituency – similarly becomes less puzzling: the geographic concentration of workers typically undermined their electoral power, or share of legislative seats.

This book also offers a general argument about new party formation that addresses a long-standing puzzle of comparative politics: Whose interests, from among all potential social, religious, ethnic, or geographic groups in a society, will be represented by political parties? This question, of course, is a more general version of Sombart's (1976[1906]), "Why is there no socialism in the United States?" Here, party systems reflect the historical opportunities created by changes in electoral geography. That is, when there are local but important changes in the distribution of electoral power, political entrepreneurs will form parties to represent the interests of newly pivotal voters. What matters for the representation of a particular group, then, is whether they are favored by changes in electoral geography. If a group is rarely pivotal in the election of legislators, office-seeking candidates will have little to gain by articulating its interests or mobilizing its members.

Measuring electoral power, however, is complicated, and requires two steps: First, for low-income voters, the income distribution within each district must be evaluated. Second, seats must be allocated as if an election had been held and low-income citizens voted en masse and as a bloc. Later chapters will provide both more detail and descriptive analysis of the electoral power of low-income voters in a variety of contemporary and historical settings. Nevertheless, this empirical work represents the culmination of significant effort to match census (or, in the contemporary period, administrative) geography to electoral geography, and, when necessary, to identify reliable sources of wage and income data that could be matched to individual-level census data on the basis of occupation or industry and location. The final contribution of this project, then, lies in the datasets that allow the electoral geography of income to be examined in real and reliable detail. These datasets, and the broadly comparative analysis to follow, provide the empirical foundation of a new explanation of the origins of cross-national differences in the quality of democratic representation, and new insight into the persistent under-representation of low-income Americans.

2

How Electoral Geography Matters

This chapter examines why and how changing electoral geography creates new opportunities for party formation. In particular, this chapter addresses the questions of *when* political entrepreneurs will form new parties, and *which groups* they will represent in a general theoretical argument. Implications from this general account will motivate a broadly comparative analysis of all new party entry in the next chapter, and then will be applied to the specific case of low-income voters: Under which conditions will political entrepreneurs recruit candidates to represent the interests of the poor? This chapter will argue that what matters, for the partisan and political representation of low-income voters, is how income groups are geographically distributed across electoral districts, and how this geographic distribution changes during crucial periods of migration and immigration.

Before proceeding, it is helpful to situate the argument presented here in the context of existing research on party formation and entry.

Stokes (1999a) addresses the question of when new parties form by distinguishing answers developed in the "comparative sociology of politics" literature from the answers developed in the institutional analysis of comparative political economists. Largely following Lipset and Rokkan (1967), political sociology explanations emphasize the long-term effects of social cleavages and alliances during crucial periods of transition, especially the Reformation and the Industrial Revolution. Parties, in this account, reflect the preferences of more-or-less well-defined coalitions in a society. More recent party formation, particularly green parties and extreme right parties, is attributed to the changing preferences of voters, and the inability of established parties to accommodate these new preferences (e.g., Aldrich 2011, Kitschelt *et al.* 1999, Inglehart 1997). Rosenstone, Behr, and Lazarus (1984) similarly emphasize changes in citizen demands in their account of American third parties. Understanding which groups are represented in party politics, in comparative sociological accounts, therefore, requires an accounting of major social cleavages, citizen preferences, and attitudes. And, within this tradition, the answer to the question of when new parties form is that they emerge when voters' preferences shift so dramatically that new cleavages arise.

One limitation of the "up-from-the-bottom" explanations, as Kalyvas (1996) and Stokes (1999a) note, are their failures to take into account the costs and strategic incentives of those who do the work of organizing and mobilizing. Boix (2009, 504) rightly notes that "the sociological literature has been too quick in positing an automatic relationship between interests and political action." By contrast, it is political entrepreneurs' potential benefits (usually, policy and office-holding) and costs of mobilization that perform the analytical work in institutionalist accounts. For example, Cox (1997, 186) explains new party formation in the following way: "[S]ome preexisting group that is already of national scope or perspective, seeks to accomplish a task that requires the help of a large number of legislators or legislative candidates; this group therefore seeks to induce would-be legislators from many different districts to participate in a larger organization." Similarly, Bawn *et al.* (2012) emphasize the policy goals of organized groups in their account of party formation (see also Hug 2001). For Bawn *et al.*, it is the preferences of "policy demanders" – not voters or citizens, as in the sociological accounts – that are most important to the formation of new parties. Interest groups and activists coordinate to organize electoral coalitions, and to ensure the nomination of candidates who will represent their best interests in the legislature.[1]

What *limits* the number of parties in the institutional accounts is their likely electoral success. Voters condition their decisions on their expectations about which candidates or parties are likely to win seats in their districts, and will not cast ballots, for example, in favor of the party they most prefer if candidates from that party are not likely to be elected in their districts. (This expectation, of course, provides the foundation of Duverger's Law.) In anticipation of strategic voting, even parties that are preferred by a national group of substantial size – whose levels of support may be broad, but shallow – may have no incentive to form or enter electoral contests. What matters, then, is the way the votes of different groups map into seats. Cox (1997) makes the more general argument that incentives for party formation reflect the overall social diversity of a place, and the permissiveness of electoral rules. Specifically, when there are many groups with divergent interests, and there are low barriers to the

---

[1] Hug (2001) presents a slightly different account, in which policy demanders approach established parties with a policy request. When the established party refuses to incorporate the policy proposal, the policy demanders may or may not organize a new party, according to the established party's expectations of the new party's ability to pose an effective electoral threat. Like other political economic accounts of new party entry, Hug (2001) emphasizes the costs of entry and benefits of office-holding (see also Tavits 2006). Hug (2001) also draws attention to the importance of new issues because, in his view, new parties are most likely to form when they are unlikely to pose a serious challenge to established parties; new issues provide this opportunity.

formation of new parties, political economists expect a large number of parties to form and enter electoral competition. In contrast, when the distribution of groups across districts is uniform, and/or the entry of new parties is difficult, fewer parties may form.[2]

What is it, though, that induces groups to coordinate on a *new* party label, rather than pursue policy goals through the existing party system? (This is really a question about the timing of party formation.) And, more importantly, *which* groups will be represented by parties? Chhibber and Kollman (2004, 16-7) frame the question this way, in their discussion of the omissions in the current political science literature: "How do voters and candidates decide among alternative strategies for winning representation and political power? How many parties will form in response to social cleavages?" As Boix (2009) and Stokes (1999a) suggest in their reviews of current explanations of party origins, political science has yet to offer an explanation of *which* groups, from among all potential social, religious, ethnic, or geographic groups in a society, will coordinate to form parties.

Although this book is about the political representation of one group – low-income citizens – the argument presented in this book bridges the institutionalist and comparative political sociology accounts of party formation, and provides general answers to the questions of *when* new parties will form, and under which conditions party leaders will be successful in recruiting candidates and mobilizing voters from a *specific group*. Here, the key to understanding cross-national variation in the representation of a specific group lies in the concept of electoral power, and an account of how changes in its distribution across groups creates opportunities for political entrepreneurs. Following Boix (2009, 594),

Politicians do not operate in a vacuum: their electoral promises and their policy-making decisions need to make sense in the context of the everyday practices and preoccupations of voters to give the former a reasonable chance to succeed at the ballot box. For politicians to successfully mobilize voters on the basis of certain ideas or programs, voters must sense some (material or ideational) affinity with the electoral platform they are offered. In short, to explain party systems we need to understand the type and distribution of preferences of voters, that is, the nature of the policy space.

---

[2] Stoll (2013) and others (Clark & Golder 2006) build on Cox (1997), and also consider how changes in the number of social groups, or the amount of social heterogeneity, affect the number of parties. In these accounts, electoral rules provide a modifying effect, in the translation of votes to seats. Stoll (2013) explicitly considers attributes of groups that might affect their likelihood of mobilization: a group's size, the type of attribute defining group membership, and its politicization.

Clark and Golder (2006) find that when electoral systems are more permissive, political entrepreneurs will be more likely to organize political parties that represent the interests of new groups who are demanding representation. If the barrier to party entry is high, neither the political entrepreneurs nor groups will find it in their interests to form new parties.

In fact, this book offers a revision of this last sentence: Rather than an understanding of the policy space that voters occupy, we need to understand the types of voters – their group memberships – and their *physical* location. By focusing on electoral geography and its implications for the distribution of electoral power (again, the share of seats that a group can elect if all members of that group turn out to vote, and they all cast ballots for the same party) this book provides insight into why legislators in some countries, but not others, may have strong incentives to represent the interests of a particular group. Because of the way groups and seats are distributed across electoral districts, a group's electoral support may or may not frequently be crucial to the electoral success of legislators, who will represent its members' interests accordingly.

The answer to the question of *when* new parties form similarly builds on the idea of electoral power, but emphasizes *changes* in its distribution. If it is costly for established parties to revise their policy positions, and local candidates are constrained by national party platforms, then opportunities for new party formation and entry are straightforward consequences of demographic change that favor one group over others.

The next section presents an analytic argument that identifies key strategic actors, clarifies their objectives, and shows how district entry decisions structure new party formation decisions. Then, this chapter distinguishes the arguments made here from other accounts of party formation, especially candidate entry models. Finally, this chapter develops clear empirical implications which are evaluated in later chapters.

2.1 ORIGINS OF ELECTORAL OPPORTUNITIES

At the center of this account of new party formation are "political entrepreneurs." These actors are similar to Bawn *et al.*'s (2012) policy demanders, or organized interest groups and activists, but may also be motivated by the goal of being elected to office themselves, ideally as part of a legislative party. Importantly, the political entrepreneurs bear the initial costs of forming a new party, often by organizing conventions, announcing platforms, and, crucially, recruiting candidates to contest elections. They are the key decision-makers and, in Olson's (1965, 177) terms, "innovator[s] with selective incentives."

Under which conditions will the political entrepreneurs bear the costs of advancing a collective good, in this case the formation of a new party? Especially a new party that represents a low-income constituency? This section will develop a general theoretical argument by focusing, first, on established parties, and then on voters in local partisan networks, in a highly stylized setting. Then, this section will turn to decisions confronting political entrepreneurs, and examine the conditions under which they will form a new party, developing general expectations, and expectations regarding when a party will mobilize a low-income constituency.

Although this chapter does not present formal notation, the argument developed here follows the logic of formal models of endogenous party formation and candidate entry (see, e.g., Callander 2005, Morelli 2004). An electoral geography is revealed (perhaps through a census; this is the result of history and nature, and is Stage 0 in Chapter 1's framework), established parties announce policy platforms, the political entrepreneurs decide whether or not to form a new party and where to recruit candidates, an election is then held, and a government is formed. Each party, and the full set of voters, have complete information about the distribution of pivotal voter preferences, and are choosing an optimal strategy (identified by backward induction), given their expectations about what each other actor will do.[3]

Established Parties

To begin, to see how electoral geography matters, imagine a country in which elections are contested in SMDs, and in which two established parties traditionally alternate in government. (Multi-member district (MMD) systems, and systems with more than two parties, will be considered later.) These established parties approach each election with the goal of maximizing their share of seats in the legislature, and do so by promising their constituencies policy benefits and, once elected, distributive benefits. Established parties contest seats in every district; for the established parties, the key decision is whether and how much to shift policy positions in response to changes in the preferences of pivotal voters.

It is difficult or costly, however, for parties to take on new positions or to change their platforms once they are established. This is because, following Callander (2005), when an established party takes on a new position, it may *undermine* its electoral success. Although the adoption of new policy positions may stave off potential challengers, including third parties, and in some districts, the new positions may also alienate established and otherwise loyal constituencies.[4]

---

3 In fact, because established parties are limited in their abilities to take on new positions, whether they or the new party announces positions first does not matter for the outcome.

4 One example of the challenges in changing position is illustrated by Przeworski and Sprague's (1986) analysis of socialist parties: In their account, socialist parties face a "magic barrier," beyond which they are unable to increase their electoral support. This barrier exists, Przeworski and Sprague argue, because when socialist parties weaken their message of class solidarity, with the goal of increasing electoral support from other occupation and class groups, working-class identity is simultaneously undermined. Working-class voters are then free to vote for other parties.

   More generally, using data from the Comparative Manifesto Project, which tracks the content of parties' policy proposals, Adams *et al.* (2004, 590) find that while parties sometimes do respond to shifts in public opinion that leave them at a disadvantage by changing their positions, generally, "parties are reluctant to alter their ideologies" (see also Budge 1994). Established incumbent parties may, however, implement electoral reforms, in response to

Political Entrepreneurs

In this framework, political entrepreneurs are faced with two decisions: First, they must decide whether to pursue their political goals within the established party apparatus or to strike out on their own and form a new party. Here, the decision to form a new party is represented by the announcement of a national platform or policy position.[5] If the political entrepreneurs decide to form a new party, they are confronted by a second decision. Specifically, they must also decide where – which districts – to recruit candidates and enter electoral contests (or, which candidates to nominate or endorse; see Cohen *et al.* 2008, Cox 1997). For Przeworski (1985; see also Przeworski & Sprague 1986), for socialist and social democratic parties, the decision to participate in elections represents the "crucial" decision.

Like the established parties, the political entrepreneurs are motivated by their desire to maximize their share of seats in the legislature. Policy-motivated political entrepreneurs will recognize that the share of seats under their control will determine the bargaining power of the party, and that voters have similar incentives to favor those parties that can win a substantial share of seats in the legislature. So, the political entrepreneurs will choose a platform that maximizes their likelihood of winning seats in as large a number of electoral districts as possible.[6] Further, particularly in founding elections when resources are limited, political entrepreneurs will aim to minimize mobilization costs while maximizing the likelihood of electing their candidates to the legislature, and entry into each specific electoral contest represents a crucial strategic decision.[7]

---

changes in voter preferences, to return pivotal votes to members of their constituencies (see, e.g., Boix 1999, Rokkan 1970).

Hirano (2008) provides another example: The legislative behavior of Democrats and Republicans is generally unresponsive to the strength of Populist electoral threats, and indeed, to changes in the policy demands of their constituents.

[5] This assumption distinguishes this analysis from models of endogenous entry, in which independent challengers can take any policy position and compete only in one district (e.g., Callander 2005).

[6] Notice that this account does not require (or exclude the possibility) that political entrepreneurs are policy motivated. If voters care about policy, political entrepreneurs can be incentivized to deliver policy goods because doing so furthers their office-seeking goals. Alternatively, if the political entrepreneurs *are* motivated by policy preferences, they must also be office seeking.

[7] This setup is similar, in this respect, to Morelli's (2004) analysis, in which leaders of (extreme) established parties are strategic actors who make offers to a third (moderate) party and potential electoral coalition partner, and candidates choose whether or not to enter. Here, of course, there is no explicit coordination between the established parties and political entrepreneurs, and the new party's policy proposal is unconstrained. Finally, it is the political entrepreneurs who bear the real costs of organization and mobilization. This is consistent with the archival material that will be presented in later chapters, and with what Chhibber and Kollman (2004) find: In Canada, India, the United Kingdom, and the United States, to form new parties, political entrepreneurs play an important role in recruiting local candidates.

Voters and Local Partisan Networks

Although voters might be ordered along some policy dimension, here they are more appropriately thought of as members of groups that, within each district, are incorporated into local partisan networks (sometimes, "machines") that are developed and cultivated by the established parties through a combination of policy and distributive benefits.[8] What this implies is that partisan identification is inherited from location, perhaps as much as from one's parents, occupation, or other social identities.

This understanding of partisanship reflects early and contemporary analysis of "neighborhood effects": simply, which party a voter identifies with is conditioned by the party preferred by her neighbors, and vice versa. Some have suggested that these local partisan networks may reflect selection into a particular place, that voters with similar preferences may live in a particular place *because* they share similar interests and preferences.[9] However, to the extent these local partisan networks provide an incumbency advantage, parties have strong incentives to develop, cultivate, and mobilize these networks as an effective way to meet their electoral goals. As we shall see, opportunities in electoral districts where large numbers of voters have not yet been incorporated into local partisan networks, perhaps because they are new arrivals or because they have been explicitly excluded, will be especially attractive to political entrepreneurs.

Incorporating Electoral Geography

To see the importance of electoral geography, imagine two cases:

First, suppose that the composition of electoral districts is homogeneous (i.e., each district perfectly replicates the national distribution of groups). Both

---

[8] Although this framework was developed with Downs's (1957) spatial voting model and subsequent analyses of party entry (especially Callander 2005, Morelli 2004) in mind, the emphasis on group membership and its connection to partisan networks is more in keeping with Przeworski and Sprague's (1986) account, in which socialist party leaders actively shape the identities and preferences of working-class voters as part of their mobilization strategy (see also Iversen 1994).

[9] To demonstrate that "geographical or natural factors have contributed very materially in creating the conditions which determine political predilections," Krebheil (1916, 432), for example, shows that the composition of the local labor force is strongly related to election outcomes. "When the laboring class is most numerous in a county constituency," Krebheil (1916, 424) writes, "the chances are that it will incline to the Liberal or Labor party." Similar district-level analysis led Tingsten (1975) to introduce a "law of the social centre of gravity," that a group's electoral participation increases with its relative size in each electoral district (see also Gosnell 1937). Johnston, Pattie, and Allsopp (1988) (see also Johnston *et al.* 2005), especially, extended this analysis in a careful treatment of neighborhood effects to show that, for example, levels of class voting in Britain depend upon the class composition of each district. That is, whether or not a particular citizen identifies as "working class" – and votes accordingly – is dependent upon whether she lives in a predominantly working-class neighborhood (Johnston & Pattie 2003, 346).

established parties will take the policy positions preferred by the national median voter (who holds the same preferences as the median of each district). Under these conditions, following Downs (1957), no third-party candidates will enter any electoral contest: they simply cannot win. And, without any hope of winning even a single seat, the political entrepreneurs will not incur the costs of recruiting new party candidates or mobilizing voters.

What if, however, electoral districts vary in their composition, and the median voter (group) prefers different policies in different districts? In this second case, as Callander (2005) suggests, established parties will take (usually different) positions that are optimal (i.e., that maximize their share of seats in the legislature) given the full distribution of district medians.[10] If we imagine the districts ordered according to the preferences of their median voters, and if some district medians take fairly extreme positions, it will be clear that any position an established party might take may be quite different from the position most preferred by the pivotal voters in at least a few districts.

To the extent that this is the case, again following Callander (2005), we may expect independent candidates to enter electoral contests in those districts where the established parties are especially out of step with the preferences of the district median. Note, however, that most of the time, the established parties will be able to take policy positions that deter new party formation. That is, established parties will take positions that ensure that the medians of the districts from which the established parties are most different have nothing in common. (Specifically, that there is no position that a new party could take that median voters in more than one district would prefer to the positions offered by the established parties.) Further, it may be the case that incumbents from the established parties are able to develop strong local partisan networks to fully deter challenger entry, even in districts where national party platforms are "far" from district medians. All of this suggests that while independent candidates may enter specific electoral district contests, most of the time we may expect two-party competition, even in systems with heterogeneous districts.

New Party Formation

Under which conditions, then, will new parties form?

The coincidence of two factors ensures that efforts to mobilize new candidates and voters will be successful: First, suppose that some large-scale (but not national) changes in the composition of districts allow new voters (and groups) to take the median position in some large number of districts. Established parties are limited in their ability to respond to these newly pivotal voters, because any gains to be made in the districts where the changes

[10] This "divergent" result, in which parties distinguish themselves in policy space, even in SMD competition, of course, conflicts with Downs's (1957) convergence.

have occurred may be offset by losses in other districts (perhaps ideological strongholds, where fewer distributive benefits were provided).[11]

Second (this is a key original claim of this research), if the newly pivotal voters are members of groups who are largely, perhaps explicitly, excluded from existing partisan networks, they may be especially easy to mobilize in support of new party candidates. These newly pivotal voters may be recent migrants or immigrants, or may have been excluded from local partisan networks through enfranchisement laws and suffrage restrictions. In any case, they may have received little from established party candidates, in terms of distributive benefits, and as a consequence may weigh policy proposals more heavily in their voting decision. Although there may be other districts in which members of the groups the new party represents form a numerical majority, without *changes* in the composition of the district, the strength of existing partisan networks will discourage the recruitment and entry of new party candidates in those districts.[12]

Notice that although new party formation and entry into electoral competition constitute separate strategic decisions, they are inexorably linked and largely determined by (mostly exogenous) demographic changes. Opportunities for new party entry lie in the new concentration of voters who share preferences, in sufficient numbers that they are pivotal in election outcomes. There are several phenomena that have the potential to cause this concentration – to disrupt the electoral market, in Boix's (2009) words – and to create the opportunity for new party formation and entry:

Internal migration is an important source of new electoral opportunities, and will feature prominently in the empirical analysis presented in the next

---

[11]   This account emphasizes changes in the composition of districts, rather than changes in preferences of voters – changes in *who* is pivotal rather than changes in the *preferences* of the pivotal voter. Why is this? Would we expect the same thing if the *preferences* of the median voter simply changed? No: local partisan networks could accommodate shifts in preferences through compensatory distributive benefits. Rather, it is the existence of voters outside of existing partisan networks that represents the opportunity for political entrepreneurs and new parties.

[12]   Why might challengers prefer to contest the election on a new party's ticket rather than as an independent, or even as a member of an existing party? If changes in electoral geography create the opportunities for party formation and entry that are described here, established party labels will offer few advantages. Further, the advantage of party membership, in terms of defrayed election costs, and the benefits of legislative party membership ensure that if challengers are recruited by the "third-party men," they will happily enter the election on that ticket. (Because recruited challengers will contest on the new party ticket with certainty, at least in the context of this analysis, they are largely excluded from the above discussion.) This account, therefore, offers a different perspective from Cox's (1997) analysis, in which access to the major parties' endorsement processes ("permeability") and value of a party's endorsement ("advantage") vary, and structure a group's decision to enter electoral competition on an established party's ticket, or to form a new party. Here, instead, political entrepreneurs recognize that the established parties' labels have limited value, at least in some districts.

few chapters. Of course, *who* moves is not random, nor is the location of *where* they go. In fact, understanding who moved where and why is the key to understanding cross-national differences in the partisan representation of low-income citizens.

Immigration has the capacity to change the distribution of electoral power across different groups in society, particularly when the acquisition of citizenship and voting rights is straightforward and large groups of immigrants cluster in geographic space. As will be especially clear in the case of the Canadian CCF, immigrant groups provided an early and important source of electoral support.

Change in local conditions will also be shown to have an important role in creating opportunities for new party formation and entry. For example, extreme droughts may change the relative standing of previously prosperous agricultural workers over a large geographic area, creating a new low-income constituency. If existing partisan networks insufficiently compensate for their recent loss in economic standing, these newly pivotal voters may also be available for mobilization by new parties and candidates.

Suffrage expansion, particularly when changes in eligibility are tied to income levels (as was the case in Sweden between 1866 and 1911), has the potential to shift local distributions of electoral power in profound ways. When increased earnings are concentrated within sectors and, as a consequence, in specific places, even unintentional expansions of voting rights also create the opportunity for new party entry.[13]

When these phenomena affect a large number of districts, especially when changes in local populations are profound, and favor one group in particular, we ought to see new parties forming and entering electoral competition. And, new parties ought to be especially likely to recruit candidates to enter contests in those districts in which members of their groups are newly arrived (and/or not yet incorporated in local partisan networks) and newly pivotal.[14]

---

[13] More generally, electoral reform and the manipulation of district boundaries may have profound implications for local distributions of electoral power. As Rokkan (1970) and others have suggested (notably Ahmed 2013, Rodden 2010, Calvo 2009, Boix 1999), the adoption of MMD rules was more often a *response* to new party entry. Similarly, strategic redistricting or "gerrymandering" might be seen as attempts to moderate changes in the local distribution of electoral power that threaten incumbent legislators. As a consequence, these explicit changes in electoral geography should only rarely represent opportunities for new party entry. The analysis presented in Chapter 3 confirms this intuition: new parties appear less likely to enter electoral competition following major electoral reforms, although the relationship is estimated with considerable variance.

[14] One might reasonably wonder about the extent to which each source of change is rightly viewed as exogenous. Later chapters will address this question explicitly, in the context of each specific source of change.

2.2 GENERAL IMPLICATIONS FOR NEW PARTY FORMATION

This chapter has presented a general argument about when we might expect a new party to form that follows from two straightforward axioms. Specifically, (1) when established parties are limited in their abilities to change or take on new policy positions, and (2) candidates are tied to national party platforms, demographic changes create new opportunities for party formation and entry. This account has several general implications for party competition and the quality of political representation, and specific implications for the partisan representation of low-income citizens.

First, this framework suggests when established parties ought to take on new positions. If there are general and uniform demographic changes, established parties can take on new policy positions without concern that these changing positions will cost them electoral support. Otherwise, parties' policy positions ought to be relatively stable, or consistent, over time.

Second, when demographic shifts change who (which group) is pivotal in only a subset of districts, established parties may not be able to alter their positions to respond to the preferences of this group without losing electoral support in other districts. As a consequence, local demographic changes create opportunities for challengers. When the same group is favored across some substantial number of districts, changes in the composition of within-district electorates create opportunities for new parties, especially when those changes involve the incorporation of groups that were previously excluded from existing partisan networks.

Third, especially when changes in the distribution of electoral power affect large numbers of districts within well-defined subnational units, opportunities for entry may create incentives for entrepreneurs to mobilize voters through ethnic or regional identities. In these cases, national multi-party competition may be sustained, even under SMD rules.

Fourth, when demographic changes are limited or unsystematic over a long period of time, party competition may appear to be "frozen," or reflect early electoral geographies. "Realignment" or the establishment of new parties reflects changes in the pivotal voters' preferences, or rather, changes in *which groups* are pivotal. As we shall see in Chapter 3, rates of local population change increased markedly during the late nineteenth and early twentieth centuries, when most low-income and workers' parties entered electoral competition.

Fifth, although the argument in this chapter was developed in the context of SMD electoral rules, the idea of electoral power provides a way to generalize the intuition to other electoral systems. To the extent that demographic changes are concentrated in MMDs that elect only a few legislators (i.e., "low-magnitude" districts), we may expect local population change to create opportunities for new party entry even under proportional representation rules. However, if large numbers of legislators are elected in each electoral district, and/or there are compensatory tiers in which seats are allocated to ensure a strictly proportional outcome, local changes in the composition of district electorates may offer only limited opportunity for party entry. This is because, in "high-magnitude" districts, the proportionate mapping of votes to seats moderates changes in electoral power across groups.[15]

The final general implication concerns how we ought to think about the distribution of political power and its relationship to electoral geography. To the extent that legislators rely on a particular group for their electoral success, policy ought to reflect the interests of that group. Further, cross-national (or cross-state) differences in policy ought to reflect differences in a group's electoral power, or the frequency with which that group is pivotal in the election of seats in the legislature.[16] If district boundaries are constructed in such a way that, given the current geographic distribution of groups, a group is almost never pivotal in the election of legislators, we should not be surprised if policy is unresponsive to that group's interests.

2.3 IMPLICATIONS FOR THE POLITICAL REPRESENTATION OF THE POOR

Most of the rest of this book applies implications of the argument presented in this chapter to the specific case of low-income citizens, and presents tests of our

---

[15] Consider this example: Suppose that a group of voters moves into a single urban area, increasing their share in each of ten SMDs from 10 to 50 percent. This new group would now be pivotal in the election of all ten representatives in this area. Now, compare this outcome to one in which all ten legislators are elected within a single multi-member district, according to a proportional representation rule. In this case, the group would have increased the number of representatives from their group from perhaps one to five. If similar demographic changes occur elsewhere, this increase may be sufficient to induce new party formation and entry, but this group's increase in electoral power is clearly moderated by the MMD electoral rules.
   A related question is about how the existing number of parties moderates opportunities for new party entry: Ksleman, Powell, and Tucker (2016) find, for example, that new parties are more likely to enter electoral competition when there are already large numbers of parties competing in an election. They attribute this finding to the potentially large effect that a new party might have on policy, when party competition is already fragmented. From the perspective of electoral geography, however, particularly when party competition is highly nationalized (see, e.g., Caramani 2004, Chhibber & Kollman 2004), even under SMD electoral rules where large majorities of district electorates are needed to win seats, multi-party competition lowers the threshold of viability. That is, smaller groups can be pivotal in elections, and as a consequence, smaller changes in the distribution of electoral power create the opportunities for new party entry. Even purely office-seeking political entrepreneurs, therefore, can be induced to enter electoral contests when there are large numbers of parties competing in elections. (That is, the political entrepreneurs need not be motivated by policy goals.)

[16] Note that the concept of a group's electoral power is distinct from the *size* of a group (see Stoll 2013). This distinction is seen perhaps most clearly in a response to Przeworski and Sprague (1986), who were motivated by the puzzling failure of socialist parties to win the majority of seats, despite that workers often comprised large shares of the electorate. In fact, because workers were concentrated "inefficiently," their electoral power was limited: they were pivotal in less than half of the seats elected to the legislature.

expectations about when, and where, we might expect political entrepreneurs to mobilize low-income voters in support of a new party and its candidates.

As suggested in Chapter 1, there are analytic advantages in comparative research to delimiting interest groups by income rather than by occupation, ethnic or racial composition, or other factors. Although the argument in support of the ideological coherence of these groups may be stronger, at least in the case of occupation groups, the mapping of group interests to policy outcomes for low-income voters can be easily assessed: To what extent does policy aim to alleviate poverty? Perhaps more important for this comparative analysis, by focusing on low-income voters, defined as those comprising the bottom third of the national income distribution, the size of the group is fixed. This allows variation in the electoral power of the group (the number of seats it can elect in the legislature) to be compared over time within and across countries without concern about the effects of differences in the size of the group. That is, countries and cases will be distinguished only in the way votes map into seats – the key independent variable of this analysis.

Building on the general argument presented above, then, we can derive some expectations about the quality of political and partisan representation of low-income voters:

First, policy ought to be more responsive to low-income voters where they are more frequently pivotal in the election of legislators. This expectation follows most clearly when elections are contested in SMDs but, as suggested above, differences in the electoral power of low-income citizens matter for social policy under MMD rules, too. Importantly, Chapter 8 will also show that some of the variance in social policy outcomes that is unaccounted for by contemporary electoral geography can be attributed to differences in the historical power of low-income peoples' parties. This implication suggests that early electoral geographies may have long-term and cumulative effects on the quality of the political representation of the poor – an explanation for the origins of cross-national differences in social policy.

Second, at least to the extent that periods of local population change increase the electoral power of one group, relative to others, these periods should be accompanied by the formation and entry of new parties. Although data limitations prevent tracking changes in the electoral power of income groups over long periods, Chapter 3 takes up this implication and examines how rates of local population change create opportunities for new party entry.

Finally, the argument presented in this chapter has implications for where new parties, once formed, ought to enter election contests. Specifically, we ought to see new low-income peoples' parties entering those electoral contests where the composition of the district has changed such that low-income voters are now pivotal. This strategic recruitment of candidates and allocation of campaign resources is examined in several analytic case studies, from the United States, Canada, Great Britain, and Sweden. In each of these cases, a new party (or, in the case of Canada, two new parties) forms and challenges two established parties, under SMD electoral rules, and under circumstances like those described above. That is, substantial, but local, changes in the composition of electoral districts created new opportunities to mobilize a low-income constituency. These new parties often recruited members of groups who were excluded from existing partisan networks, including recent migrants and immigrants. In several cases, the opportunities were rural, and the political entrepreneurs developed platforms that incorporated the interests of a low-income, agrarian constituency. Elsewhere, it was the concentration of low-income citizens in industrial districts that created the opportunities, and party platforms crafted by the "third-party men" reflected the preferences of an industrial working class. Finally, in the case of Sweden, we will see the impact of electoral reform on the long-term distribution of electoral power across income groups. Together, these cases contribute a different and important explanation for the origins of cross-national differences in the quality of political and partisan representation of the poor.

2.4 SUMMARY AND CONCLUSIONS

This chapter began with two straightforward axioms about electoral competition – that established parties are limited in their abilities to change positions, and local candidates are at least somewhat tied to these positions – and developed an argument about the conditions under which new parties will form and recruit candidates for electoral competition. Specifically, if districts are heterogeneous, and some experience important changes in their social and demographic composition, established parties may be unable to respond to changes in the preferences of pivotal voters in these districts. To the extent that these changes in the composition of districts favor one group across some number of districts, political entrepreneurs may recognize an opportunity for new party formation, and recruit candidates to contest elections in those districts.

This explanation for new party entry provides an important, but so far missing, account of which groups, from all groups that might be mobilized within society, may be represented in partisan competition. Simply, political entrepreneurs will form parties to represent the interests of those groups that are favored by changes in electoral geography, especially when those groups are not yet incorporated into local partisan networks. Further, following changes in electoral geography that favor low-income voters, we may expect political entrepreneurs to form parties that represent a low-income constituency. If the newly pivotal low-income voters reside in rural districts, the political entrepreneurs will craft platforms that are responsive to agrarian workers. If, on the other hand, as was more often the case in Europe, the newly pivotal low-income voters are industrial workers, the platforms of the new parties will reflect the interests of labor. In either case, as we shall see, it was the change in the composition of districts that created the opportunity for new party formation and entry, and political entrepreneurs developed platforms that reflected the interests of the newly pivotal voters.

3

New Parties and the Changing Electoral Geography of Contemporary Democracies, 1880–2000

This book presents a general theory of party formation and entry in which demographic changes present political entrepreneurs with important opportunities. When a particular group becomes pivotal in legislative elections across some number of districts, and especially when this group is excluded from local partisan networks because of its recent arrival or because of suffrage restrictions, political entrepreneurs can pursue their office-seeking goals by mobilizing this group as a core constituency. While most of this book will test this claim by examining the conditions under which political entrepreneurs will mobilize a low-income constituency, this chapter will present a broadly comparative analysis that will show that new parties *generally* enter electoral competition following major changes in electoral geography. Specifically, for a large number of developed democracies, the analysis presented here will track local population changes from around 1880 through 2000, and show that all new parties are more likely to enter electoral competition during those periods in which we observe the largest changes in district electorates. By estimating the magnitude of local population change – evidence of internal migration or immigration – this analysis will focus attention on key periods in which new electoral opportunities likely presented themselves to political entrepreneurs.

The following section summarizes the earlier argument about why concentrated demographic changes represent electoral opportunities for new parties. Then, drawing on data for a large number of countries, and an extended period of time, this chapter develops a measure of local population change. Finally, this chapter uses data on the total number of new parties entering electoral competition in a particular decade as the dependent variable in an analysis that links local population change to electoral opportunity and new party formation.

3.1 LOCAL POPULATION CHANGE AND OPPORTUNITIES FOR PARTY ENTRY

Chapter 2 developed an account of party formation in which political entrepreneurs are faced with two decisions: (1) whether or not to form a new party (i.e., announce a policy platform), and (2) where to recruit candidates (i.e., enter electoral competition). When the political entrepreneurs face an established party system and a stable distribution of voters, the barriers to entry are high. The established parties have adopted platforms that maximize their share of seats in the legislature, and cultivated local partisan networks that sustain their electoral success. When there are important changes in the composition of a (non-trivial) subset of districts, however, the established parties may be constrained in their abilities to respond to the preferences of newly pivotal voters. Simply, the adoption of new policy positions may alienate their existing constituency, and threaten their electoral success. Political entrepreneurs may seize this opportunity to form a new party that better reflects the preferences of these newly pivotal voters, and recruit candidates in those districts where changes in the composition of the district are profound. The opportunities for new party formation and entry may be especially appealing to political entrepreneurs when, rather than simply recognizing a change in the preferences of pivotal voters, they see an opportunity to take advantage of newly pivotal voters who are not yet incorporated into local partisan networks and, as a consequence, are "ripe" for mobilization.

Note that this argument applies generally: Political entrepreneurs may mobilize *any* sufficiently large group as a potential partisan constituency when they are favored by changes in electoral geography. (Which groups count as "sufficiently large" likely varies with the size of electoral district, and the ways in which seats are allocated.)[1] Here, I track local population changes for (mostly) stable geographic units, over the 1880–2000 period, and examine the timing of *all* new party entry. If the account of party formation and entry presented above, and in more detail in Chapter 2, is correct, then it ought to be the case that periods of concentrated population change (i.e., resulting from immigration or internal migration) will be followed by the formation of new parties representing those groups favored by the population change.

---

[1] Cox (1997, 142) suggests that groups that are "organized, that have leaders who can speak for their interests in an authoritative and public fashion, and that are perceived as usually voting as a bloc" are especially ripe for partisan mobilization. Stoll (2013) similarly emphasizes a group's politicalization. The bar here is somewhat lower. Specifically, to the extent that political entrepreneurs (in and outside of established parties) are successful, they may politicize a group's identity in the process of mobilizing that group, and indeed, may generate a voting bloc where none had previously existed. For example, support for the Republican party has increased dramatically among Evangelical Christians, who now overwhelmingly support Republican candidates, and whose leaders are now sometimes important Republican party insiders (see, e.g., Williams 2010).

The analysis presented in this chapter will also justify later attention on changes in the electoral geography of income during the 1880–1930 period. Although dramatic and relatively widespread changes in local conditions (i.e., local economic shocks that change the relative standing of concentrated populations in the national income distribution) will not be evident in the analysis presented in this chapter, this strategy will identify periods in which internal migration and immigration have the capacity to change the vote-to-seat mappings of different income groups. Then, the analytic case studies presented in later chapters will examine in more detail how changes in the distribution of electoral power across income groups, specifically, created new opportunities for party entry.

What are the other, established, accounts for party entry, against which we can evaluate the explanatory power of demographic change? Cox (1997) and others (e.g., Stoll 2013, Clark & Golder 2006) have emphasized the roles of institutional barriers to entry, especially in established party organizations and candidate selection procedures, and social heterogeneity, in determining the *number* of parties that will compete for office within a particular system.

Certainly, where there are dramatic changes in the social heterogeneity of the electorate, as Stoll (2013) shows in her analysis of African American suffrage expansion and the formation of African American sectarian parties during the period of Reconstruction, political entrepreneurs may recognize opportunities to form new parties. However, outside of periods of suffrage expansion, the overall level of diversity in most electorates changes only slowly. To the extent that changes in the composition of local electorates represent real opportunities for political entrepreneurs, and are independent of suffrage expansion (i.e., migration and immigration), the measure used in this analysis will reflect these changes.

The analysis presented later in this chapter, therefore, will incorporate indicators of electoral reform that may signal a change in the system's permissiveness, and indicators of periods of suffrage expansion, as well as measures of local demographic change.

3.2 MEASURING LOCAL POPULATION CHANGE

This first empirical section develops the measure that will be the key independent variable in a broadly comparative analysis of new party formation and entry. (This measure will also be used to identify periods of significant local population change and will justify later attention on the late nineteenth and early twentieth centuries for examining new electoral opportunities.) As we shall see, periods of especially intense local population change tended to occur early in this period. Second, this section suggests a reason why the entry of new low-income peoples' parties occurred only rarely after 1930. Because local population change was more limited after 1930, especially in the US, electoral opportunities for new parties were likely to be equally limited. In combination with districts that were increasingly heterogeneous – that is, the vote-to-seat mapping became increasingly biased against low-income voters – incentives for party entry weakened. (Chapter 8 will focus more rigorously on this observation.)

Tracking changes in the electoral geography of income over long periods of time is complicated by frequent and concurrent electoral reform and redistricting. As suggested above, changes in the electoral geography of income – the vote-to-seat mappings for different income groups – are generated by three factors, in addition to electoral reform: internal migration, immigration, and local shocks. The changes induced by any of these factors must be geographically concentrated in order to alter the vote-to-seat mappings of national income groups. For example, if low-income citizens are just as likely as high-income citizens to relocate, and all relocate in a random way, we would not expect changes in the frequency with which each income group is pivotal in the allocation of legislative seats. Alternatively, if low-income citizens are more likely to move, and tend to relocate in geographically concentrated areas (because of similarly concentrated economic opportunities, for example), then even without income data, we would expect localized population changes to signal changes in the electoral power of low-income voters.[2] This approach, therefore, likely includes changes in the electoral power of low-income voters, along with changes in the electoral power of other groups, to the extent that their members move cohesively and systematically.

Here, therefore, I calculate population changes in small, stable geographic units, relative to national population changes, and identify periods and regions that experience significant local population changes. Specifically, I estimate

$$\delta_t^d = \text{Local Population Change}_t^d$$
$$= \left(\frac{Population_t^d - Population_{t-1}^d}{Population_{t-1}^d} - \frac{Population_t^N - Population_{t-1}^N}{Population_{t-1}^N} \right)^2, \quad (3.1)$$

where *Population* levels are reported for $d = 1,\ldots,D$ districts (actually, subnational units), at time t (coinciding with the census in each country, or each decade if other data are used), and N designates the national population. *Population* estimates are generally derived from census data (for Europe, these data are reported in Rothenbacher 2002, Rothenbacher 2005), and are reported for the smallest geographic area that remains consistent over the twentieth century. In the US, for example, the boundaries of counties remain relatively consistent over time. In other countries, provinces or states are small and

---

[2] To be clear, the measure developed below is not intended to approximate changes in the electoral power of low-income voters or, actually, any specific group. Instead, it is meant to identify changes in the distribution of electoral power across any and all groups in each society. To the extent that local population changes do not reflect movement of (potentially mobilizable) groups, this measure exaggerates opportunities for new party entry.

numerous enough to provide useful information about local population change. (In one country, Canada, rather large provinces are used because there are no smaller stable geographic units). When major administrative boundaries shift over time, or new subnational units are created, observations from earlier years are matched to these new boundaries to allow, as much as possible, for stable unit observations throughout the 1880–2000 period. Sub-national units are included in the analysis for as many periods for which δ_t^d can be calculated; the number of observations varies as states or provinces are created or combined. Finally, when data are not available for a particular year (e.g., 1940), estimates for the next decade (e.g., 1950) are based on changes over the previous two decades (i.e., since 1930).

To generate a national summary for each decade, I calculate

$$\delta_t = \sqrt{\frac{\sum_d \delta^d}{D_t}}, \tag{3.2}$$

which provides an estimate of the rate of local population change and gives a measure that is similar to a standard deviation: it will be approximately zero when local population change mirrors national (average) population change consistently across the country. Values larger than zero will indicate the average rate at which local population change deviates from national population change. For example, a value of $\delta_t = 0.10$ implies that local populations were changing, in this case, by an average of about ten percentage points more than the national population as a whole. Appendix 3.A provides a summary of the data used in this analysis. (Note that estimates for the 1940s and 1950s should be interpreted with caution: data from 1940 are not available for five of the fifteen countries. When 1940 observations are simply missing, estimates for these countries for 1950 reflect average changes in local populations since 1930. Later analysis will be replicated excluding wartime observations, e.g., 1920, 1940, and 1950.)

Figures 3.1 and 3.2 report the distribution of estimated values of "average local population change" (δ), by decade, for each country. Often, the values estimated for the 1880–1940 decades are larger than later values, reflecting rates of local population change that are quite different from national patterns of growth during this early period. This suggests that electoral opportunities for party entry created by population movement were especially frequent early in the century, at least in these countries. In a few cases, including Great Britain as well as Denmark and France, there is some evidence of increased rates of local population change during the 1970s and 1980s – a period that corresponds with party "realignment" and the entry of green and radical right parties (e.g., Franklin, Mackie, & Valen 2009, Dalton *et al.* 1984).[3]

---

[3] In fact, as Franklin, Mackie, and Valen (2009, 20) write, the realignment of parties' systems followed the dramatic changes in cleavage structures, often by considerable periods of time;

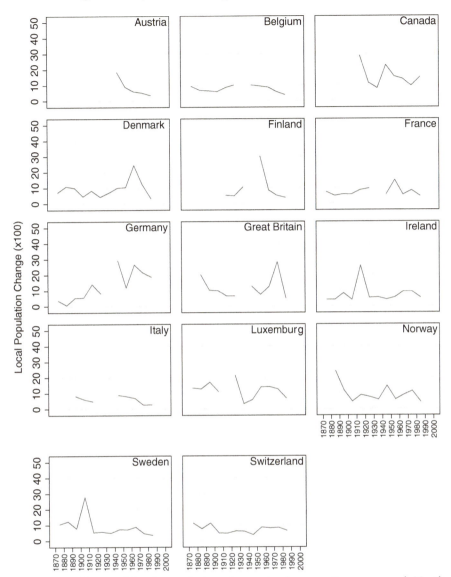

FIGURE 3.1. Rates of local population change in fourteen European and North American countries, 1880–2000.

Note: This figure reports values of local population change (δ_t) for each country and decade.

Sources: Sources vary by country; please refer to Appendix 3.A for details.

"why did the effects occur so late?" The explanation presented here that emphasizes the necessity of changes in electoral geography can account for this delay: changes in social cleavages may not have been immediately accompanied by the changes in electoral geography that create opportunities for new party entry.

(a) County-Level Estimates, by Region

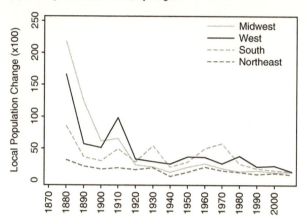

(b) Top- and Bottom-Coded County-Level Estimates, by Region

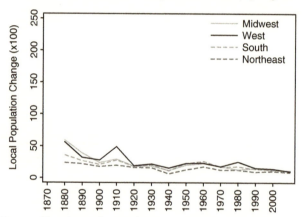

FIGURE 3.2. Rates of local population change in the US, 1880–2000.

Note: This figure reports values of local population change (δ_t) for each American region, estimated for each decade, using the original county-level estimates (top panel) and top- and bottom-coded county-level estimates (bottom panel) as the unit of analysis.

Source: Minnesota Population Center – National Historical Geographic Information System: Version 2.0 (total population by state, and county.)

To provide further understanding of how this measure of local population change reflects population movement, Figure 3.2 reports estimates of local population change for four regions in the US. Notice that in the top panel, which reports estimates based on the original data, the rates of local population change in the US throughout the period are considerably higher than those we estimate for Europe. To limit the influence of high-leverage observations (i.e., very small counties that experienced dramatic growth at rates many, many times the national growth rate during decades in which, in the US at least, many new parties entered electoral competition), the estimates used in this analysis are top- and bottom-coded to values at the fifth and ninety-fifth percentiles (reported in the bottom panel of Figure 3.2). In both panels, we observe dramatic changes in local populations at the end of the nineteenth century and beginning of the twentieth century that generally slow over the next few decades.

The series in Figure 3.2 also draw attention to periods of local population *decline*, as well as periods of local population growth. The relatively high values observed for the American South, especially during the 1960s and 1970s, corresponds to movement out of counties in this region. (Many parts of the Midwest also experienced population decline during this period, but other regions, particularly counties surrounding the major urban centers, experienced dramatic growth rates that were not found in the South.) To the extent that local population decreases, as well as increases, change the distribution of electoral power, districts where populations have declined may also represent opportunities for new party entry: Established parties may be unable to respond to the consequent changes in the preferences of the newly pivotal voters. Further, large departures may have dramatic effects on the structure and strength of local partisan networks. Because political entrepreneurs facing districts with significant population loss may not have the same advantages as those where there are large numbers of newly arrived voters who have not yet developed party loyalties, by treating local population losses as equivalent to population gains, the measure used in this analysis provides an inclusive measure of potential changes in the distribution of electoral power. (Treating reductions and increases as equivalent in the calculation of national averages also introduces variance, and likely weakens the empirical relationship between local population change and new party entry.)

The estimates of average local population change reported in Figure 3.1, and a national (top- and bottom-coded) summary of the American case, will provide measures of the key independent variable in the analysis that follows. To the extent that geographically concentrated changes in the distribution of electoral power represent new opportunities for party entry, average rates of local population change – which, with electoral reform and local shocks have the capacity to change the distribution of electoral power – should be positively associated with new party entry. That is, where we see higher rates of local population change, we should also observe the more frequent formation of new parties.

3.3 WHEN DO NEW PARTIES FORM?

Are new parties more likely to form and enter electoral competition following major changes in electoral geography that shift the balance of electoral power? This section evaluates the relationship between local population change and new party entry.

Before proceeding, however, this section addresses important empirical challenges associated with this task. For example, *which* new parties ought to be included in the analysis? Here, I use an inclusive count of the number of new parties, with the goal of explaining the decision to *enter* electoral competition: if decisions to coordinate across districts and form parties are structured by incentives related to likely success, a more limited set of parties, perhaps selected with criteria related to success (e.g., seat thresholds, etc.), would exaggerate the relationship between changes in electoral geography and new party entry.

Instead, ideally, this analysis would identify new parties by the behavior of candidates. Is there evidence, for example, of a coordinated decision to contest the election, as a direct challenge to established parties? Can the decision to form a party be attributed to a specific date? Is there evidence of cross-district coordination in campaigns? Does the new party field at least, say, three candidates in at least two districts in the first election following the decision to establish a party? In practice, most of the parties listed in Caramani (2000), for Europe, or the Constituency-Level Elections Archive (CLEA: Kollman *et al.* 2014), for Canada and the US, meet these criteria: a clear origin date, and minimal cross-district coordination of candidates in original elections, although Caramani uses a success-based threshold, and includes only those parties that earn at least 5 percent of votes cast within one territorial unit. This analysis includes, therefore, all parties Caramani (2000) identifies as competing in legislative elections, as well as all Canadian and American parties included in CLEA that meet the criteria outlined above.[4]

Figure 3.3 reports the numbers of new parties formed in each decade between 1880 and 2000, for each country. There are three features of the rate of party entry that are important to this analysis: First, notice that new parties are absent in a large number of elections (about 30 percent of country-decades overall, although new parties always enter contests in Great Britain and the US, and in about half of the decades in France). Second, in a casual comparison of Figures 3.1, 3.2, and 3.3, new parties appear to form following decades of local population movement. The pattern of new party entry in Great Britain, for example, follows the inverted U-shape trend in local population movement.

Finally, notice that rates of all new party formation are typically much higher in the SMD systems (Canada, France, Great Britain, and the United

---

4   For each country, Caramani lists all parties that secured at least 5 percent of votes cast in any one territorial unit. My attempts to limit the numbers of parties to those for whom a "founding" date could be determined, and to those parties that competed for at least three seats in at least two districts (indicating cross-district coordination of candidates), generated a more restrictive list.

The CLEA data are more comprehensive, and include all candidates and parties contesting elections in Canada and the US, listed by district. Here, the three-seats-in-first-election rule excludes all but 104 of 749 (14 percent) of parties entering in US House of Representative elections. In Canada, these criteria exclude 67 of 122 parties entering elections to the House of Commons (59 percent). In most cases (560 in the US, 60 in Canada), these parties entered only a single district, and are more properly considered insurgent challengers rather than parties per se.

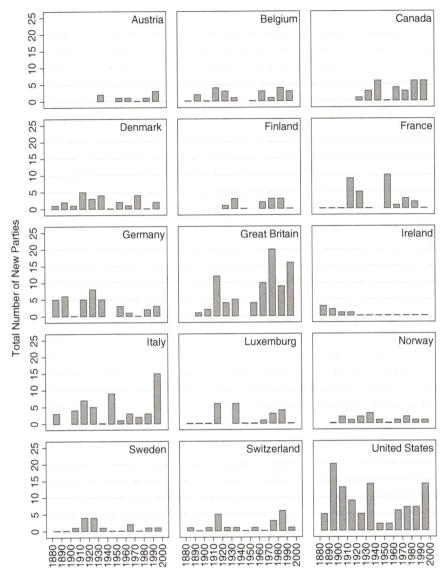

FIGURE 3.3. New party entry in fifteen European and North American countries, 1880–2000.

Note: This figure reports the total number of new parties entering electoral competition, for each decade and country.

Sources: Caramani (2000), Kollman *et al.* (2014).

States). In fact, this pattern of association between SMD electoral rules and new party formation applies to low-income peoples' parties, as well. As Table 3.1 reports, the major social democratic, workers', or agrarian parties for each country included in this analysis typically (17 out of 28 parties) contested their first elections under SMD rules.[5] This finding sits uneasily with arguments about the importance of low thresholds for representation under MMD rules, and the ease of party entry. Instead, it appears that the disproportionality of SMD rules may facilitate the entry of new parties when their constituents are geographically concentrated.[6]

The multivariate analysis that follows will allow the relationship between new party formation and local population change to be assessed more rigorously than the casual analysis presented above. Specifically, let the number of new parties that enter in each decade be a function of the average local population movement *in the previous decade*, described by Eq. (3.2), for each country. Then, factors that represent change in policy preferences or demands (i.e., change in national economic conditions) or the quality of existing representation can be evaluated, along with local population change, in their contribution to the variance in the timing of party entry. Notice that to the extent that political entrepreneurs are able to respond more quickly to local population changes (i.e., between census reports), the estimated relationship between local population change and new party entry will be underestimated, and estimated with more variance.[7]

Table 3.2 reports coefficients from (ordinary least squares) regression analyses in which the dependent variable is the number of new parties entering each system, each decade. Each column corresponds to different specifications, or different measurements of key independent or dependent variables. (Additional specifications are included in Appendix 3.A). As suggested above, this analysis also attempts to control for the effects of potentially confounding variables – those that might be associated with the formation of new parties *and* local population change. Especially dire economic conditions, for example, might drive local population movement, and generate demands for new forms of political representation. This analysis includes measures of change in per

---

[5] While this list attempts to be inclusive, it probably misses smaller low-income peoples' parties that had only limited electoral success. Also, several listed are no longer parties that represent low-income constituencies as their core constituency, and their inclusion may seem odd. This table attempts to include all those social democratic, labor, communist, or agrarian parties that had at least some electoral success (their candidates contested a large number of districts, and some were elected, in two or more elections), and appealed to a low-income constituency in their founding elections.

[6] This finding is consistent with Ksleman, Powell, and Tucker's (2016) analysis, in which they find that indicators of proportionality are generally negatively associated with new party entry (although, in one case, they observe a positive, but high-variance, relationship).

[7] Implicit here is an argument that census-taking provides a crucial information-providing role to political entrepreneurs. Following the census, and as a consequence of national conversations about who lives where, political entrepreneurs recognize whether and where opportunities for entry might be.

TABLE 3.1. *Electoral rules and the entry of low-income peoples' parties.*

Country	Entry under SMD rules		Entry under MMD rules	
	Plurality	Majority	Plurality	PR
Austria		SPÖ (1891[a])		
Belgium			BWP/POB (now BSP; 1894)	KPB/PCB (1925)
Canada	CCF-NDP (1935) Social Credit (1935)			
Denmark	A (1872[a])			DKP (1920)
Finland		SDP (1898[b])		Agrarian League or Maalaisliitto (now K; 1907[b]) SKP (as SSTP in 1922[b])
France	SFIO (now PS; 1906[c]) PCF (1924[c])			
Germany		SPD (1871[d]) BB (1893)		KPD (1920[b])
Great Britain	Labour (1900[a])			
Ireland				Labour (1922[a,b]) Farmers' Party (1922)
Italy		PSI (1895[a])		PCd'I (1921)
Luxembourg			LSAP (1902[b])	

(continued)

TABLE 3.1. *continued*

Country	Entry under SMD rules		Entry under MMD rules	
	Plurality	Majority	Plurality	PR
Norway	A/Ap (1903[c]) Landmandsforbund (now Sp; 1918[c])			
Sweden	SAP (1902[a])			Bondeförbundet (now C; 1911[b])
Switzerland	SP (1887)			
United States	People's Party (1892) Progressives (1912)			
Total	12	5	2	9

Notes: This table lists major low-income peoples' (labor and agrarian) parties and the dates of their first electoral contests, classified by the rules governing these elections. Splinter parties are omitted.

[a] These parties entered electoral competition prior to universal male suffrage.

[b] These parties were founded under SMD electoral rules, although their first electoral contests were governed by MMD rules.

[c] Elections held in these systems at the time of the left party entry were contested in two rounds: to win on the first ballot, an absolute majority was necessary. However, the second ballot was open to all candidates, and only a simple plurality was required to win.

Sources: Bartolini (2000), Caramani (2000).

TABLE 3.2. *Predicting new party entry.*

	DV: Number of new party entries			
	(1)	(2)	(3)	(4)
Local population change (δ_t)	10.396[a]	7.888[b]	9.803[a]	7.776
	(3.518)	(3.436)	(3.702)	(5.067)
SMD electoral rules		2.248[a]		
		(0.591)		
Suffrage expansion		2.261		
		(1.147)		
Electoral reform		−0.391		
		(1.159)		
Change in GDP per capita			−2.483	−3.862
			(1.831)	(1.975)
Change in top 1% income share				3.565
				(1.900)
Intercept	1.898[a]	1.023[b]	2.669[a]	3.418[a]
	(0.482)	(0.512)	(0.687)	(0.861)
N	155	155	140	70
Adjusted R^2	0.048	0.130	0.050	0.101

Notes: This table reports coefficients, estimated in a series of regression models in which the dependent variable is the number of new parties entering electoral competition in each decade, as a function of local population change, electoral rules governing elections, and changing economic conditions in each decade.
[a] $p < 0.01$.
[b] $p < 0.05$.

capita GDP as well as change in the share earned by the top 1 percent of the income distribution, as a measure of changing income inequality, for a smaller sample of countries. This analysis also includes indicators of electoral reform, specifically the extension of suffrage rights to include women in the electorate, and major electoral reforms (usually, the adoption of PR rules). Finally, this analysis includes an indicator of elections contested under SMD rules where, as seen in Figure 3.3, parties generally form more frequently.

In each of these specifications, the estimated effects for the key independent variable, local population change (δ_t), are consistently positive and (except in one case, Model 4, which is based on a restricted sample) meet conventional standards of statistical significance. Model 4, which incorporates measures of income inequality, is based on a considerably smaller sample of nine countries, with only a few countries included in early decades.[8] A conservative estimate

---

[8] Any country for which more than half of the time series was missing income inequality data was excluded.

(from Model 2) suggests that an increase in the rate of local population change, i.e., from an estimate of $\delta = 0.035$ (the fifth percentile), indicating an average rate of local population change that is three and a half percentage points greater than the national rate of population change, to $\delta = 0.278$ (the ninety-fifth percentile), is associated with an increase of almost two new parties entering electoral competition. This is a fairly substantial effect, that generally persists even when other factors thought to encourage new party formation are taken into account.

Periods of electoral reform, which most obviously change vote-to-seat mappings (intentionally), do not contribute to new party entry, possibly because existing elites may implement changes in electoral rules *in response* to the entry of strong challengers (e.g., Boix 2010). However, in those decades following the extension of suffrage rights to women, new parties frequently form. In fact, the strong effect of the extension of suffrage rights to women is maintained even in an analysis that includes an indicator for the 1920s, when most countries held their first universal-suffrage elections: this is a more general effect (see Model 2). On one hand, to the extent married couples sort on class or other social characteristics when they marry, the incorporation of women into the electorate does not obviously change the distribution of electoral power in a country. On the other hand, if political elites see the mobilizing of newly eligible voters, who are excluded from existing partisan networks, as a way to pursue their office-seeking goals, then extensions of franchise rights may represent real opportunities.

Other variables, like those that reflect changes in economic conditions, and which might signal changes in aggregate policy preferences, have more ambiguous effects (see Models 3 and 4). Decreases in GDP per capita, and increases in income inequality, appear to be associated with new party entry, but both relationships are estimated with considerable variance. Coefficients describing the effect of local population change, however, remain fairly consistent in magnitude in models that include these economic variables (even if their standard errors are increased in the smaller sample), suggesting that the opportunities created by changes in electoral geography are sustained, independently of potential changes in voter demands.

Appendix 3.A reports alternate specifications of the analysis presented in Table 3.2, including a negative binomial specification (which is appropriate for analysis of count measures) and probit specifications, in which the dependent variable is a binary indicator of whether more than two parties entered electoral competition in each decade. Again, in each specification, coefficients are positive, suggesting that higher rates of local population change are associated with new party entry (although the coefficients describing this key relationship are, in at least one case, estimated with considerable variance).

Although the concurrent trends towards less local population change, and fewer parties entering, are not especially stark (i.e., Great Britain deviates from both), one might worry that something else is contributing to both

TABLE 3.3. *Predicting new party entry (by decade).*

Decade	DV: New party entries			
	Local population change (δ_t)	Intercept	N	R^2
1880	4.392	1.188	10	0.180
	(3.319)	(0.773)		
1890	34.393[b]	−1.449	11	0.397
	(14.128)	(2.399)		
1900	52.577[a]	−3.463[b]	12	0.604
	(13.460)	(1.581)		
1910	9.238	4.699[a]	12	0.086
	(9.502)	(1.365)		
1920	−6.638	3.985[a]	13	0.057
	(8.151)	(1.121)		
1930	45.653[a]	−0.721	14	0.475
	(13.869)	(1.453)		
1940	22.742	−0.591	9	0.100
	(25.826)	(1.929)		
1950	−1.161	1.859	14	0.001
	(10.017)	(1.456)		
1960	5.567	1.725	15	0.021
	(10.465)	(1.449)		
1970	8.716	2.358	15	0.011
	(21.331)	(2.873)		
1980	19.435	1.165	15	0.248
	(9.377)	(1.194)		
1990	21.229	2.893	15	0.034
	(31.172)	(2.602)		
Full peacetime sample (excl. 1920, 1940, 1950)	12.474[a]	1.954[a]	119	0.074
	(1.954)	(0.571)		

Notes: This table reports coefficients, estimated in a series of regression models in which the dependent variable is the number of new parties entering electoral competition in each decade, as a function of local population change.
[a] $p < 0.01$.
[b] $p < 0.05$.

features of the developed democracies included in this analysis. As a way to demonstrate the robustness of the general result – that higher rates of local population are generally associated with more frequent party entry – Table 3.3 reports estimates from a series of regression models, one estimated for each decade. The strength of the relationship varies over time, but it is generally positive (although often estimated with substantial variance; note the small sample sizes), suggesting that recent local population change creates new opportunities for party entry. Further, the magnitude of the estimate for

1980, for example, implies a substantively large relationship (i.e., larger than the overall relationship), suggesting that local changes in the distribution of electoral power continue to structure incentives for political entrepreneurs. Those cases in which negative coefficients are estimated – 1920 and 1950 – correspond, of course, to the decades after the major world wars. Estimates of local population change for the previous decade are less reliable, and sometimes based on the previous two decades. Of course, it is also the case that these periods were not characterized by "normal" party politics. The restriction of the analysis to peacetime observations approximates the general bivariate result.

3.4   IMPLICATIONS

This chapter has provided evidence that is consistent with the idea that office-seeking elites appear to recognize electoral opportunities in those demographic changes that may also change the distribution of electoral power in their countries. Specifically, when population changes are concentrated – here, the proximate measure of a changing distribution of electoral power – new parties form more frequently. This empirical relationship is generally robust to the inclusion of other short-term changes that might contribute to demand for new political parties.

A skeptical reader might worry that the analysis presented in this chapter proceeds at a rather high level, that system-level measures of local population change and the inclusion of all new parties provides only a limited explanation of the origins of low-income peoples' parties. In fact, the analysis presented in this chapter has important implications for the analytic case studies presented in the next few chapters.

First, this chapter draws attention to the period around the turn of the twentieth century when there is significant local population change, at least in the cases considered here (the US, Canada, Great Britain, and Sweden).[9] Recall that, as Table 3.1 demonstrates, low-income peoples' parties often entered their first electoral contests during this early, pre-1940 period. Further, notice that a large proportion of these parties also contested their first elections under SMD electoral rules, when the implications of electoral geography (i.e., deviations from proportional vote-to-seat mappings), and perhaps the opportunities resulting from changes in local distributions of electoral power, are especially dramatic. Each of the following chapters examines the strategic entry decisions of low-income peoples' in SMD systems, following periods of important changes in the local distributions of electoral power.

Second, while the measure of local population change used in this chapter can be calculated for a fairly large number of countries, its generality may

---

[9]   One could imagine conducting a similar analytic case study on, for example, the strategic entry decisions of the Social Democratic Party, and eventually the Liberal Democrats, in the 1980s, in the UK.

obscure actual changes in the local distribution of electoral power. As suggested above, opportunities for new party entry exist only when local population changes concentrate members of a group in a way that alters the distribution of electoral power. It will be important, therefore, in the analytic case studies presented in the following chapters, to examine changes in the electoral power of low-income citizens, specifically. The general relationship between new party entry and local population change established in this chapter provides promising empirical support for this book's main argument about the importance of electoral geography to new party entry. By demonstrating that new parties enter where local population changes favor *their specific constituency*, the next few chapters will provide comparatively low-level understanding of the ways political entrepreneurs respond to changes in the distribution of electoral power.

The next four chapters, therefore, focus on new party entry decisions in several of the countries included in the broadly comparative analysis presented in this chapter. Specifically, in a series of analytic case studies on the American People's Party, Canadian CCF and Social Credit, British Labour, and the Swedish Social Democrats, Chapters 4–8 evaluate the formation and entry of these low-income peoples' parties: Where did these new parties recruit candidates in their first elections? How did their leaders allocate campaign resources? More generally, how did electoral geography structure their strategic entry and mobilization decisions?

While each of these case studies offers a unique perspective on the implications of changing electoral geography for the development of party systems, importantly, in each case, we see political entrepreneurs responding to very similar incentive structures. That is, in federal and unitary systems, in a presidential and in parliamentary systems, in systems with and without universal suffrage rights, and in systems with quite different patterns of migration, political entrepreneurs form parties in periods of local population change, and enter electoral competition in those districts where changes in local distributions of electoral power are most profound. These country case studies, then, are not meant to be contrasted in a way that is more common in comparative research. Rather, the end of this chapter marks a shift in the unit of analysis to the electoral district, properly seen as nested with each electoral contest. And, because district-level entry decisions reflect similar incentive structures, despite quite different electoral contexts, the accumulation of evidence presented in the following chapters is offered as strong support for the important role played by electoral geography in the development of party systems.

3.A APPENDIX: SUPPORTING MATERIALS

Calculations for European countries are based on data reported in Rothenbacher (2002) and Rothenbacher (2005). US state- and county-level estimates

TABLE 3.A.1. *Estimates of local population change.*

Country	Coverage period	Unit of analysis (D)	Mean (std. dev.)
Austria	1930–2000	State (9)	0.12 (0.16)
Belgium	1880–1930, 1950–2000	Arrondissement (43)	0.07 (0.02)
Canada	1910–2000	Province and territory (12)	0.15 (0.07)
Denmark	1880–2000	Region (14)	0.09 (0.06)
Finland	1920–1940, 1960–1990	Län (10)	0.06 (0.03)
France	1880–1930, 1950–2000	Department (85)	0.07 (0.03)
Germany	1880–1940, 1960–2000	Regierungsbezirk, Land (38)	0.13 (0.09)
Great Britain	1890–1930, 1950–2000	England: County. Scotland and Wales: Standard Region. (52)	0.12 (0.07)
Ireland	1880–2000	County (28)	0.07 (0.06)
Italy	1880, 1900–2000	Region (19)	0.06 (0.03)
Luxemburg	1880–1920, 1930–2000	Canton (13)	0.12 (0.05)
Norway	1890–2000	Amte/Fylke (19)	0.09 (0.06)
Sweden	1880–2000	Län (25)	0.08 (0.06)
Switzerland	1880–2000	Canton (26)	0.07 (0.02)
United States	1880–2000	County (3,411)	0.26 (0.16)

Notes: This table reports the countries and periods included in the analysis of local population change. The number of districts reported (i.e., D) is for 2000, or the latest year for which data are available.

are based on data reported by the Minnesota Population Center – National Historical Geographic Information System: Version 2.0 (total population by state, and county). Estimates for Canada are based on Statistics Canada (2014), "Table A2-14. Population of Canada, by Province, census dates, 1851–1976" and "Annual of Estimates of Population for Canada, Provinces and Territories, from July 1, 1971, to July 1, 2014."

TABLE 3.A.2. *Predicting new party entry (alternate model specifications).*

	(1) Negative binomial	(2) Probit (≥ 2 parties)	(3) Probit (≥ 2 parties)	(4) Probit (≥ 2 parties)
Local population	2.713^a	2.605^a	1.772	6.171^a
change (δ_t)	(1.009)	(1.402)	(1.397)	(2.614)
SMD electoral rules			0.554^b	
			(0.213)	
Suffrage expansion			0.600	
			(0.430)	
Electoral reform			0.257	
			(0.417)	
Change in GDP per capita				−1.453
				(1.001)
Change in top 1%				−0.088
income share				(0.874)
Intercept	0.782	−0.184	$−0.407^a$	−0.014
	(0.155)	(0.176)	(0.193)	(0.392)
α	1.050			
	(0.174)			
N	155	155	155	70
Pseudo R^2	0.009	0.041	0.061	0.086

Notes: This table reports coefficients, estimated in a series of regression models in which the dependent variable is the number of new parties entering electoral competition in each decade, or an indicator of whether two or more new parties entered electoral contests, in each decade as a function of local population change, electoral rules, and changing economic conditions.

[a] $p < 0.01$.

[b] $p < 0.05$.

4

The Populists and "Third-Party Men" in America

This chapter is about how American electoral geography changed during the late nineteenth and early twentieth centuries in the US, and how these changes created electoral opportunities for political entrepreneurs. The analysis presented in the previous chapter focused our attention on a key period – 1880 to 1900 – when local population change in the US was substantial. Of course, demographic changes, resulting from both internal migration and immigration during this period, receive ample academic attention. The demographic changes that are considered here, however, are more specific than the well-documented trends of movement towards the frontier, and of immigration to the cities of the American Northeast. How do these patterns of migration and immigration affect the distribution of electoral power across income groups? Where are low-income voters pivotal in the election of Representatives, and how does this change during this period? Is there evidence that the Populists – the most significant third party in the US – saw opportunities in the changing distribution of electoral power, and entered those districts where the changes were most profound?

This chapter considers these questions, and explores the circumstances under which political entrepreneurs coordinate across districts to form a new party and enter electoral competition, or will work within existing party networks to achieve their office-seeking and policy-making goals. Here, as suggested in Chapter 3, demographic changes created the electoral opportunity: when (1) low-income voters became increasingly concentrated, through migration and immigration as well as local economic shocks, and (2) such that they were pivotal (i.e., decisive in elections, forming the numerical majority) in a substantial number of electoral districts, political entrepreneurs were incentivized to coordinate across districts, form a new party, and enter electoral competition.

To provide some justification for the rigorous empirical analysis presented towards the end of this chapter, the next two sections first draw on historical materials to describe the electoral context as it was seen by the leaders of the Populists, arguably the most successful party that has challenged the American two-party system and elected seats in the House of Representatives. As we shall see, the Populists took positions that reflected the interests of a national low-income constituency. Further, the decision to enter electoral contests occurred on a district-by-district basis, and party leaders were seen as "third-party men". That is, the early party organizers were political entrepreneurs who organized the party as the optimal way to pursue their office-seeking goals and recruited candidates in those districts where the balance of electoral power had recently changed in favor of low-income voters.

This chapter begins with a brief overview of the American political economy at the end of the nineteenth century, and then provides a fairly detailed account of the empirical foundation of this analysis, and the construction of the datasets that describe the electoral geographies of income, for 1880 and 1892. Then, drawing largely on historical and newspaper accounts of the "third-party men" who bore the costs of establishing and mobilizing the People's Party, this chapter provides a qualitative analysis of their strategic decision-making. Finally, estimates of the changing electoral power of low-income voters are incorporated, in the final section, into an analysis of the strategic entry decisions of People's Party candidates.

4.1 THE AMERICAN POLITICAL ECONOMY, 1880–1900

When the People's Party announced their Omaha platform in 1892, they confronted a highly regionalized economy, with industrialization occurring rapidly, predominantly in the North, and the southern and western regions dominated by cotton and grain production, respectively. As Bensel (2000, 21) writes, the differences between the North and elsewhere, at least with regards to economic structure, are hard to overstate:

Imagining for a moment the national economy as one in which industry and agriculture were the only two pursuits, regional specialization at the turn of the century was nothing short of spectacular. At one end, Rhode Island's per capita production of manufactured goods was almost twenty-nine times as great as the state's agricultural output. At the other end, North Dakota's agricultural production stood at more than seven times the state's industrial production.

But North Dakota and the other western states shared only their reliance on agricultural production with the southern states. The per capita value of agricultural goods in the West, for example, far exceeded the per capita value of agricultural production in the South. These regional differences generally coincide with variation in other economic attributes, including value added in manufacturing, rates of technological innovation and adult literacy, as well as wealth and income. When Bensel (2000) combines indicators of these several dimensions of economic well-being to develop a broad index of economic development estimated for each county, familiar regions emerge. Although there is some variation within each region, and for each measure, most counties in the Northeast are ranked among the "most advanced," with counties in the West taking values of three or four (out of five). Counties in the Midwest typically rank one or two, while southern counties take values consistently below the national average on each dimension, and score zero on Bensel's index of economic development. In her analysis of the role of the agrarian movement in the development of the modern American state, Sanders (1999, 19) similarly describes the cotton South as the "most truly peripheral to the modern industrial economy."

Regional variation in form of economic production had important implications for the structure of class conflict, and ultimately for national party politics. Although this summary is brief, and perhaps oversimplifies the complex nature of American politics at the end of the nineteenth century, it will be helpful in illustrating the nature of the Populists' strategic decisions. In the Northeast and industrial Midwest, political conflicts reflected the interests of industrial labor and capital. In the South, cleavage structures reflected the legacy of slavery and the continued production of cotton. Black sharecroppers and tenants had significant reasons to mistrust white plantation owners and merchants, on whom they relied for the provision of supplies and support until their crops could be brought to market. Finally, where single-family farms dominated, typically in the West, political conflict was structured by agricultural workers' complaints of exploitation by eastern banks and railroad owners.

These political economic conflicts mapped uneasily into national party politics, in a way that corresponds to class or income group cleavages. For example, while the Republican party was seen as the major agent of northern industrialization, the Republicans also served as the (largely symbolic) guarantor of civil rights for southern blacks. As a consequence, the Democrats typically aligned with labor in the north, but upper class whites in the South. In the West, where agricultural workers depended on the well-being of eastern families who would purchase their products, and where low-income families benefited from what Bensel (2000, 235) refers to as the "cross-cutting elements of the Republican program," including pension payments to Union veterans and local infrastructure development, support for the Republicans was generally widespread.

Because of these regional differences in their bases of support, Republicans and Democrats represented complicated coalitions that varied in composition, in different parts of the country, but not in a way that was strongly correlated with levels of economic development. Bensel (2000) finds, for example, that average levels of support for the Republican presidential candidate in 1892,

Benjamin Harrison, range from 44 to 49 percent, when counties are grouped into his top five levels of economic development. Only in the "least advanced" category (i.e., typically in the South), does the average level of support drop to about 26 percent. Variation in support for the Democratic candidate, Grover Cleveland, across levels of development, is slightly more systematic, with strongest levels of support observed in the lowest and highest economic development categories, but never below 38 percent (observed in the "middle low" category). A further consequence of the complicated partisan coalitions is that neither party formed a national majority, and electoral competition was intense. "The culmination of the 1892 election season," Brewer and Stonecash (2009, 47) write, "found America's two major parties in an uneasy stalemate. Both could attain power nationally, and both had a chance to win elections in every region except for the South, where the Democrats were firmly in control. But each could also just as easily lose elections and power. Uncertainty existed for both the Democrats and Republicans, contributing further to the close partisan divide."

The intensity of the electoral competition was reflected in local party organizations, as well. Jensen (1971, 165) writes, "The parties were army-like organizations, tightly knit, disciplined and united. All the voters, save for a few stragglers and mercenaries," – possibly migrants and immigrants fell into these categories – "belonged to one or the other army, and the challenge of the campaign was the mobilization of the full party strength at the polls on election day." This competitiveness likely heightened the established parties' costs associated with responding to changes in American electoral geography, and to changes in the distribution of electoral power. Note that it was not the case that parties were rigid in their ideologies (see, e.g., Sanders 1999).[1] Rather, it was the strength of local partisan networks – the groups to which they were affiliated – that may have limited their abilities to respond to newly pivotal low-income voters. For example, Jensen (1971, 165) describes the importance of German immigrants, who had "emerged as a large, cohesive bloc of voters" in the 1892 election, "organized and united, but uncontrolled."

As we shall see in the next few sections, in fact, the late nineteenth century is marked by important economic and demographic changes that dramatically altered at least local distributions of electoral power, and created important opportunities for new party entry. The leaders of the People's Party would recognize these opportunities, recruit candidates in those districts where there were profound changes in which groups were pivotal, and attempt to build a national constituency of low-income voters.[2]

---

[1]   Indeed, as Hirano (2008) shows, incumbent House members (from both parties) failed to alter their legislative behavior either in response to formal Populist entry or in response to the economic changes that Bensel (2000) and others (e.g., Brewer & Stonecash 2009, Sanders 1999) identify with latent demand for populist candidates.
[2]   James (2006), in particular, has argued that Democratic presidential candidates in particular attempted to build a national farmer–Northern worker coalition, but as Stonecash and Silina

The next section will walk through the development of a map that characterizes the electoral geography of income at the end of the nineteenth century, and identify districts where low-income voters became pivotal in election outcomes. Specifically, the next section will show where electoral opportunities for new parties emerged through the demographic and economic changes of the 1880s, and will provide the measure of the key independent variable in this analysis.

4.2 MAPPING EARLY ELECTORAL GEOGRAPHIES OF INCOME

Individual-level census data, in combination with data describing elections, provide the empirical foundations of the analyses presented in the next few chapters. Without the individual-level data, it would be extremely difficult to track the changes in the electoral geography of income that create the electoral opportunities for new party entry, for several reasons:

- First, the levels of aggregation used in official *reports* rarely coincide with electoral districts. American census data from this period are often reported at the level of counties, for example, or wards within cities, which have boundaries that only sometimes coincide with congressional district boundaries. Individual-level data, however, usually include low-level geographic information (enumeration districts that, in cities, roughly correspond to blocks) and can be matched to electoral districts with a high degree of accuracy. (More on this below.)
- Second, census reports are usually more inclusive than electorates. The 1880 electorate, for example, officially included all men over the age of twenty-one. However, because sometimes formal and often informal suffrage restrictions limited the electoral power of African Americans, political entrepreneurs may have had few incentives to mobilize African American communities, even with their exclusion from local partisan networks. Individual-level census data allow this analysis to be replicated for the population as a whole, therefore, as well as more restrictive electorates.
- Finally, with historical information about wages and salaries, individual-level census data can be used to examine the composition of electoral districts, including the concentration of poverty *within* districts, and overall and within-district levels of income inequality.

Individual-level census data, like those made available through the University of Minnesota Population Center (the North Atlantic Population Project and IPUMS) and the Canadian Century Research Infrastructure, therefore,

---

(2005) report, prior to 1896 the class basis of the established parties was uncertain. Others (especially Jensen 1971) have suggested that other cultural or ethnic identities were more important to the definition of partisan electoral coalitions.

provide a new opportunity to study the implications of electoral geography for political economics: They provide information that more closely approximates the on-the-ground view of contemporary strategic actors than the official census reports.

Beginning with these individual-level data, this analysis followed four steps to generate maps of the electoral geography of income in each country: First, for each census period, census geography is matched to electoral geography, and census datasets are restricted to eligible voters. Second, using historical and archival resources, income and wages are estimated as precisely as possible for occupation or industry groups. Then, the electoral power of low-income voters is assessed for each electoral district, and for each census period. Finally, this analysis concludes by examining the relationship between the change in the electoral power of low-income voters and new party entries into local electoral contests.

This section provides a fairly detailed description of this process in a context that will likely be familiar to the reader, with the goal of identifying challenges associated with this strategy, and the ways in which these challenges have been addressed. Future chapters will limit this description to sections on supporting material, highlighting only those challenges that are unique to each case. In the end, this section will provide a more detailed picture of the American political economy at the end of the nineteenth century, and will specifically identify those districts that represented an electoral opportunity for the recruitment of new party candidates.

Step 1. Matching Census Geography to Electoral Geography

The first step in this analysis involves matching the smallest geographic units in each case to their corresponding electoral district boundaries. For each individual appearing in the 1880 US census, this geographic unit is their enumeration district. Enumeration districts are typically those areas covered by a single census enumerator, are unique within counties, and vary in size across censuses. For most of the country, during the late nineteenth century, congressional district boundaries coincided with county boundaries, and so the allocation of individuals to congressional districts was relatively straight-forward. For example, the first district of New York, for the Forty-Seventh Congress (1881–1883, elected in 1880) was comprised of Suffolk, Queens, and Richmond counties.

In cities, however, congressional district boundaries often correspond to local political boundaries (e.g., wards and assembly districts), or are defined by streets: New York's eighth district included wards 9, 15, 16, and "that portion of 18 lying within 14th St., 26th St., and Fourth and Sixth Aves." (Martis 1982, 248). In these cases, maps or descriptions of enumeration districts were used to match households to this and other urban districts; enumeration districts were small enough – often only a city block – that they rarely straddled congressional

TABLE 4.1. *Matching US census geography to electoral geography.*

	1880	1900
Census units	255 counties	269 counties
	18,381 enumeration districts	24,000 enumeration districts
Electoral units	293 congressional districts	352 congressional districts

Note: This table reports the numbers of nested census geographic units which matched to the corresponding electoral units for the 1880 and 1900 censuses.

districts' boundaries.[3] In the end, almost 99 percent of the potentially voting eligible populations were allocated according to the boundaries that defined the Forty-Seventh and Fifty-Third US Congresses. (Very rarely, a household cannot be allocated to a specific congressional district, and is excluded from the analysis.)

As suggested above, a second important advantage that comes from working with individual-level census data is the ability to restrict analysis to eligible voters. Suffrage was nationally restricted to male citizens, aged twenty-one and older, until 1920. Registration requirements, white primaries, literacy tests, and poll taxes, however, combined to dramatically restrict the suffrage rights of African Americans and poor whites in the South; individual-level census data makes it possible to investigate the implications of this disenfranchisement by restricting the analysis to white native-born citizens. Table 4.2 reports the characteristics of the full (or sample) individual-level dataset, and the size of smaller samples, reduced by various suffrage restrictions.

Step 2. Estimating Historical Wages

Once eligible voters were allocated to their electoral districts, the second task in generating a map of the electoral geography of income required estimating their earnings and incomes. Here, information about each individual's industry or occupation, and, in a few cases, their geographic location, provided the basis of these estimates. Although there was significant interest in the characteristics of national income distributions on both sides of the Atlantic during the late nineteenth century (see, e.g., Wright 1900), income data were not routinely collected by censuses. (Canadian censuses began collecting income data in

---

3   The timing of redistricting can complicate the allocation of city wards and assembly districts to congressional districts. The ward and assembly district boundaries that were used to define the forty-seventh congressional district boundaries in New York, for example, were revised before the census, which describes enumeration districts with reference to the new boundaries. In cases like New York in 1881 (also, St. Louis), old boundary maps also provided an important link between American census and electoral geography.

TABLE 4.2. *Defining the American electorate in 1880 and 1900.*

	1880 100% census	1900 5% sample
Adult men, aged 21 and over per congressional district	8,782,473 42,483 (30,250–66,450)	843,849 2,350 (1,538–3,777)
White native-born men Votes cast in presidential election[a]	5,991,623 9,210,420	701,825 13,970,470

Notes: This table reports estimates of the total national electorate, based on the US 1880.

[a] Rusk (2001).

1910.) Instead, the primary source for American wage data is *The First Annual Report of the Commissioner of Labor* (1886), which reports data collected through surveys of firms. In 1885, the Bureau of Labor dispatched fifteen field agents to gather data about wages and the costs of living and production from "about forty industries, seven hundred and fifty-nine establishments, and about one hundred and fifty thousand employees" (although only 582 reported wage data) with the goal of understanding the variation of wages in different parts of the country. Because of this extensive coverage, and because the data are reported separately for men, women, and children, with the average number of days and hours worked in each occupation category, the Bureau of Labor Statistics (BLS) data are generally recognized as the best available for this period (Long 1960, 9). Nevertheless, the BLS wage data are available only for those in manufacturing jobs.

For this analysis, earnings estimates for other trade and service occupations were compiled from a second BLS report (Wright 1900) that standardized and reported all wage data included in other national or state-level official reports from 1886 to 1900. This second resource offers two important advantages: First, wage data are often reported at the state level, allowing better estimates of national averages; when estimates are reported for enough states, state-level estimates of wages for a particular occupation and year are used instead. (This allows for some cost-of-living differences to be accommodated in estimates of income.) Second, wage data are reported for narrower occupation-industry categories (rather than industry categories, which provide the basis of data reported in the first BLS report). For those industries in which industry-wide averages are not available, this analysis estimates wages for the most frequently held occupation in each industry category.

To make wage imputations for agricultural workers, this analysis draws on the US Department of Agriculture Bureau of Statistics report, *Wages of Farm Labor*, which lists average monthly earnings, with board, for farmers and agricultural workers, by state. These data were originally collected and reported by crop correspondents (volunteers who would write reports on local weather and crop conditions); Holmes (1914) then standardized the measures and periods to provide averages for each state and year. One might worry that the use of wage data would be especially misleading for agricultural workers: they may have had access to resources that are not reflected in reports of annual wages. In fact, it is more likely that cash incomes of agricultural workers are *overestimated* – and yet, as will be discussed, they often still fall short of estimates of poverty thresholds from this period.[4]

Finally, information on the salaries of professionals, teachers, and public servants from this period comes from a variety of resources. For professionals (not clerks or bookkeepers) in finance, insurance, and real estate, this analysis uses the salary of members of the House of Representatives ($5,000). Similarly, the average salary of federal district judges ($3,391) serves as an approximate estimate for legal professionals. Estimates of teachers' salaries are state specific, and are based on the Annual Report of the Commissioner for Education.

In sum, this strategy yields at least 170 distinct wage or salary estimates for each census period. All wage data are reported as (real) annual salaries, and are calculated only for full-time male workers. Figure 4.1 reports the average wages for each industry category; Appendix 4.A provides more technical details.

Three aspects of the data reported in Figure 4.1 should be noted: First, this strategy yields reasonable wage estimates for over 90 percent of the male, economically active population for each census period. Those occupations without wage and salary data typically represent small proportions of the adult male population – and very small proportions of any congressional district. Further, most of the occupations without wage data are relatively high-earning, and are unlikely to complicate estimates of low-income voters' electoral power.

Second, just over half of the American labor force works in the agricultural sector, and with very low earnings. This share of agricultural workers in the

4 As late as 1940, there was "considerable overlap among the three classes of agricultural workers – operators, unpaid family workers, and hired workers. Sharecroppers and share tenants are customarily grouped in the operator category, although in terms of economic status there is often little difference between them and wage workers" (Ducoff 1945, 21). Further, Ducoff (1945, 22) reports that "many agricultural workers do not remain in any one category during the course of a year. Operators of low-income farms may also work for wages on other farms, and unpaid family workers may work for pay for a while on the family farm or on another farm." Agricultural workers may also receive use of dwelling and gardens, as well as a stable and feed for livestock, food, firewood, and so forth (Holmes 1914, 49). For all agricultural workers, this analysis uses "average wages of outdoor labor of men on farms, per month, in hiring by the year, with board" (Holmes 1914, 30, 32). Annual earnings are calculated by multiplying monthly wages by twelve, rather than eight, which is more standard for agricultural workers, to capture the flexibility in position and near-cash benefits agricultural workers receive. Although these data are available only for 1909, Holmes (1914, 52) estimates the average cash values of in-kind benefits to range from about $7 to about $21 each month – between about a third and one full month of the national average monthly wage.

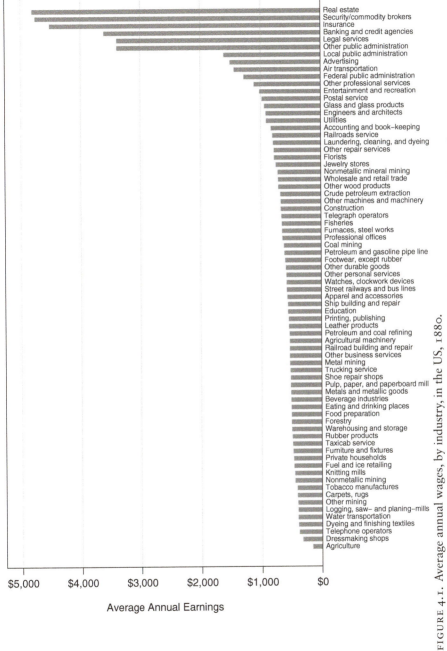

Real estate
Security/commodity brokers
Insurance
Banking and credit agencies
Legal services
Other public administration
Local public administration
Advertising
Air transportation
Federal public administration
Other professional services
Entertainment and recreation
Postal service
Glass and glass products
Engineers and architects
Utilities
Accounting and book-keeping
Railroads service
Laundering, cleaning, and dyeing
Other repair services
Florists
Jewelry stores
Nonmetallic mineral mining
Wholesale and retail trade
Other wood products
Crude petroleum extraction
Other machines and machinery
Construction
Telegraph operators
Fisheries
Furnaces, steel works
Professional offices
Coal mining
Petroleum and gasoline pipe line
Footwear, except rubber
Other durable goods
Other personal services
Watches, clockwork devices
Street railways and bus lines
Apparel and accessories
Ship building and repair
Education
Printing, publishing
Leather products
Petroleum and coal refining
Agricultural machinery
Railroad building and repair
Other business services
Metal mining
Trucking service
Shoe repair shops
Pulp, paper, and paperboard mill
Metals and metallic goods
Beverage industries
Eating and drinking places
Food preparation
Forestry
Warehousing and storage
Rubber products
Taxicab service
Furniture and fixtures
Private households
Fuel and ice retailing
Knitting mills
Nonmetallic mining
Tobacco manufactures
Carpets, rugs
Other mining
Logging, saw- and planing-mills
Water transportation
Dyeing and finishing textiles
Telephone operators
Dressmaking shops
Agriculture

$5,000 $4,000 $3,000 $2,000 $1,000 $0

Average Annual Earnings

FIGURE 4.1. Average annual wages, by industry, in the US, 1880.

Notes: This figure reports average annual wages for each industry category. Details of sources are provided in the main text.

TABLE 4.3. *Characteristics of the American national income distributions, 1880, 1900, and 2010.*

	1880	1900	2010
Gini index	0.421	0.494	0.469
Income ratios of selected percentiles			
90/10	6.21	8.25	11.67
95/50	3.96	3.11	3.66
50/10	1.72	3.67	4.15
Shares of household income quintiles			
Q1	6%	4%	3%
Q2	10%	7%	9%
Q3	10%	14%	15%
Q4	36%	36%	23%
Q5	48%	39%	50%

Notes: This table reports characteristics of the national income distributions for the US in 1880 and 1900. For comparison, the same statistics are reported for the current American income distributions.
Source: US (2010): Current Population Reports, Series P60-204. "Table A-3. Selected Measures of Household Income Dispersion: 1967 to 2010."

American labor force, of course, far exceeds the proportion of British workers (about 10 percent) devoted to agriculture, for example, but is similar to the proportion of agricultural workers in Canada and Sweden.

Finally, Table 4.3 provides a summary of the national income distributions, and indeed, measures of the levels of inequality for each census period, alongside contemporary measures of income inequality. Note the remarkable similarity in the historical and contemporary estimates of income inequality for each period. There is some evidence that earnings increases have recently been concentrated among the highest quintile of income earners. However, the structure of the income distribution that we observe in the late nineteenth century data, in quintile shares and in the income level ratios, is replicated in the current income distribution (see also Piketty 2014).

Step 3. Estimating Electoral Power

A key challenge in analyzing changes in electoral geography – that is, changes in the way a group's votes map into seats – lies in the number of different ways groups can be identified. Absolute poverty thresholds (e.g., the official US poverty line) complicate comparisons of the number of seats that, for example, a low-income voting bloc might elect, because the size of the group might vary over time and across cases. To facilitate a comparative analysis of the implications of electoral geography, low-income citizens are defined here as the first third of the national (market) income distribution. In the US, this corresponds to an annual salary of less than $166 in 1880 and about $200 in 1890. Note that these estimates are quite a bit lower than Hunter's (1904, 52) "most conservative" poverty thresholds of $300 per year[5] for an average-sized family in the South and $460 in the North.[6] In fact, other observers estimated that about half of the American population would be considered "very poor," and another 38 percent would be "poor" (Spahr 1900, cited in Hunter 1904, 45). The thresholds used here, therefore, undoubtedly focus attention on the most desperate families during this period – a group with significant grievance, but with how much electoral power?[7]

To estimate the electoral power of low-income citizens during this period, Figure 4.2 builds on the first two steps in this analysis, matching electoral and census geography and estimating wages on the basis of occupation, industry, and location, to calculate the share of low-income voters in each electoral district, and changes in this share over time. Figure 4.2(a) reports the percentage of each congressional district electorate earning low incomes in 1892; Figure 4.2(b) reports estimates of how much this percentage changed over the previous decade, and therefore identifies changes in local distributions of electoral power – or, if the argument presented here is correct, opportunities for new party entry.

Two cautionary notes are in order: First, almost all of the individual records collected in the 1890 census were destroyed in a fire in 1921. To estimate the geographic distribution of low-income voters in 1892, this analysis assumes that most of the movement observed between 1880 and 1900 occurred between 1880 and 1892 – as is suggested by county-level census data – and that most individuals did not change their occupations between 1890 and 1900.[8] Then, individuals observed in the 1900 census were matched to 1892 congressional

---

5 This income amount corresponds roughly to the sixty-fifth percentile of the income distribution in Southern states in 1900
6 This amount corresponds to the thirty-fifth percentile in Northern states.
7 One might worry that, by using a threshold based on the national income distribution, differences in the concentration of low-income citizens merely reflect differences in the cost of living. As noted in the text, however, state- or region-specific estimates of wages are used whenever data were sufficient. Consequently, some of these differences are incorporated into estimates of national income distribution.
8 Although individual-level records were destroyed, official census-level reports remain, including county-level population estimates. At least the rank order of county-level population estimates is stable between 1890 and 1900, with correlation estimates of approximately 0.97. (This correlation is slightly lower between 1880 and 1900, at 0.96.) In those counties with the largest population increases (those in the upper quartile), an average of about 57 percent of the increase occurred between 1880 and 1890; in those counties that saw their populations decline, about 74 percent of the change occurred between 1880 and 1890.
  The assumption of stability in occupations is also generally reasonable. Using the North Atlantic Population Project (NAPP) linked census data, about 55 percent of those who were working in 1880 were working in the same industry in 1900. This percentage is higher among

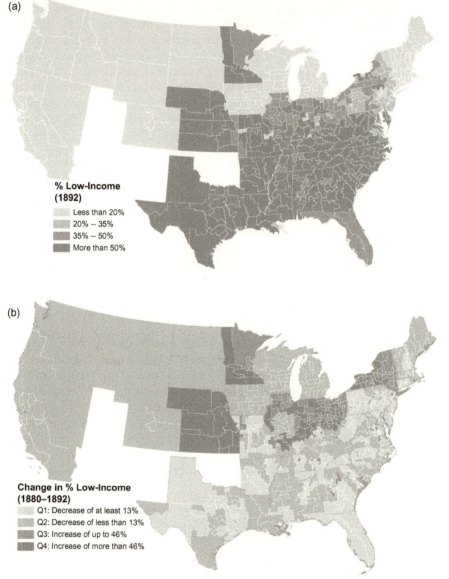

FIGURE 4.2. The changing electoral geography of low-income voters in the US, 1880–1892.

Sources: See the main text for details of how the wage data were collected. Congressional district boundary file: Lewis *et al.* (2013). State boundary file: National Historical Geographical Information System (NHGIS).

district boundaries. To estimate the electoral geography of income, I have used wage data reported for 1890, allowing for local shocks in earnings to be accommodated. While this strategy likely overestimates population movement between 1880 and 1890, to the extent that this bias exists, it introduces variance into later analysis. If parties enter where local population changes most favor low-income voters, and local changes in population are, in some places, exaggerated, this should reduce the predictive value of my measure of change in the electoral power of low-income voters, and increase the variance with which coefficients describing this relationship are estimated.

The second challenge, evident in the data presented in Figure 4.2, concerns the calculation of changes in local distributions of electoral power when district boundaries change along with demography. During this period, states redrew electoral district boundaries according to their own (often irregular) schedules, and sometimes several times within a decade (see Martis 1982). To estimate changes in the electoral power of low-income voters between 1881 and 1892, this analysis used Lewis *et al.*'s (2013) digital shape files of congressional district boundaries to generate (area-) weighted estimates of the change in the proportion of low-income eligible voters, between 1881 and 1892.[9] In Figure 4.2(b), 1,892 district boundaries are reported with white lines; variation in shading, within districts, identifies cases of changing district boundaries.

With these challenges noted, we can begin our analysis of the changing electoral geography of income. In Figure 4.2, we see very clear geographic concentrations of low-income citizens in the South, and also in the Midwest in 1892 – Sanders's (1999) periphery, and precisely the areas Bensel (2000) identifies as least developed. What is also clear, however, is that *changes* in the electoral geography of income were also geographically concentrated. For example, we observe substantial increases in the percentage of low-income citizens, especially in the Midwest. In most congressional districts in the South, however, the concentration low-income citizens *decreased* between 1880 and 1892.

By focusing on the changing electoral power of low-income voters within districts, this analysis is especially well suited to evaluate how political entrepreneurs assessed entry decisions: Are political entrepreneurs taking advantage of *new* opportunities when they coordinate across districts and form new parties? Are political entrepreneurs, for example, mobilizing movers and immigrants who may come without strong party ties? Or, do political entrepreneurs see advantages in mobilizing groups with long-standing

the 67 percent who did not move during this period – about 62 percent – and lower among those who moved to a new state, about 40 percent.

9 An alternative approach using linked census data, in which individuals could be located within overlapping district "fragments," provided weights for estimates of change in the percent of low-income voters. In practice, however, large numbers of district fragments with small numbers of eligible voters undermined the success of this approach.

grievances and new electoral power? These questions may be best addressed
with the qualitative evidence of party strategy presented below, but it is helpful
to consider as well what drives the changes to the electoral power of low-income
voters that we observe in Figure 4.2.

Several districts in Michigan, for example, observe a dramatic increase in
the share of men with earnings that fall in the first third of the national income
distribution: almost no one falls into in this category in 1880, but in 1892,
about 50 percent of adult men have low incomes. Partly, this reflects the
changing fortunes of Michigan's farmers, who were doing considerably better
in 1880 relative to the national average earnings for agricultural workers than
they were in 1900. Holmes (1914) estimates that average monthly earnings
in 1880 for agricultural workers in Michigan and nationally were $16.58
and $11.70, respectively. In 1890, Michigan farmers earned an average of
$16.75, while the national average had increased to $14.59. Note that these
earnings estimates put Michigan farmers above the poverty threshold in 1880
(i.e., in the second third of the national income distribution), but below the
1900 low-income threshold. Similar changes in local conditions contribute to
changes in the electoral power of low-income voters in Kansas, as well.

How does internal migration correspond to changes in the local distribution
of electoral power during the late nineteenth century? Because income
is estimated for occupational categories, and migrants tended to take on
occupations with higher earnings, assessing the relationship between migration
and low-income status is complicated. Linked census data, however, provide
some leverage on this question. Overall, about 30 percent of men who were
of voting age in 1900 reported living in a different county or state in 1880;
about a quarter of these had relocated to a different region. In districts where
low-income voters formed the numerical majority in 1900, recent migrants
accounted for an average of 32 percent of eligible voters – and formed the
clear majority in 21 of these 130 districts. Put slightly differently, in districts
in which low-income voters were pivotal, low-income migrants composed
about 20 percent of the electorate; elsewhere, low-income migrants represented
only 4 percent of eligible voters. All of this suggests that internal migrants
represented an important source of the changing electoral geography that
created opportunities for new party entry. (See also the later analysis of the
People's Party strategic entry in 1896.)

The third source of changing electoral geography during this period, of
course, is immigration. Like internal migrants, immigrants tended to hold
occupations with higher earnings, making the relationship between immigration and low-income status difficult to assess (see Abramitzky, Boustan, &
Eriksson 2014). Nevertheless, during this period, the proportion of immigrants
earning low incomes in 1900, by my estimates, was quite high in the Midwest
(about 17 percent) and in the South (39 percent). In districts where the electoral
power of low-income voters increased between 1880 and 1900, immigrants

comprised about 18 percent of the total district electorate, compared to 7 percent elsewhere.

Finally, American electoral geography was also intentionally altered between 1880 and 1892 when, after the Tenth Census, the size of the House of Representatives was increased by thirty-two seats, and again in 1891 by twenty-four seats. Seats were also added as North and South Dakota, Montana, Washington, Idaho, Wyoming, and Utah were admitted as states. These changes in the size of the chamber coincided with an increase of *eighteen districts* in which low-income voters were pivotal, for a total "delegation" of 138 Representatives. Although the total electoral power of low-income citizens – that is, the share of the seats a low-income bloc can elect – remained at about 40 percent, these new districts nevertheless represented an opportunity for party entry and for the mobilization of low-income voters.

Summary

This section of the discussion has described, in considerable detail, the construction of district-level datasets that characterize the electoral geography of income in the US during this early period. Similar procedures were followed for each of the other countries included in this analysis; technical sections at the end of each chapter will summarize the technical aspects of each case, as well as general data processing notes. Hopefully, the detail offered here is sufficient to persuade a skeptical reader that these historical electoral geographies have been carefully constructed from primary, usually contemporaneous, sources and provide meaningful and reliable descriptions of the electoral context that would-be political entrepreneurs faced.

What is clear, in the American case and for the Populists, is that major changes in low-income voters' electoral power were concentrated primarily in the Midwest, as well as a few districts in the Northeast. Changes in the distribution of electoral power in the South – where we might expect a low-income people's party to enter if new parties simply responded to voter demands – tend to favor *other* income groups, with a few exceptions. That is, if the political entrepreneurs who established the People's Party recognized electoral opportunities in those places where changes in distributions of electoral power are most profound, we should expect them to most often recruit candidates more frequently in the Midwest, West, and some parts of the Northeast, but less frequently in the South.

The next section of this chapter introduces these "third-party men" and provides some more qualitative evidence of their strategic decision-making. Their recruitment and entry decisions are then evaluated more rigorously in an analysis that also accommodates other explanations for Populist entry decisions, before this chapter concludes with a discussion of the Populists' ultimate collapse and the few other third parties that have entered American electoral competition.

4.3   THE FORMATION OF THE PEOPLE'S PARTY

In his analysis of the formation of the Populist Party, Hicks (1928, 219) describes the task of political entrepreneurs in this way:

Those who have tried within recent years to found a new political party in the United States will be quick to agree that the task is not a light one. It is not merely that the inertia of the American voter is great and his adherence to party tradition firm; there are yet other obstacles to be overcome. The mere business of getting convinced reformers together in sufficient numbers to justify formal organization; the problem of inducing men who are notably contentious to agree upon any common platform or plan of action; the creation of a party machine by which candidates may be named, campaigns conducted, and elections carried—these things constitute some of the initial difficulties that the would-be reformers must confront.

In fact, the formation of the People's Party resulted from the explicit and strategic decisions of "third-party men" – office-seekers, who worked carefully to build a national coalition, mobilized three constituencies: confederated labor, the "silver men," and especially the Farmers' Alliance. Over the course of 1891 and 1892, a series of conventions – labor in St. Louis, the silver men in Denver, and the Alliance in Cincinnati – consolidated the purpose and organization of each group, so that when delegates representing each interest finally convened in Omaha, Nebraska in July 1892, "the new People's Party [was] a unit in its aggregation and combination of the tremendous organized forces." An Alliance leader stated that each of "those several conventions ... were all preliminary steps in an admirably-formulated plan for effective action in the coming campaign" ("Nimble Rainbow Chasers," *The New York Times*, July 3, 1892). This series of conventions led not only to the establishment of a national council, through which Ignatius Donnelly, an early organizer and "third-party man," and others who were committed to a third party, simply assumed leadership positions – "they were in on the ground floor" (Hicks 1928, 238) – but also to the announcement of a party platform that would serve to mobilize the People's Party.

What becomes clear in a careful reading of accounts of the People's Party development is that this "plan" proceeded in a way that was sensitive to local distributions of electoral power. Especially in the Midwest, where the electoral power of low-income voters increased by an average of 25 percent across districts, party leaders worked hard to coordinate and mobilize the often newly pivotal voters in support of the new party. In St. Louis, in June 1891, the People's leadership "decided to make a special fight in Ohio, Mississippi, Kentucky, and Iowa" ("Just as Hopeful as Ever," *The New York Times*, June 14, 1891). About a year later, Ignatius Donnelly, described the organization in this way:

The country is awake on this third party, as it has not been on any questions since the war. Some compare it with the Greenback movement. The situation is different.

The movement is more widespread. We have now 5,000,000 voters in the Alliance. We are sure to carry several States in the next election, and I anticipate that the party will carry the national election in 1892. The growth of the party is rapid. In Minnesota there are now 1,338 Alliances, which have grown up in two years. We have in that State 50,000 voters. I believe we shall carry the State. We are sure of Kansas.

The movement is growing in Wisconsin, where more than a hundred Alliances have been started within a year. Nebraska is strongly Alliance and, I expect, will be carried at the next election by our party. In Ohio the movement is new, but has grown remarkably. ("Just as Hopeful as Ever," *The New York Times*, June 14, 1891)

Clearly, the People's Party benefited from existing Alliance organizations as it tried to mobilize its supporters. But the party leadership also invested heavily in local party organizations – newspaper accounts document Donnelly's extensive travels and mobilization efforts, for example – and had substantial opportunities to exercise discretion over local candidates. As Hofstadter (1955, 101) and others write (e.g., Hall 1967), the local People's candidates were rarely farmers, but more often were "a ragged elite of professional men, rural editors, third party veterans, and professional reformers." They were, in Chhibber and Kollman's (2004) terms, "local notables." And, incentives to recruit local elites may have been enhanced by the relatively limited People's Party funds (Hofstadter 1955, 102).

The Populists' mobilization efforts were also deeply earnest in their attempts to mobilize industrial laborers. As Sanders (1999) writes, "By virtue of the dominance and exploitation of large corporate and financial interests, farmers and workers occupied similar positions in the social and economic order. The redemption of the state to serve the interests of ordinary people, and its use to affect the democratization of the industrial and commercial economy, would serve both" agricultural and industrial workers – an idea, while less prevalent in the writings of contemporary trade union leaders, that featured prominently in the arguments of Populist leaders. In their call to "Laboring men of America!" the political entrepreneurs who founded the People's Party quite clearly had a national, low-income constituency in mind (see, e.g., Knoles 1943).[10]

Like the cases of British Labour and the Swedish Social Democrats, as we shall see, the political entrepreneurs who established the People's Party also confronted the question of whether to work within established parties. In fact, Donnelly and other Populist leaders were explicitly rejected by the established party leadership (the Democrats, in Donnelly's case), despite attempts at "fusion" (Hicks 1931, 258). They approached entry into each state's contest deliberately, and in some cases were successful in working within local Democratic or Republican parties. While in the South the Populists

---

10 American Federation of Labor President Samuel Gompers (1892, 93) refuted these efforts of "*employing* farmers," noting that their interests diverged from the interests of "*employed* farmers." Nevertheless, Gompers suggests that the People's Party offers more to workers than "any similar party heretofore gracing the Presidential political area."

sometimes mobilized black voters to challenge Democratic white supremacy, the Southern Alliance men more often took control of the Democratic Party and used their organization as its own. "[They] will take no chances whatever, by dividing the Democratic vote, and so, while the Farmers' Alliance will exist as an organization, its members will vote with *their old parties*" ("Democrats will be Democrats," *The New York Times*, April 9, 1891; emphasis added). Another observer made the point more explicitly: "The Democratic party at the South is something more than a mere political organization striving to enforce an administrative policy. It is a white man's party" (*People's Party Paper*, August 26, 1892, quoted in Hicks 1931). At least partly because the strength of local partisan networks was reinforced by ethnic identity, and migration was fairly limited, the Populists recruited relatively fewer candidates to their own label in Southern districts (at least, compared to the Midwest): few voters were ripe for mobilization. Instead, office-seeking Populists more frequently attempted to work within the Democratic apparatus.

It is important to note, however, that Bensel's (2000) analysis of state party platforms suggests the Populist co-optation of the southern Democrats met with very limited success, at least with regards to policy. With the exception of calls for federal pensions for Union soldiers, Democratic platforms in the South generally conformed to Democratic platforms elsewhere. Even in the South, the Democratic platforms remained distinct from Populist platforms on issues related to tariffs, some monetary policy, labor, the distribution of land, income tax, the direct election of senators, women's suffrage, and temperance. Where fusion was successful, and candidates contested the election on joint Democratic–Populist platforms, Southern low-income and agricultural workers may have shared the interests and demands articulated by the Populists but were already well incorporated into the local Democratic partisan networks.

One might also worry, in the US, that the People's strategic entry decisions were structured by the presidential contest. This seems not to be the case. Although the People's Party nominated James Weaver and James Field to head their ticket, leaders of the People's Party did "admit that their only object in placing an Electoral ticket in the field in Virginia and other Southern States is to strengthen the chances of success for their candidates for Congress. They argue[d] that they could not have hoped to make any headway in this movement without presenting a Presidential candidate to be voted for. The whole fight is being made with the view of securing as many members of the House as possible, thus enabling them to hold the balance of power in that branch of Congress" (*The New York Times*, September 9, 1892). Even though national focus generally shifted to presidential elections during this post-Civil War period, for the People's Party, and the 1892 election, congressional elections and the cumulation of power in Congress structured the party's strategic allocation of candidates and resources.

Finally, it is quite clear that the political entrepreneurs who bore the costs of mobilization were office-seekers. In fact, Donnelly and others worked quite hard to establish the third party, and often encountered resistance among members of the founding organizations. Some in the Farmers' Alliance and other organizations felt that policy reform could best be achieved through independent, non-partisan action (Hicks 1928). Further, as suggested above, white political elites in the Democratic South were especially concerned that the formation of a third party would facilitate a Republican victory. But the creation of a non-political organization, Donnelly suggested, was like making a gun "that will do everything but shoot" (quoted in Hicks 1928). Through the strategic manipulation of an early convention (Ocala) agenda, Donnelly ensured a third party; the People's official support of the subtreasury bill there was also admitted to be an attempt to divide Southern Democrats, and make way for the new party ("The Alliance Their Tool," *The New York Times*, December 14, 1890). One keen observer described the Cincinnati Convention as a meeting of the "discontented and the ambitious, the latter seeking to lead the former" ("The Third-Party Movement," *The New York Times*, May 19, 1891). Another observer suggested that "[t]hese third-party bosses are in politics for the money only, and they will sell out to the side that offers them the most" (*The New York Times*, July 23, 1892). Hofstadter (1955, 102) also saw deep and profound ambition in the leaders of the People's Party, describing them as "cranks and careerists who had failed to find a place for themselves within the established political machines...They hungered for success as major-party leaders knew it."

In the end, the Populists' decisions to recruit candidates in each state, and indeed, each district, were the result of careful strategic calculations, largely structured by expectations about the geographic distribution of electoral support, and motivated by office-seeking candidates who were willing to bear the costs of party formation and voter mobilization. The map in Figure 4.3 indicates those districts in which People's candidates entered electoral contests (dark gray), as well as those in which candidates contested on "fusion" tickets, as joint Populist–Democrat candidates. As suggested above, the decision to enter electoral contests clearly proceeded on a district-by-district basis. Although there were some states where the Populists contested every district, this was not generally the case.

A casual comparison of Figures 4.2 and 4.3 suggests that, in fact, Populists were especially likely to enter electoral contests in those parts of the country where we observe large changes in the electoral power of low-income voters. While this section has provided some qualitative evidence of the strategic nature of Populist decision-making, the next section will use quantitative evidence about the changing distribution of electoral power to evaluate the Populists' strategic entry decisions more rigorously.

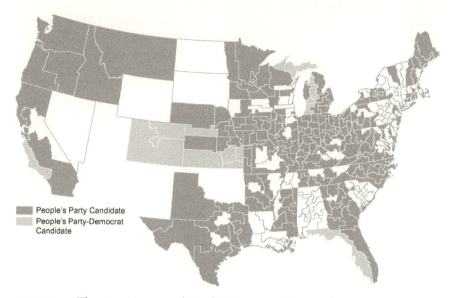

FIGURE 4.3. The strategic entry of People's Party candidates, 1892.
Sources: Election data: Swift *et al.* (2009), revised according to Dubin (1998). Congressional district boundary file: Lewis *et al.* (2013). State boundary file: NHGIS.

4.4 CHANGING ELECTORAL GEOGRAPHY AND NEW ELECTORAL OPPORTUNITIES

Table 4.4 reports coefficients from several probit regression analyses in which the dependent variable is an indicator of whether a candidate contested the election in that district on the People's Party ticket. The key independent variable, of course, is the measure of changes in concentration of low-income voters in congressional districts between 1880 and 1892, developed in Section 4.2, which provides a robust prediction of where People's candidates contested elections. The analyses increase in complexity across the columns, and in the last column are replicated for states outside of the South, where the Populists less frequently recruited candidates for reasons other than changes in local distributions of electoral power. The first column only includes the percentage of low-income voters (observed in 1880[11]) and the total change in the percentage of low-income voters. In this basic specification, we see that while the overall level of low-income voters does not reliably predict which districts People's Party candidates will contest, the change in the electoral power of low-income voters *does* explain the strategic entry decisions. In the specification reported in the second column, the difference in the percentage

---

[11]   To avoid post-treatment bias, this analysis includes covariates measured in 1880. As the reader might expect, the percentages of low-income voters, industrial, and agricultural workers observed in 1880 and 1900 are highly correlated, at 0.68, 0.90, and 0.88 respectively.

of low-income voters is grouped into quartiles, and included as indicator variables. (One might worry that, for reasons other than electoral opportunity, the Populists avoided Southern districts, which also experienced decreases in the proportion of low-income voters, and therefore might create the appearance of a linear relationship.) This specification shows that the apparent relationship between People's Party entry and the change comes primarily from the decision to enter electoral contests where the percentage of low-income voters has *increased*.

The analysis reported in the third column includes measures that approximate two features of Bensel's (2000) index of economic development that might have been especially important for Populist entry decisions: the percentage of agricultural and industrial workers among eligible voters. In fact, neither of these variables account for variance in the entry decisions of People's candidates, and the indicators of changing local distributions of power maintain their robust effect.

One might reasonably be concerned by limited variance accounted for by the models specified in Table 4.4. (Indeed, were this the only analytic case study included here, the case for the importance of electoral geography in new party entry would be weak.) The fourth column of Table 4.4, however, provides an opportunity to focus on the mechanism linking changes in electoral geography to the viability of a Populist candidacy in each district. Specifically, did People's candidates contest those districts in which the electoral power of low-income voters increased sufficiently to make them pivotal? This is a test with clear implications: to the extent that changes in the electoral power of low-income citizens represented an electoral opportunity for the People's Party, its candidates should have been most likely to enter electoral contests in districts where low-income citizens were newly pivotal.

In fact, this seems to be the case: To put the analysis reported in column (4) in substantive terms, in the thirty-five districts in which low-income voters were pivotal in 1892 (but were not in 1880), People's candidates contested all but eight (79 percent; four of the remaining districts were contested by a fusion candidate). This rate of candidate recruitment contrasts with those districts in which the electoral power of low-income voters decreased, and where low-income voters were not pivotal: People's candidates contested less than half of these sixty-four districts.[12]

---

[12] I suspect that even this relatively high rate of contestation in districts where low-income citizens were neither favored by recent changes nor the numerical majority may reflect measurement error, rather than inconsistent Populist decisions. Notice, for example, that thirty-seven of these districts, for example, were in the Northeast. As seen in Figure 4.3, the districts contested by the Populists in New Jersey, New York, or Pennsylvania were predominantly the rural districts towards the western border of each state. Because income for agricultural workers, however, is based on state-level estimates, it may be the case that income profiles in these districts more closely resemble those of districts in neighboring Ohio, for example. That is, the measurement

Finally, as suggested above, the People's Party may have been discouraged from contesting at least some districts in the South for fear of dividing the white Democratic voting bloc that sustained white racial status. Because these Southern districts are also districts in which low-income voters have limited electoral power, and saw few new arrivals during the 1880s, the inclusion of these districts has a potentially confounding effect, potentially generating the appearance of a relationship between changes in electoral geography and the strategic entry of People's candidates. To investigate evidence of this confounding effect, the model reported in column (5) excludes Southern districts, and replicates the strategic entry analysis of column (4). In fact, even in this smaller sample we see Populist candidates most likely to enter those congressional districts in which changes in local distributions of electoral power dramatically favored low-income voters, such that they formed the numerical majority.

This analysis, therefore, has shown that the Populists were especially likely to enter electoral contests where dramatic changes in the local distribution of electoral power favored low-income voters. This pattern persists even when other potentially confounding features of the district, including features others have thought to be important to Populist entry decisions, are incorporated in the analysis.

4.5 SUMMARY AND CONCLUSIONS

Ultimately, of course, the 1892 election represents both the entry and, at least, the beginning of the People's slow retreat from American politics. Despite entry in nearly two-thirds of House contests, the Populists would win only eleven seats in the House of Representatives (plus two additional fusion members). Disheartened with his own poor showing, Donnelly would declare that "the People's party afforded no reward for me or any other man" (quoted in Hicks 1931, 261). In 1896, Donnelly profoundly resisted the Populist fusion with the Democrats, and the People's endorsement of the Democratic candidate William Jennings Bryan. Supported by so-called "middle-of-the-roaders," Donnelly pursued his own nomination to the top of the ticket at the Populist convention, but he was shut out of crucial leadership positions, including a position on the platform committee (Hicks 1931). Most scholars have attributed the ultimate collapse of the Populists to the Democrats' succesful co-optation of the silver issue (see, e.g., Rosenstone, Behr, & Lazarus 1984), but the disenchantment and exclusion of those who bore the costs of mobilization also likely played a role.

A full treatment of the People's collapse is beyond the scope of this analysis. One might worry, however, that the changes in local distributions of electoral

strategy likely overestimates income for these districts, generally, and probably underestimates increases in the electoral power of low-income citizens.

TABLE 4.4. *Strategic entry of People's Party candidates, 1892.*

	DV: People's Party candidate entry				
	(1)	(2)	(3)	(4)	(5) South excluded
Proportion low-income (1880)	0.339 (0.234)				
Low-income district (47th Congress)		0.537^b (0.222)	0.303 (0.297)		
Change in proportion low-income, 1880–1892	1.000^a (0.337)				
Quartile 2 [−0.13,0]		−0.194 (0.203)	−0.201 (0.203)		
Quartile 3 [0,0.07]		0.275 (0.240)	0.235 (0.242)		
Quartile 4 [0.07,0.81]		0.740^a (0.252)	0.566^b (0.288)		
Proportion in agriculture (1880)			0.137 (0.582)		
Proportion in industry or manufacturing (1880)			−1.083 (1.410)		
Low-income district (47th & 53rd Congress)				0.535^a (0.204)	0.405 (0.215)
Increase in low-income voters, not a low-income district (53rd Congress)				0.431^a (0.190)	0.430 (0.470)
Increase in low-income voters, low-income district (53rd Congress)				0.844^a (0.277)	0.967^a (0.309)
Intercept	0.236^a (0.109)	−0.030 (0.205)	0.144 (0.464)	−0.039 (0.156)	0.000 (0.185)
N	343	343	343	343	231
Pseudo R^2	0.021	0.030	0.034	0.026	0.035

Notes: This table reports coefficients estimated in probit analyses, in which the dependent variable is a binary indicator of whether or not a People's Party candidate contested the election. Standard errors reported in parentheses.
[a] $p < 0.01$. [b] $p < 0.05$.
Source: Election data: Swift *et al.* (2009), revised according to Dubin (1998).

power reflect, predominantly, local economic shocks, rather than opportunities created also by migration or immigration. From this perspective, the collapse of the Populists could have resulted from an improvement in economic conditions, and more typical economic voting: voters rejected the established parties, especially the incumbent Democrats (House and Presidency), only to return to them in 1896 when local conditions had somewhat improved.[13] If this were the case, the importance of strategic entry decisions would be difficult to distinguish from accounts of party formation and entry that emphasize voters' demands. Because this analysis relies on decennial census data, the effects of short-term changes in local electoral power distributions on entry decisions are difficult to evaluate. Nevertheless, an examination of which districts Populists contested in the 1896 elections can be helpful, both for demonstrating the strategic nature of their entry decisions, and possibly for rejecting changes in voter demands as an explanation for the ultimate collapse of the party.

Table 4.5 reports the percentage of districts in which Populists recruited candidates to contest the 1896 election. Unlike the period between 1880 and 1892, and with the exception of districts in Illinois, Indiana, and South Carolina,[14] congressional district boundaries were stable between the 1892 and 1896. As a consequence, changes in the size of the electorate can estimated directly. If Populist entry decisions reflected changes in local preference, rather than opportunities created by voters who were ripe for mobilization (either newly arrived, or otherwise excluded from local partisan networks), Populist entry decisions would not be structured by simple demographic changes. Instead, what Table 4.5 shows is that Populists were especially likely to contest those districts in which low-income voters were pivotal in 1892, *and* in which the size of the electorate had increased substantially between 1892 and 1896. (Five of these thirty-two districts were new districts, added in an election in which the Populists *reduced* the number of their contests by 148 districts.) One might reasonably worry that the increased size of the electorate reflects the parties' efforts, but in fact this would corroborate the importance of demographic change to the electoral opportunities: there were significant numbers of voters available for mobilization in these districts.

(In the later analysis of the Swedish Social Democrats, we will see the new party enter electoral contests where economic *good* times generated changes in local distributions of electoral power by extending suffrage rights to those whose earnings had increased substantially. As in the case of the Populists, the Social Democratic geographic pattern of entry is difficult to reconcile with changes in voter preferences that are consistent with economic voting.)

---

[13] Of course, the Populists also suffered in 1894 as a consequence of the Panic of 1893, which resulted in hundreds of bank closures and deep poverty taking hold throughout the country, and actually *gained* seats in 1896.

[14] Massachussetts and New Jersey also altered some boundaries in their urban areas, and North Carolina reallocated Mitchell county from its eighth to its ninth district.

TABLE 4.5. *Strategic entry of People's Party candidates in 1896.*

	Change in electorate, 1892–1896	
	[−13,112, 4,217]	[4,340, 19,643]
Not a low-income district	24%	25%
	(71)	(69)
Low-income district (1892)	53%	61%
	(45)	(51)

Notes: This table reports the proportion of districts in each category that were contested by People's Party candidates, and excludes districts in Illinois, Indiana, and South Carolina.
Source: Election data: Swift *et al.* (2009).

A natural question – indeed, a motivating question for this project – concerns the general absence of other parties who formed with the intention of representing the interests of a low-income constituency.[15] While new parties have challenged the established Democrats and Republicans, none of those entering elections in the post-Civil War era have surpassed the Populists in the extent of their initial entry into electoral competition,[16] nor, arguably, their success. Hirano and Snyder (2007) suggest that support for, especially, third parties of the left has declined because the Democrats have co-opted the progressive policy space, particularly following the adoption of the New Deal. In fact, what we saw in Chapter 3 is the coincidence of two phenomena. After 1930, rates of local population change generally declined, and new parties entered electoral competition less frequently.[17] To the extent that changes in the distribution of electoral power create opportunities for new party entry, these opportunities occurred less frequently after 1930, new parties formed more rarely, and indeed, voters had fewer opportunities to vote for new parties.

---

15 A reasonable case might be made, of course, that the Progressives or the Socialists took positions that were favored by many low-income voters. Sanders (1999, 159), for example, suggests that many of the major policy reforms of the Progressive era were, in fact, "agrarian" agenda items. But as Rosenstone, Behr, and Lazarus (1984) suggest, there is little evidence that the Progressive Party began with the goal of mobilizing a national low-income constituency. Instead, although every "previous third party began with a party, which in turn selected a nominee ... in 1912 Roosevelt was the party. Had he not run, it is unlikely there would have been a Progressive challenge that year." The Socialist Party, and its predecessors, were almost exclusively urban organizations and confined their early mobilization efforts to industrial workers, who only rarely fell among the nation's low-income voters (see, e.g., Kipnis 2004).
16 The Progressives contested 153 districts in their first contest; the Prohibitionists contested less than 100 seats for their first decade; the Greenbacks contested 43 seats in their first election; and, finally, the Socialist Party of America would not contest more than 100 seats until 1902, nearly 20 years after the original Socialist Labor Party was founded.
17 Also, parties forming after 1930 typically enter fewer district contests.

Chapter 8 develops this argument further, in an effort to link party entry decisions to the absence of a major third party in the US.

Where the Populists were successful in 1892, however, the importance of electoral geography is hard to underestimate: of the eleven districts where Populist candidates won, ten were districts in which the electoral power of low-income voters had increased (by an average of about 31 percent) and where, in 1892, low-income voters comprised about 45 percent of the electorate. Overall, the Populists won about 13 percent of votes cast in those districts where low-income voters had recently become pivotal, compared to about 3 percent of ballots cast where low-income voters were neither pivotal nor had increased their electoral strength.

The next few chapters replicate the analysis presented here, but in settings or for cases that vary in important ways from the US at the end of the nineteenth century. In Canada, a case that often serves as a natural comparison to the US, new parties of the left and right form and enter electoral contests, often in the same districts. In the UK, which, like Canada, is a parliamentary, rather than a presidential, system, the new Labour Party enters elections and mobilizes a primarily industrial constituency. In Sweden, again, a parliamentary system, but one in which the changing electoral geography results from (exogenous) suffrage expansion, I focus on the strategic entry decisions of the Social Democratic Party. In each case, a small group of political entrepreneurs play crucial roles in establishing the party, announcing its platform, recruiting candidates, and mobilizing voters. Importantly, *where* each party enters electoral contests suggests that these entrepreneurs recognize opportunities in changing local distributions of electoral power.

4.A APPENDIX: SUPPORTING MATERIALS

The North Atlantic Population Project

Individual-level census data, available through the University of Minnesota's North Atlantic Population Project and Integrated Public Use Microdata Series, provide the empirical foundation for the analysis presented in this chapter (and in Chapters 6 and 7).

Complete censuses are available for the US (1880), the UK (1881), and Sweden (1890 and 1900). The analysis of the US in 1900, presented in this chapter, is based on a 5 percent sample of the full census.

In each case, the NAPP data provide datasets with full documentation and standardized coding of individual-level and household-level variables. The datasets typically include variables for most of the fields collected by census enumerators (e.g., a household's characteristics, and demographic and economic characteristics of its members), as well as geographic location information.

Matching Census and Electoral Geography

The US 1880 and 1900 censuses and NAPP data report enumeration district numbers, as well as street addresses, for each household enumerated. Enumeration districts are unique within, but vary in size and population, across counties and censuses.

During this period, many congressional district boundaries correspond to county boundaries. In cities and a few other places, however, congressional district boundaries are defined with reference to other administrative or political boundaries (e.g., cities, wards, or assembly districts). To allocate census enumeration districts to these congressional districts, enumeration districts first had to be matched to these alternate sets of boundaries (which sometimes had been revised between censuses). To facilitate this allocation, this analysis relied on Morse and Weintraub's (2007) digital transcriptions of enumeration districts, digital shape files made available through the Urban Transition Project (Logan *et al.* 2011), and a series of microform enumeration district maps (US Census Bureau 1950).

Martis (1982) and Parsons, Dubin, and Parsons (1990) provide congressional district boundary descriptions; the maps presented in this chapter are based on Lewis *et al.*'s (2013) digital shape files.

Estimating Wages and Earnings

Estimates of income are drawn primarily from Wright (1886, 1900, 1904), and are generally based on industrial categories (the NAPP variable, IND1950,

TABLE 4.6. *Missing wage data.*

Occupation or ptindustry	1880		1900	
	National	District	National	District
Welfare and religious services	1%	4% (Nebraska 3)	1%	2% (Kentucky 4)
Transportation services	<1%	2% (New York 8)	1%	3% (Illinois 9, 15)
Bowling alleys and billiard, pool parlors	<0.1%	<1% (Massachusetts 2)	<0.1%	<1% (New Jersey 4)
Total	5% $n = 9,925,625$	15% (Connecticut 2)	2% $n = 843,849$	4% (Illinois 3)

Notes: This table reports the largest occupation groups for which wage or salary data are not available, as a percentage of the national economically active population, and as its largest share of an electoral district.

which classifies transcribed occupations on the basis of the 1950 US Census Bureau industrial classification system).

Estimates of earnings are based on the closest year for which data are available, and are adjusted for inflation. In most cases, estimates are based on average daily wages; Wright (1886) also reports the average number of days worked per year. When these data are not available, annual earnings estimates are based on 312 days worked per year.

For those who hold occupations in manufacturing, but in industries not included in Wright (1886), this analysis uses Long's (1960) industry-weighted average for manufacturing workers.

Wright (1900) more frequently reports earnings by occupation than by industry. For 1892, estimates of earnings therefore reflect the earnings of the occupations most frequently held within each industry.

When possible, estimates of earnings are reported for each state: Wright (1900) provides state-level averages for machinists, teamsters, and laborers (for at least some states) for 1892. Lebergott (1964, 539) provides average monthly earnings estimates for agricultural workers, for each state and region, for 1880 and 1892. The analysis here is based on twelve months of work for workers with room and board. (See footnote 4 for more discussion.) The annual Reports of the Commissioner of Education report average monthly earnings for male teachers (see Table I, xv; Eaton 1882).

Finally, Table 4.6 reports the largest occupation groups appearing in the 1880 and 1900 censuses for which wage data are unavailable, and the congressional districts most affected by these omissions.

N.B. *Fully documented tables, reporting wage and earnings estimates for each IND1950 occupation code will be made available as supplementary resources.*

5

Strategic Entry of the CCF and Social Credit in Canada

Canada has often provided a natural comparison to the US in explanations of why no American labor party emerged. Certainly, this was the case for Lipset (1968, ix), who "was interested in learning why an avowedly socialist party, the Cooperative Commonwealth Federation, was winning elections in Canada, when comparable efforts had brought no such success to the United States." To Lipset, "it seemed that many of the social conditions that various commentators had cited to explain 'why there is no socialism in the United States' were also present in Canada." For example, Canada shares with the US an open land frontier, the absence of a feudal past, higher rates of social mobility than were present in Europe, and preindustrial democratic and party system development. Indeed, Canada also shares important institutional features – SMDs and a federal structure of government – that have been emphasized by Chhibber and Kollman (2004) and others in explanations of the development of party systems.

Like Chapter 4's analysis of the US at the end of the nineteenth century, the focus here is on changes in local distributions of electoral power, and the opportunities these changes created for political entrepreneurs. To the extent that the established parties and their candidates were tied to national platforms, changes in the composition of a subset of districts that favor one group over others created opportunities for new party entry.

What is especially interesting about the Canadian case is the nearly simultaneous formation of parties with very different ideological commitments. Here, I evaluate the extent to which changes in the electoral power of low-income voters in Canada created opportunities for the Cooperative Commonwealth Federation (CCF) and Social Credit parties. The CCF and Social Credit – parties of the left and right, respectively – formed in the early 1930s and recruited candidates to contest the 1935 federal election. That they contested largely the same districts – of the forty-five districts contested by Social

Credit, the CCF contested forty-two (and seventy-one more) – and aimed to mobilize largely the same groups of voters suggests that the party leaders' decisions were shaped by incentive structures that were similar and in which locally-emerging policy preferences played a subordinate role. Further, the evidence of strategic recruitment and entry of candidates is difficult to reconcile with an "up-from-the-bottom" account of party formation that emphasizes citizen demands. Instead, narratives of the formation of CCF and Social Credit are consistent with accounts of party formation that focus attention on the strategic behavior of office-seeking political entrepreneurs and the opportunities presented by changes in electoral geography.

This chapter begins with an analysis of Canadian political economic conditions in the early 1930s, and then, using strategies similar to those developed in the US case, maps the distribution of income and its changes in anticipation of the formation of the CCF and Social Credit. Drawing on archival as well as secondary historical analysis, this chapter then tracks the formation of the CCF and Social Credit parties and their organizations, and especially how leaders of the CCF and Social Credit thought about their electoral viability. Finally, this section will conclude with a focused and rigorous district-level analysis of the relationship between the changing electoral power of low-income citizens, and each party's strategic entry decisions.

In the end, this chapter will provide evidence that electoral geography, and changing distributions of electoral power, structured the strategic entry decisions of CCF and Social Credit party leaders. Both parties were most likely to recruit candidates in districts where the electoral power of low-income voters had dramatically increased, and crafted electoral appeals to mobilize this newly pivotal constituency.

5.1 THE CANADIAN POLITICAL ECONOMY IN THE EARLY 1930S

Although a full treatment of the Canadian political economy during the early part of the twentieth century is beyond the scope of this project, an understanding of three features and their implications for Canadian politics provides important context for the strategic decisions of the CCF and Social Credit party leaders.

First, like the American economy, the Canadian political economy was highly regionalized, but had developed much more slowly than the American economy. Lipset (1968, 40), for example, suggests that, at the time of his writing, the prairie provinces, Saskatchewan and Alberta, were comparable to "the frontier areas of Kansas and Nebraska in the late 19th century when these states were the stronghold of Greenbackism and Populism." Although Winnipeg, Saskatoon, and Calgary had emerged as important urban centers, the prairie economy remained mostly agricultural and largely dependent on wheat produced for export. (Other important exports included lumber and paper.) Lipset (1968, 44) writes,

To a unique extent, the economic history of Saskatchewan is that of wheat. No other governmental unit in the world attempting to maintain a modern civilization is so completely dependent on the production and marketing of one commodity—a commodity which under even normal conditions is subject to wide variations in production and price.

Partly because of this extreme dependence, Green and MacKinnon (2012, 354) report that the Great Depression was "imported to Canada": the Canadian economy was highly integrated into the international economy, and was deeply affected by the collapse of the world's commodity market.

By 1929, the economies of Ontario, and especially Quebec, in contrast, were much more diversified, and well established as the economic and industrial – and the political – center of Canada. While industries that contributed to exports (including industries in support of transportation, like iron and coal production) would be similarly affected by the Great Depression, this industrial core was less generally dependent on agricultural exports than was the West, and period of economic decline was less painful and shorter in duration for central Canada. Strikwerda (2012, 44), for example, reports that while per capita incomes fell about 44 percent between 1929 and 1933 in Quebec and Ontario, per capita incomes fell by 72 percent in Saskatchewan.

The second feature of the Canadian political economy that structured the entry incentives of the CCF and Social Credit, as the next section of this discussion will demonstrate with more precision, was profound demographic change that occurred during the 1920s. (We saw this, as well, in Chapter 3.) Overall, the western provinces, Saskatchewan, Alberta, and British Columbia, in particular experienced dramatic growth during the 1920s, where local populations grew by 22, 24, and 32 percent, respectively. Population increases were solid but more moderate in Ontario and Manitoba (14 and 16 percent). The Maritimes, particularly Nova Scotia and Prince Edward Island, experienced population *decreases* during the 1920s.

Parts of Quebec also experienced the dramatic effects of internal migration and immigration. For example, Olssen (1973, 19–20) reports that, "as Canada's largest metropolis, Montreal was the main beneficiary of the rural-urban migration. Her population rose from 618,506 in 1921 to 818,577 in 1931, a growth of 31 per cent for the decade. Two-thirds of Quebec's population lived in Montreal and its immediate suburbs. From 1924 to 1930, 5,800 families, or roughly 27,300 persons, moved to Montreal and its suburbs of Verdun, Westmount and Outremont." For comparison, Olssen (1973) notes that, "Quebec, the capital and second city, had only 130,000 inhabitants." The population of the district of Mont Royal increased from about twenty-three thousand to over thirty-two thousand – a *40 percent* increase. The electorate in the federal electoral district of St. James almost doubled, from about sixteen thousand in 1924 to over thirty thousand in 1935 (Canada. Dominion Bureau of Statistics 1935, 52). In addition to rural-to-urban migration, increases in local population reflect large numbers of immigrants arriving in Montreal. Of the sixty thousand residents of Verdun, for example, about one-third were born outside of Canada. (Most of these were British.) In Montreal proper, about 140 thousand – about 18 percent – were born outside of Canada (Canada. Dominion Bureau of Statistics 1935, 192).

Some parts of Canada, therefore, particularly the West, but also urban centers generally, experienced the absence of "strong, settled ties to a traditional pattern of economic, political, and social behavior" because of the mass migration and immigration, particularly in the 1920s. As late as the 1960s, the Canadian West still lacked a "static social structure, and in this respect [was] characteristic of frontier areas." In fact, as Lipset (1968, 41) notes, large proportions of prairie farms were, in fact, established by members of the migrant and immigrant working class. More than half of farm operators surveyed in Alberta and Saskatchewan reported no previous agricultural experience. This served to unsettle traditional class status, and with the economic devastation of the early 1930s, exacerbated in Saskatchewan by drought and pests, migrants and immigrants in the west and in cities were ripe for mobilization in a way that those living in other parts of Canada were not.

Finally, the major conflict structuring electoral competition was – and of course, in an important respect, continues to be – the role of Quebec in the Canadian federation. Most of Canadian history has been structured by two-party (or more) competition between the long-governing Liberal Party and the Progressive Conservatives (and its several post-1992 successors). But unlike in the American case, where each party had cultivated reliable local partisan networks throughout the country in a way that heightened the electoral competition (everywhere outside of the South) and the intensity of partisan commitments, Canadian political competition was highly regionalized. Because of their association with the British, conscription during the First World War, and the hanging of Louis Riel,[1] the Conservatives remained unable to mobilize the support of French Canadian voters living in Quebec. As a consequence, Quebec became as solidly Liberal as the South was Democratic, with similar effects: the Liberals were able to form the legislative majority, often without an electoral majority, and usually with limited support outside of central Canada. Further, this created incentives for established parties to "aim appeals at the nerve centers of particular provinces or regions, hoping thus to capture a bloc

---

[1] Riel was a leader of the Métis, and was tried for treason after leading militarized rebellions against the Canadian government, and on behalf of those living in what would become Manitoba and Saskatchewan. His claims were made especially on behalf of the francophones living in these provinces, and were championed throughout Quebec. When he was sentenced to death by an English-speaking jury in 1885, his conviction was upheld by Prime Minister John A. Macdonald, who was famously quoted as saying "He shall die though every dog in Quebec bark in his favor."

geographical vote," rather than launch national campaigns (Scarrow 1965, 72). As Cairns (1968, 68) writes,

The extra-parliamentary structures of the two major parties have been extremely weak, lacking in continuity and without any disciplining power over the parliamentary party. The two major parties have been leader-dominated with membership playing a limited role in policy making and party financing. Although there are indications that the extra-parliamentary apparatus of the parties is growing in importance, it can be safely said that for the period under review both major parties have been essentially parliamentary parties.

Party identifications, therefore, were tied to geographically and culturally defined groups, with the Conservatives associated with Ontario and the British, and the Liberals representing the interests of French-speaking Canadians, in and outside of Quebec. The newly arrived immigrants who settled in Canada's western provinces were not well incorporated into these existing partisan networks. In combination with the profoundly regional effects of the Great Depression on the distribution of electoral power across income groups, migrants and immigrants living in the Prairie provinces – then, the Canadian periphery – may have been an especially attractive constituency for office-seeking political entrepreneurs.

The next section will make this general discussion of Canada's political economic context more precise, and, using the strategy outlined in the previous chapter, will generate a map of Canada's changing electoral geography. District-level estimates of the changing electoral power of low-income voters will then serve as the key independent variable in an analysis that evaluates the strategic entry decisions of the new parties, CCF and Social Credit.

5.2 MAPPING THE ELECTORAL GEOGRAPHY OF INCOME IN CANADA, 1921–1931

In his account of the CCF, Lipset (1968) emphasizes the role of the "economic and climatically vulnerable wheat belt" as the "back bone" of all protest movements in Canada and the US. The Canadian West and prairies are important to this account, too, not so much because of their economic vulnerability, but rather because this region (with parts of Quebec) experienced the most dramatic population growth during the 1920s. (Districts in the Maritime provinces, New Brunswick, Nova Scotia, and Prince Edward Island, for example, had similar concentrations of low-income voters.) Importantly, large numbers of immigrants and migrants reported relatively low incomes in the 1931 census, and as this section will demonstrate, their presence dramatically increased the electoral power of low-income voters in this region.

To map the changing electoral geography of income in Canada, this analysis draws on 4 and 3 percent samples of the Canadian 1921 and

TABLE 5.1. *Characteristics of the Canadian national household income distributions, 1921, 1931, and 2013.*

	1921	1931	2013
Gini index	0.38	0.40	0.44
Income ratios of selected percentiles			
90/10	5.66	7.52	15.55
90/50	2.84	2.75	2.46
50/10	1.99	2.73	6.37

Notes: Calculations based on household market income (1921 and 1931) and economic families (2013).

Source: Canada (2013): Statistics Canada. CANSIM Tables 206-0033 (Gini index) and Table 206-0031 (income deciles).

1931 censuses, respectively, that were developed as part of the Canadian Century Research Infrastructure (CCRI), and are available for analysis in Statistics Canada Research Data Centres. For each household included in the 1921 and 1931 datasets, enumeration divisions and subdivisions were also reported, allowing individuals to be matched to the boundaries of the 1933 Representation Order.[2] By matching both census datasets to the 1933 electoral boundaries, this analysis is able to examine changes in the composition of the districts over time, without concern for concurrently changing district boundaries.

As suggested in Chapter 4, the mapping of Canadian income is more straightforward than the other countries included here because, in addition to information about workforce participation and occupation, the 1921 and 1931 censuses also collected information on wages and earnings. That is, rather than relying on regional estimates of wages for each occupation group, income was recorded by census enumerators for about one third of the adult population. These data were then used to generate estimates for the wages and earnings of those working in the same industry, in the same province, and of the same gender. (Women's suffrage rights were extended in 1918.) Then, earnings were tabulated within households to generate estimates of the national household income distribution. Appendix 5.A provides the details of each step of this analysis; Table 5.1 reports summary characteristics of the 1921 and 1931 household income distributions, and Figure 5.1 provides average annual wages for each industry category.

---

[2] The Canadian census report suggests that census divisions and subdivisions correspond to electoral divisions; in fact, this is not the case. Although most of the enumeration subdivisions could be accurately allocated to electoral divisions, in some cities this allocation is more imprecise.

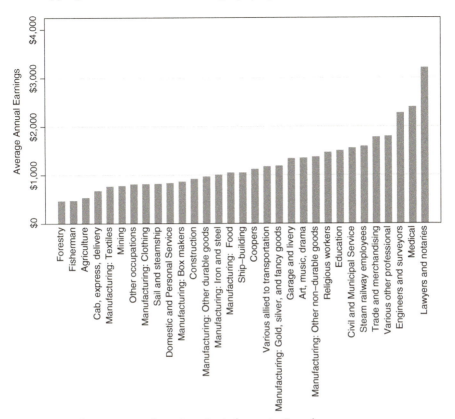

FIGURE 5.1. Average annual earnings, by industry, in Canada 1931.
Notes: This figure reports average annual earnings for each industry category. See Appendix 5.A for further technical detail.

In 1931, the lowest third of the national market income distribution included those households that were earning less than (CAD) $1,000. This amount includes farming households, in which agricultural workers earned a national average of $535, although there is some important regional variation, ranging from $482 in Manitoba to $569 in British Columbia. In single-earner households, those earning "low incomes" also included many of those working as fishermen and miners, as well as in some manufacturing industries.

The occupations associated with low incomes correspond to the clear regional patterns in the Canadian electoral geography of income that were anticipated in the previous section – agricultural and forestry, in the west, but also mining (and fishing) in the Maritimes. This geographic distribution of income voters (again, those with household earnings in the first third of the national market income distribution) appears quite clearly in Figure 5.2(a), where low-income voters frequently form the majority in the western provinces, and the Maritimes. There is more variance in the electoral power of low-income voters in districts in Ontario and Quebec.

There are also strong regional patterns in the *changes* in the electoral power of low-income citizens – Figure 5.2(b) – although there is more variation within each province. For example, and as anticipated by the discussion above, low-income voters increased their concentration especially in Manitoba, Alberta, and Saskatchewan. With the exception of Nova Scotia, the Maritime provinces (and Quebec) saw comparatively small decreases, or more often, increases in median incomes.

How did this changing electoral geography of income structure the incentives of political entrepreneurs? Which districts did the CCF and Social Credit candidates contest? If changes in electoral geography structure party entry decisions by creating new opportunities to mobilize unconnected but often pivotal groups, then it ought to be the case that the CCF and Social Credit candidates contest those districts that experienced the most dramatic increases in the electoral power of low-income citizens just prior to the 1935 election – in Saskatchewan and Alberta, but also in some parts of Ontario. The next section will examine support for this account, drawing on archival and secondary material, for CCF and Social Credit candidates' recruitment decisions, before turning to more rigorous district-level analysis in the final section of this chapter.

5.3 NEW ELECTORAL OPPORTUNITIES: THE ELECTION OF 1935, THE CCF, AND SOCIAL CREDIT

In their attempts to mobilize a newly pivotal, low-income constituency, political entrepreneurs crafted two responses to the desperate economic conditions: On the left, the leaders of the CCF drew on socialist ideas and saw the socialization of the banks and railways as a solution to the social and economic exclusion of agricultural workers. On the right, the leaders of what would become the Social Credit party advocated instead for monetary reform, and the provision of a $25 dividend per month for every adult to alleviate the general lack of purchasing power. In their defense of capitalism and commitment to private enterprise, the leaders of Social Credit confronted socialism directly, and indeed, although the parties would coordinate on candidates in some places, and party organizers would sometimes switch parties, their members more often saw each other as competitors for the same low-income constituency. Ironically, it was Social Credit, the party of the right, that had more success in organizing the urban working class, at least in Alberta. However, as the following discussion details, the leaders of *both* parties sought to organize and mobilize the newly pivotal low-income urban and agricultural workers of the Canadian prairie provinces.

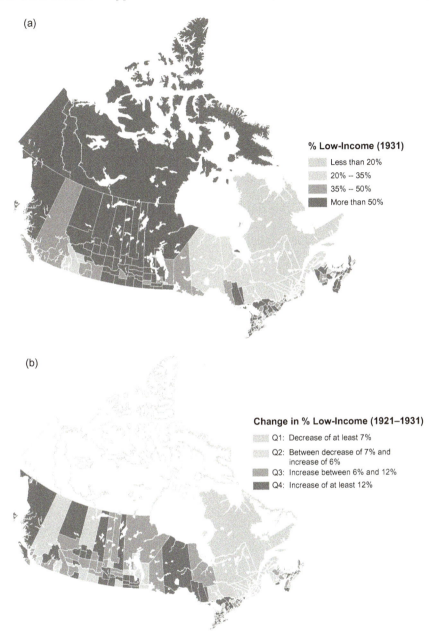

FIGURE 5.2. The changing electoral geography of low-income voters in Canada, 1921–1931.

Notes: District boundaries correspond to the 1933 Representation Order.

Sources: Refer to text for discussion of income estimates; technical details reported in Appendix 5.A. District boundary files are based on revisions of CCRI Reference Maps.

The Formation of the CCF

Several features of the CCF's formation resemble the history of the American People's Party: First, the CCF was founded at a convention of farmers' alliances and organized labor, that was organized by an elite group of office-seekers. Its federal structure explicitly incorporated democratic practices, but these, as Young (1969, 140) argues, in fact created "a degree of leadership control and manipulation which, given the nature of party factions, would not have been possible under any other kind of structure." Although James Shaver Woodsworth is usually identified as the founding leader of the CCF, he typically emphasized what he saw as the greater, educative, role of the party, rather than its electoral purpose; he was generally seen as uninterested in the politics of electoral competition (see Young 1969). Instead, it was M.J. Coldwell and David Lewis who took on the strategic leadership of the party. Of Coldwell and Lewis's efforts in the early-to-mid 1930s, Young (163) writes, "It is difficult to exaggerate Coldwell's role in building the party at this stage; it is hardly possible to exaggerate that play by Lewis." Coldwell would provide the parliamentary leadership, and Lewis, the party's first national chairman, would develop the broader CCF organization through the explicit electoral strategy.

Were the CCF founders the Canadian equivalent of the "third-party men," who were so active in the early days of the People's Party? Certainly, they were organizers, and probably office-seekers. Often, Lipset (1968) finds and Courtney (2007) recounts that the CCF leadership drew on their earlier experiences as members and leaders of the British Labour Party, the Fabian Society, the Socialist Party of the United States, and even the People's Party. Writing about the early CCF, Zakuta (1958, 41) recalled that a minority "warned that a party of conventional form would either become mired in a parliamentary morass, or if it escaped that trap, would be defenceless against the ruthlessness of its now desperate foes. Political 'realism' dictated the creation of a more effective instrument, towards which Lenin's model of tightly disciplined elites might be a useful guide."

The CCF's federal structure implied a strategic investment in local party organizations that was generally absent, or weak, in Canada in the early 1930s. Although the strength of party identification during the early decades of the twentieth century, especially in Ontario and the Maritimes, impressed foreign observers (see Scarrow 1965, 74), it was not because they were reinforced by active local party organizations. Rather, Epstein (1964, 50) writes that "[n]either major Canadian party has a large mass-membership (dues-paying not being a standard practice), neither has a heavily class-conscious base, neither has a clear-cut ideological or even programmatic position, and neither has an apparatus (outside parliament) claiming authority to establish policy for the party's publicly elected legislators." The CCF party leaders, by contrast, recognized the importance of local mobilization efforts, and built the party organization from voting polls (or precincts), to constituency organizations,

Provincial Councils and a national Executive. But the extensive involvement of local organizations should not be seen as lack of national leadership: As Engelmann (1956, 166–7) writes,

Leaders must be relied upon to determine strategy in electoral contests, and this need is recognized in the CCF. While the organization of electoral activity and the issuing of propaganda is in the hands of a few people, the party takes pride in employing voluntary labour in campaigns, a necessity become a virtue. This spontaneous participation at the menial level of electoral process does not constitute co-determination of election policy.

Part of this election policy was, of course, crafting and refining the CCF message to appeal to the voters it hoped to mobilize. Although the Regina Manifesto, CCF's founding document, committed the party to a socialist program after winning only eight seats in the 1935 election, the party leaders quickly confronted a question fundamental to their organization's success: "Should the CCF continue as an independent socialist party preaching that socialism is the only hope for a decent society, until the pressure of events brought the majority over to them? Or should the party compromise its program by modifying its radicalism in order to win an electoral majority for a program of immediate reforms that would put the party in power?" (Lipset 1968, 141). In fact, the CCF compromised, and the program developed for the 1936 convention documents omitted the CCF's original commitments to socialism and the nationalization of land.

In its early years, the CCF also confronted the question of the role of agricultural workers in its electoral coalition. When the party was established, urban intellectuals, mostly from Toronto and Montreal, who compromised the League for Socialist Reconstruction, became the "brain trust" of the CCF (Young 1969, 70). For them, more was needed to address the ills of capitalism than the agrarian isolationism promoted by some early CCF leaders. However, the CCF leadership also recognized that the "CCF provided a vehicle for the active involvement denied the farmers by the old parties, an involvement they lacked in economic and social spheres as well" (Young 1969, 75). Further, "the political necessity of keeping close touch with agrarian questions was never overlooked, for the obvious reason that the party won seats in the farm belt and generally had more rural members in the parliamentary caucus than urban" (Young 1969, 75).

That the CCF confronted existential questions about its commitment to socialism so early in its history, on the one hand, and about agricultural workers on the other, is especially hard to reconcile with an "up-from-the-bottom" account of party formation: What did the Canadian voters want, exactly? Rather, it seems more likely that political entrepreneurs struggled to resolve tension between their own policy objectives and the realities of electoral geography. Indeed, Young (1969, 59) writes, "The strain between these two aspects generated tensions within the party and hostility towards those who seemed to be either ignoring the party's role in the Canadian party system or subverting principle in order to win office or the support of some segment of Canadian society, for example, the trade unions."

This tension between policy objectives and the leaders' office-seeking goals was probably exacerbated by the fact that, like the People's Party "third-party men," the CCF party leadership, and ultimately the candidates they would recruit, were quite well off compared to typical agricultural workers (Lipset 1968). Rather than an organization of members mobilized by their grievances, the party was sustained by its leadership. The CCF National Treasurer and Organizer, Donald MacDonald, suggested that "[o]ur members are too often a collection of lost political souls who rarely see each other from one year to another, let alone get together to discuss and plan the work of the political party they believe in"(Engelmann 1954, 95–6). Anticipating a more general argument made in *Political Man* (1983), Lipset (1968, 204) characterized the "Saskatchewan situation" this way:

[W]ithin an exploited economic group, such as the prairie wheat farmers, those who possess economic and social status within the class are most resentful of a threat to their security. The poorer, socially outcast groups, when they are seriously affected by economic reverses, are likely to be politically apathetic rather than rebellious. In Saskatchewan this group did not organize for remedial action, but had to be organized from the outside by leaders of the more prosperous farmers.

Does the relatively high status of the CCF leadership and early supporters (see, e.g., Lipset 1968, 201), suggest that the CCF was something other than a low-income people's party? This perception is difficult to reconcile with later empirical analysis that shows that the CCF entered those electoral districts where shifts in electoral power had favored low-income voters. Further, the nature of political appeals, particularly during the "early radical period," were clearly addressed to the "extremely poor farmers" of the Canadian prairies, even if they did not typically belong to the organized farmers' movements that contributed to the CCF's early momentum (Lipset 1968, 203–4).

Of course, some of the CCF's difficulty in mobilizing those with very low incomes at least partly results from the coincidence of their Catholic identity and the (largely mistaken) impression of the CCF's commitment to socialism.[3] As Lipset (1968, 210) writes, even outside of the predominantly Catholic province of Quebec, "Catholics are generally afflicted with a deep-rooted, though unconscious, prejudice against the CCF." Because of the Church's opposition to socialism generally, and the CCF in the Canadian context, Catholic identity may have reinforced established partisan networks, perhaps

---

[3] Olssen (1973), for example, describes the CCF's efforts to respond to criticisms offered by Catholic clergy. Lipset (1968, 210) also notes the "terribly distorted view of the CCF *reality*" with regards to religious tolerance and commitment to socialism.

especially where immigrant communities were mostly Catholic, but changes in local distributions of electoral power favored low-income citizens. In Quebec, in addition to the Church's opposition, French Canadian identity also served to reinforce local partisan networks. There, the CCF met with additional resistance to its advocacy of greater federal authority and centralized economic policy-making. Further, the CCF's failure to accommodate French language rights, for example, led one observer to note that "the CCF lacked success in the beginning [at least in Quebec] not because of its socialist content but because of its Canadian nationalism" (Olssen 1973, 102).

In the end, the entry decisions of the CCF varied province-to-province, and district-to-district within provinces (see Figure 5.3): the CCF contested every district only in Saskatchewan. Otherwise, CCF entry decisions within provinces were clearly deliberate. And, while the CCF generally avoided electoral contests in Quebec, it recruited candidates in Mont Royal, St. James, and Verdun – districts that experienced the dramatic changes in the composition of their electorates described above. Similarly, the CCF contested slightly more than half of the districts in Ontario, particularly those in the north and around Lake Ontario. The CCF generally avoided districts in New Brunswick, Nova Scotia, and Prince Edward Island, and this likely reflects the strength of existing partisan networks, in combination with the region's population decline, noted earlier. Maritime districts where Woodsworth and the CCF attempted to make inroads – including those in Cape Breton (Earle & Gamberg 1989) – are those districts in the region that experienced the largest changes in the proportion of low-income voters, and in fact would be contested by the newly formed Communist and Reconstruction parties. Like the People's Party, therefore, it seems that the CCF's strategic decisions to enter electoral contests largely proceeded on a district-by-district basis.

The CCF's formation and strategic entry decisions, therefore, correspond well to the account of party formation offered in Chapter 2. A casual comparison of Figures 5.2 and 5.3 suggests that, in fact, the leaders of the CCF recognized in Canada's changing electoral geography electoral opportunities to mobilize a new national low-income constituency. As we shall see below, this account of endogenous party formation and entry fits well with the history of Social Credit, a party that promoted quite different policies, but responded to similar electoral incentives. Then, this chapter's final section will use the measures that describe Canada's changing electoral geography to rigorously evaluate the relationship between the changing electoral power of low-income citizens and CCF and Social Credit's entry in Canada's 1935 federal election.

The Formation of Social Credit

The formation of Social Credit and the recruitment of candidates to contest elections on the Social Credit label also corresponds well to the general outline presented above. Social Credit was formed by a small group of political

FIGURE 5.3. The strategic entry of CCF candidates, 1935.
Sources: District boundary files are based on revisions of CCRI Reference Maps. Electoral data: CLEA.

entrepreneurs who were strategic in the construction of their platform, and in the recruitment of Social Credit candidates. William Aberhart, in particular, bore the costs of establishing and mobilizing the party, and in structuring its ideological platform. As suggested above, unlike CCF, Social Credit adherents saw solutions to the profound poverty of the early 1930s in the market, and characterized the real challenge of society in terms of providing better access to the benefits of an advanced technological society. Aberhart crafted and promoted a platform in Canada based largely on the ideas of Major Clifford Douglas, an English engineer: notably, a social credit or dividend to which everyone would be entitled, and an explicit rejection of socialism, which would imply a further concentration of economic and political power.

Despite early ideological commitments, there is evidence that Social Credit party leaders, Aberhart included, were quick to revise their electoral appeals in order to maximize their office-seeking success. Early party materials, for example, notably the *Douglas System of Economics* published in 1933, and referred to as the "Yellow Pamphlet," excluded what would become an important part of Social Credit's policy platform. A commitment to "just price," or fair return on agricultural products, was featured prominently in the earlier publication, the *Social Credit Manual* (1935). Hannant (1985, 109) identifies the incorporation of "just price" as Aberhart's explicit attempt to broaden the Social Credit constituency, and especially to mobilize agricultural workers. Further, as MacPherson (1953, 151) writes,

Very early in his political campaign, and more emphatically as the campaign went on, Aberhart preached the necessity of the people's uniting to demand results and forgoing the divisive discussion of methods and technical theory ... the aim is "to obtain a mass expression of the will of the people, i.e. a mobilization of the nation's most urgent desire—the abolition of poverty in plenty."

"What was needed," Aberhart claimed and MacPherson (151) reports, "was not 'educators' but 'campaigners,' no matter how 'technically unsound.' "

Key party leaders also established themselves as office-seekers, whose ideological commitments may have been less complete. Hannant (1985, 114) draws our attention to the case of Fred Anderson, who was "really a socialist and [did] not believe in the social credit proposals at all." Apparently, Anderson had joined the CCF shortly after it was founded, and worked hard as an early organizer. After a prolonged period of unemployment, however, Anderson would soon abandon the CCF, and in fact was elected to Alberta's provincial legislature on the Social Credit ticket. Hannant (1985) also notes that J.F. Maloney and Eric J. Poole had similar political conversions. Both early supporters of CCF, Maloney and Poole were elected to the House of Commons as members of the Social Credit caucus. This flexibility led one observer to conclude that "[w]hatever idealism there may be in this social credit movement which has swept the province of Alberta, there is certainly a great deal of paltriness and self-seeking and an utter lack of principle on the part of many" (Norman Priestly, quoted in Hannant 1985, 115).

Finally, Social Credit, like the CCF and other parties considered here, carefully and deliberately invested in the recruitment of candidates and organization of voters. Social Credit invested in local organizations and established study groups throughout Alberta. Aberhart and other party leaders would frequently tour even remote areas of the province. Nevertheless, as Hannant (1985, 106) writes, "the importance of leadership emanating from Calgary cannot be denied." One way in which this leadership was expressed was through the recruitment of local candidates. As Irving (1959, 141) recounts, Aberhart and the national executive committee would select candidates from the three or four chosen by constituency organizations. When confronted with a set of possible candidates that did not meet Aberhart's criteria – he preferred "reliable, honorable, bribe-proof businessmen" and "socially prominent newcomers" – Aberhart's committee would simply choose its own candidates, including, for example, two men who had been defeated by local nomination procedures and one candidate who had not been nominated at all. These selections, Irving (1959, 143) suggests and Hannant (1985) recounts, were deliberate attempts to win over the more well-heeled parts of Calgary, who could provide valuable support for the party.

How did Social Credit party leaders think about its electoral viability, and its potential constituency? In fact, as suggested above, Social Credit often focused its mobilization efforts on voters also sought after by CCF. One activist, for example, recounts her efforts to mobilize the working-class districts of east Calgary:

So I went over to the Labor Temple where ... was in charge, preaching Socialism and Communism to the poor working men. I found out I could hold meetings there, so for over three years all my groups met as a large group in this Labor Temple. The time we were taking the straw vote [January 1935] I had over 8,000 names signed up in that district. I took those people right away from Socialism and Communism and sold them on Social Credit. (Irving 1959, 270, quoted in Hannant 1985, 105)

Further, Social Credit focused its mobilization efforts on Calgary, a city which had experienced tremendous growth over the previous decade. The districts in Northern Alberta, however, including Edmonton, received much less attention from early Social Credit organizers.

In the end, Social Credit would enter far fewer federal electoral contests than the CCF, and these contests were exclusively in the western provinces of Manitoba, Saskatchewan, Alberta, and British Columbia (see Figure 5.4). Although Social Credit would recruit candidates in every district in Alberta, where their hold on the provincial government likely created an important advantage,[4] there is evidence that Social Credit was more strategic in its recruitment of candidates in the other provinces. In Manitoba, for example, Social Credit recruited candidates in the high-growth districts of Winnipeg. Similarly, Social Credit would enter electoral competition in the Burrard district of Vancouver, which also experienced relatively large increases in the electoral power of low-income voters.

---

4 Particularly in the case of Social Credit, which was elected and formed Alberta's provincial government early in 1935, one might wonder about the strategic investment in provincial as well as federal party organizations. As noted above, the CCF also established a federal structure linking provincial organizations under a national committee, and would compete in early provincial elections. MacPherson (1953, 24) suggests that "there are obvious advantages to the national organizers in having the same machine for both federal and provincial elections. It is easier to keep up party enthusiasm and party loyalties" – that is, sustain local partisan networks – "if the voters can be mobilized on party lines at both federal and provincial elections; the more frequently a party machine is actively used, the more smoothly it is able to run." Further, if a party is able to capture the provincial government, its members will benefit from the additional spoils, deepening the bond to the party and aiding the national party in its purpose.

FIGURE 5.4. The strategic entry of Social Credit candidates, 1935.
Sources: District boundary files are based on revisions of CCRI Reference Maps. Electoral data: CLEA.

Summary

This section has drawn on historical analysis of the CCF and Social Credit parties to evaluate evidence in favor of the account of party formation presented in Chapter 2. In both cases, we see parties formed and mobilized by office-seeking political entrepreneurs who were political outsiders. They established the CCF and Social Credit parties as highly centralized and exerted important levels of influence over the activities of local party organizations, including the recruitment of candidates and development of electoral appeals. There is also evidence that each party was careful and deliberate in the electoral contests it entered. In fact, that there is significant overlap in the districts contested suggests that the party leaders likely were responding to similar opportunity structures, in spite of important ideological differences between the parties. In combination with the flexibility of each party's platform and the movement of leaders and candidates between parties over the course of a single election campaign, this evidence is hard to reconcile with an account of party formation that emphasizes "up-from-the-bottom" cleavage structures, or changes in voter demands.

The next section of this chapter will make precise the role of changing electoral geography in explaining the strategic entry decisions of the CCF and Social Credit. It will use the measure of the changing electoral power of low-income citizens to predict the entry of new party candidates. In each case, there is strong evidence that the CCF and Social Credit were responding to new electoral opportunities created by changes in the local distributions of electoral power.

5.4   PREDICTING CCF AND SOCIAL CREDIT ENTRY

Table 5.2 reports an analysis of the relationship between where CCF candidates contested seats in the 1935 federal election and changes in the composition of local electorates. If earlier arguments about the importance of changes in local distributions of electoral power are correct, then it ought to be the case that CCF candidates are more likely to enter electoral contests in those districts that have experienced real increases in the electoral power of low-income voters. In fact, this is exactly what we see: the analysis reported in each column suggests that the CCF more frequently recruited candidates in those districts where changes in electoral geography favored low-income citizens. Each column reports an increasingly complex analysis that incorporates potentially confounding variables, including those that describe the composition of the labor force and the prevalence of Catholic and francophone identities in each district. Column (4) replicates the analysis of the People's Party strategic entry decisions, and examines whether the CCF was especially likely to enter those districts in which changes in electoral geography had favored low-income voters such that, in 1935, they formed the numerical majority.

The first column reports an analysis in which CCF entry is predicted by the percentage of low-income voters, and the change in the percentage of low-income voters. Here, we see a strong positive relationship between the increase in the electoral power of low-income voters and the likelihood of CCF entry – even when the overall strength of low-income voters in each district is taken into account.[5]

In a way that is similar to the case of the People's Party, where the politics of race and ethnicity reinforced local partisan networks and presented a real challenge to the Populists, and coincided with a geographic region in which there was limited change in local distributions of electoral power, we might worry that the relationship observed in Column (1) results, not from the CCF's

---

[5]   Here, as in Chapter 4, I have included the 1921 proportion of low-income voters to avoid post-treatment bias.

entry decisions, but from its decisions to avoid specific districts. Specifically, the coincidence of those districts that have experienced exceptional economic growth (and where the percentage of low-income voters declined) and those districts where the CCF faced unusual resistance because francophone and/or Catholic identity reinforced the local partisan networks of the established parties could create the appearance of a relationship between the changing composition of districts and CCF entry. To explore this possibility, the second column breaks the measure of the change in the percentage of low-income voters into quantiles, and includes an indicator for each category. (The omitted baseline category corresponds to those districts where the share of low-income voters decreased between 41 and 7 percent of the electorate between 1921 and 1931.) If it were simply the case that the linear relationship observed in Column (1) reflected CCF's avoidance of the relatively well-off districts in Quebec, the indicators corresponding to those districts in which the electoral power of low-income voters increased, Quantiles 3 and 4 would offer little explanatory power. In fact, what the analysis in Column (2) implies is that while the CCF entered only four of the districts in which the electoral power of low-income voters declined (about 7 percent), the CCF recruited candidates and contested almost two thirds (64 percent) of the districts where the electoral power of low-income voters increased. (Nationally, the CCF contested just less than half of Canada's federal districts.) This pattern of competition – the CCF entering those contests where changes in electoral geography favored low-income voters – holds even when other factors that are thought to be associated with CCF support, including labor force characteristics and religious and linguistic measures, are incorporated into the analysis (see Column 3).[6]

Column (4) reports the results of analysis that distinguishes districts according to whether or not the changes in electoral geography were sufficient to make low-income voters pivotal in the district (i.e., those districts where they formed a new, numerical majority), and looks at CCF patterns of entry across districts. What we see, first, is that CCF candidates are unlikely to enter districts where the electoral power of low-income voters did not increase – even if they were pivotal. The CCF entered only 29 of the 102 contests where low-income voters were a decreasing minority, and just six of the fourteen contests where low-income voters formed a decreasing majority. Where the electoral power of low-income voters increased, however, the CCF was much more likely to enter. The reader might naturally worry about the relative magnitude of the coefficients estimated for districts where the electoral power of low-income voters increased, but not to a sufficient extent to make them pivotal, and the last group of districts, where low-income voters were newly pivotal. Actually, in those districts where the electoral power of low-income voters increased,

---

[6] Not surprisingly, this analysis confirms that the CCF was unlikely to enter electoral contests in districts where there were large Catholic communities, as anticipated by Lipset (1968) and others.

TABLE 5.2. *The strategic entry of CCF candidates, 1935.*

	DV: CCF candidate entry			
	(1)	(2)	(3)	(4)
Proportion low-income (1921)	−1.936ᵃ			
	(0.653)			
Low-income district (1921)		0.056	0.939ᵃ	
		(0.246)	(0.321)	
Change in proportion of low-income voters, 1921–1931 Quartile 1 [−0.42, −0.07]	5.036ᵃ (0.838)			
Quartile 2 [−0.06, 0.06]		1.605ᵃ	1.055ᵃ	
		(0.300)	(0.359)	
Quartile 3 [0.06, 0.12]		1.943ᵃ	1.545ᵃ	
		(0.303)	(0.395)	
Quartile 4 [0.12, 0.37]		1.854ᵃ	1.667ᵃ	
		(0.303)	(0.394)	
Proportion in farming, forestry, or fishing (1931)			−9.251ᵃ	
			(2.065)	
Proportion in mining, construction, or manufacturing (1931)			−8.526ᵃ	
			(4.052)	
More than 20% French-speaking (1931)			0.141	
			(0.255)	
More than 10% Catholic (1931)			−1.058ᵃ	
			(0.275)	
Low-income district (1921 & 1931)				0.390
				(0.362)
Increase in low-income voters, Not a low-income district				1.512ᵃ
				(0.244)
Increase in low-income voters, low-income district (1931)				0.609ᵃ
				(0.205)
Intercept	0.477	−1.506ᵃ	0.937	−0.570ᵃ
	(0.258)	(0.257)	(0.685)	(0.137)
N	232	232	232	232
Pseudo R^2	0.212	0.200	0.323	0.136

Notes: This table reports probit coefficients for an analysis in which the dependent is a binary indicator of whether or not a CCF candidate contested the election in that district. Standard errors are reported in parentheses.

ᵃ $p < 0.01$.

ᵇ $p < 0.05$.

Source: Election data: Kollman *et al.* (2014).

low-income voters comprised an average of 38 percent of each district – and likely represented an important opportunity for the CCF, even without forming a numerical majority.

What about Social Credit? Did Social Credit's strategic entry decisions similarly acknowledge opportunities created by changes in local electoral power distributions? Again, if earlier arguments about changing electoral geography are correct, then it ought to be the case that Social Credit candidates are more likely to enter electoral contests in those districts that have experienced real increases in the electoral power of low-income voters. In fact, this is exactly what we see: the first column reports an analysis in which Social Credit entry is predicted by the percentage of low-income voters and the change in the percentage of low-income voters. Here, we see a strong positive relationship between the increase in the electoral power of low-income voters and the likelihood of Social Credit entry. In fact, we see evidence of this relationship – increasing concentration of low-income voters and Social Credit entry – in each of the specifications reported in Table 5.3, which alternately include different measures of the change in the percentage of low-income voters, potentially confounding covariates, and in Column (4), indicators of whether the increase in low-income voters' electoral power was large enough so that they likely formed the numerical majority in 1935 and were pivotal in the electoral contest.

Because Social Credit contested many of the same districts as the CCF, mostly in Alberta and Saskatchewan (although the CCF also contested many districts in Ontario and British Columbia, as well as a few in Quebec), the similarities between Tables 5.2 and 5.3 are not unexpected. Like the CCF, the rate at which Social Credit contested elections increases with increases in the electoral power of low-income citizens, from one out of the fifty-nine districts where the electoral power of low-income voters decreased, to about one third of the districts where the electoral power of low-income voters increased – actually, about 60 percent (twenty-three out of thirty-nine) of those districts, west of Ontario.

5.5 SUMMARY AND CONCLUSIONS

This chapter has presented evidence that the CCF and Social Credit recognized important opportunities in Canada's changing electoral geography, and entered electoral competition in those districts where the electoral power of low-income voters had increased dramatically. This analysis bolsters this book's more general argument about the importance of electoral geography to party formation and party system development in several ways.

First, of course, this analysis replicates Chapter 4's analysis of the strategic decision-making of the American People's Party, in a different national and temporal context, and with a different source of empirical support. That the political entrepreneurs who formed and mobilized the CCF and Social Credit

TABLE 5.3. *The strategic entry of Social Credit candidates, 1935.*

	DV: Social Credit candidate entry				
	(1)	(2)	(3)	(4)	(5) Western provinces only
Proportion low-income voters (1921)	1.468^a (0.707)				
Low-income district (1921)		0.986^a (0.268)	0.699^b (0.334)		
Change in proportion of low-income voters, 1921–1931 Quartile 1 [−0.42, −0.07]	4.686^a (1.041)				
Quartile 2 [−0.06, 0.06]		1.025^a (0.464)	0.882 (0.482)		
Quartile 3 [0.06, 0.12]		1.844^a (0.447)	1.763^a (0.459)		
Quartile 4 [0.12, 0.37]		1.864^a (0.454)	1.949^a (0.475)		
Proportion in farming, forestry, or fishing (1931)			−5.554^a (1.995)		
Proportion in mining, construction, or manufacturing (1931)			−20.174^a (4.580)		
More than 20% French-speaking (1931)			0.767^b (0.329)		
Low-income district (1921 & 1931)				1.523^a (0.425)	1.581^b (0.776)
Increase in low-income voters, not a low-income district (1931)				1.274^a (0.312)	1.224 (0.644)
Increase in low-income voters, low-income district (1931)				1.529^a (0.296)	1.499^b (0.630)

TABLE 5.3. *Continued*

	DV: Social Credit candidate entry				
	(1)	(2)	(3)	(4)	(5) Western provinces only
Intercept	−1.679	−2.476[a]	−0.630	−1.890[a]	−1.150[b]
	(0.258)	(0.425)	(0.782)	(0.305)	(0.568)
N	232	232	232	232	53
Pseudo R^2	0.138	0.194	0.325	0.170	0.099

Notes: This table reports probit coefficients for an analysis in which the dependent is a binary indicator of whether or not a Social Credit candidate contested the election in each district. Standard errors are reported in parentheses.

[a] $p < 0.01$.

[b] $p < 0.05$.

Source: Election data: Kollman *et al.* (2014).

were responding to similar incentive structures as the Populist "third-party men" – in spite of important differences between Canada and the US, that include general system characteristics, suffrage restrictions, ballot access, and so on – is remarkable.

Second, as suggested throughout this chapter, the simultaneous entry of the CCF and Social Credit into federal politics – in many of the same districts – is difficult to reconcile with accounts of party formation that emphasize voters' demands. Indeed, in both cases, the party leaders revised their ideological commitments to mobilize newly pivotal low-income voters whose support would further their own office-seeking goals.

Chapter 6 will focus on British Labour, and again will show that the political entrepreneurs who organized the new party recognized opportunities for entry in England's changing electoral geography. In this case, however, it is primarily migration from agricultural to industrial regions of the country that alters the distribution of electoral power and creates a newly pivotal constituency that was ripe for mobilization. As a consequence, the Labour party elites faced quite different incentives in the construction of their party's platform, with important long-term consequences for the political representation of low-income voters in their country.

5.A APPENDIX: SUPPORTING MATERIALS

The Canadian Century Research Infrastructure

Through the CCRI initiative, individual-level samples from the 1921 and 1931 Canadian censuses (4 and 3 percent, respectively) are available for analysis at

Statistics Canada Research Data Centres. Samples are based on dwellings, and include all individuals within dwellings. The individual-level datasets include geographic information, as well as information about each person's social and demographic characteristics. As noted in the main text of this chapter, the Canadian censuses from this period also collected data on annual earnings, employment status, occupation, and industry.

To preserve the anonymity of individuals included in the census datasets, Statistics Canada established extensive regulations for the release of any descriptive analysis based on these data, particularly for detailed geography (regions with less than 25,000 total population). The regulations affected the analysis presented in this chapter in the following ways:

First, for any cross-tabulation (including proportions of low-income voters, French-speaking residents, Catholics, agricultural workers, and so forth, by federal electoral district), it was required that each cell include at least five unweighted cases. Some cultural variables did not meet this threshold, and so binary indicator variables (e.g., identifying those districts in which more than 20 percent of eligible voters were French-speaking) were created and used in place of more continuous measures.[7] This criterion also introduced some imprecision in the allocation of census subdivisions to federal electoral districts, which in a few cases were reallocated to neighboring electoral districts when their inclusion in a particular district would have prevented the release of the tabulation.

Second, because federal electoral districts are typically classified as "detailed geography" (i.e., they have total populations less than 25,000), all descriptive analysis, including key independent variables used in the analysis, is based on weighted samples (with weights inverse to sample probabilities), and rounded to a base of fifty. This implies that estimates of, for example, the proportion of low-income voters, are less precise than estimates based directly on individual-level data.

Matching Census and Electoral Geography

The CCRI datasets report Canadian census divisions, subdivisions, and subdivision parts for the 1921 and 1931 censuses. To characterize the electoral geography of income, these were matched to the 1993 Representation Order (see Table 5.A.1) according to the descriptions reported by Library of Parliament (N.d.).

In addition to the formal descriptions of federal electoral district boundaries, several series of maps were helpful for the allocation of census units to electoral districts, notably Office of the Surveyor General (1933–1934) and the GIS digital shape files and "Reference Maps" prepared as part of the CCRI project.

---

7 The proportion of Catholic residents could not be reported for districts in Quebec, for this reason. Instead, the provincial average (86 percent) was imputed for all districts in the province.

TABLE 5.A.1. *Canadian census and electoral geography.*

	1921	1931
Census geography		
Divisions	220	231
Subdivisions	4,633	5,153
Subdivision parts	15,286	18,670
Federal electoral districts (1933 Representation Order)	245	245
Average voters per district	886	872

TABLE 5.A.2. *Estimating wages and earnings for Canada, 1921 and 1931.*

	1921	1931
Reported annual earnings		
Average	$984	$913
(Std. dev.)	(1,399)	(981)
N	82,425	86,601
Estimated annual earnings (Full sample of eligible voters, reporting occupations with earnings)		
Average	$995	$879
(Std. dev.)	(1,169)	(848)
N	124,853	135,055
Estimated annual household earnings (Full sample of eligible voters)		
Average	$2,475	$2,461
(Std. dev.)	(5,411)	(5,232)
N	214,323	211,257

Estimating Wages and Earnings

As noted in the main text of this chapter, the Canadian 1921 and 1931 census enumerators were instructed to collect data on annual earnings from all individuals. In fact, in 1921, data were reported by 82,425 individuals (86,601 in 1931). Using gender, occupations, and, where possible, provinces, annual earnings were estimated for a further 42,428 individuals (48,454 in 1931).

(Province-specific estimates of earnings were generated when earnings were reported by at least fifty people of the same gender within a province; otherwise, gender-specific national estimates were used.) Estimates of earnings were then aggregated within households, and individuals were ranked according to their position in the national household income distribution. Table 5.A.2 provides a summary of the implications of this strategy.

6

The Implications of Electoral Geography for British Labour

The case of British Labour might seem quite different from the American and Canadian parties. To the extent that opportunities in subnational governments structure the incentives of political entrepreneurs and encourage the formation of regional parties, for example (see Chhibber & Kollman 2004), party entry in Great Britain, a unitary state, ought to reflect different (at least moderated) incentive structures. Further, one might expect the importance of the presidency to structure American party formation incentives quite differently from the incentives of British political entrepreneurs, who can focus exclusively on the legislature.[1] This chapter will show, however, that the early leaders of British Labour structured their decisions in ways that were similar to the decisions of political entrepreneurs in Canada and the US. They recognized opportunities for entry in districts where the composition of voters had changed dramatically, and in ways that favored low-income citizens. And, they crafted a platform that reflected the interests of these newly pivotal voters – although these voters were predominantly industrial workers, rather than agricultural. Finally, they entered those electoral contests in which low-income voters were likely to be pivotal, and especially where large numbers of migrants were concentrated.

The main contribution of this chapter, therefore, lies in the demonstration of the importance of changing electoral geography in the origins of parties that represent, primarily, the interests of *industrial* low-income voters. If cross-national variance in the quality of political responsiveness to poverty can be attributed to the historical dominance of left parties (the "Power Resources" account; see Huber & Stephens 2001), then understanding the implications of early electoral geography for the formation and entry of social democratic and labor parties is a crucial part of this explanation. Further evidence in support

---

[1] In fact, all parties considered so far were "national" in their aspirations, even with some earlier experience in provincial government.

of this argument will be presented in Chapter 7, which examines the entry of
the Swedish Social Democrats, as well as the implications of electoral reform.
Here, I focus on the changing electoral geography of Britain between 1881 and
1906, and show how it is different from the electoral geography of the US in
the same period, and Canada in the 1920s and 1930s, but that the political
entrepreneurs – the "third-party men" – faced similar opportunities for the
formation and entry of a new party.

The next section of this chapter will provide an overview of Britain's political
economics at the turn of the twentieth century. Then, as in previous chapters,
this chapter will provide an overview of the strategies used to map the electoral
geography of income in England during this period. Section 6.3 will draw on
archival and secondary material to provide an analytic account of the formation
of the Labour Party, and its strategic entry in 1906 electoral contests. Finally,
this chapter will conclude with a rigorous empirical analysis of Labour's entry
decisions.

In the end, this chapter will show – in a context that is quite different from
the US, Canada, and indeed, Sweden – that political entrepreneurs responded
to similar incentive structures in the formation of British Labour, and for the
recruitment of candidates and mobilization of voters. The evidence presented in
this chapter, therefore, will provide further confidence in the important role of
changing electoral geography in determining which groups will be mobilized as
partisan constituencies, and how this contributes to the quality of their political
representation in the long term.

6.1 THE BRITISH POLITICAL ECONOMY AT THE END OF THE NINETEENTH CENTURY

When the Labour Representation Committee (LRC) was formed in 1900,
Britain was a highly industrialized and generally integrated, but working-class,
economy. "In 1901 about 85 percent of the total working population were
employed by others, and about 75 percent as manual workers" (McKibbin
1990, 2). While each region cultivated some expertise in a specific trade –
textiles, for example, in the North West cities of Manchester and Clitheroe, and
iron and steel along the perimeter of the North Eastern coalfields – over half
of adult men in every region were employed in manufacturing or construction
industries. There were two exceptions to this generally integrated labor market
structure. First, agricultural development was generally limited – "almost
exiguous," writes McKibbin (1990, 2) – and agricultural workers tended to live
in the South East, South West, and Midlands regions. Second, miners comprised
more than 30 percent of eligible voters in only thirty-five of more than four
hundred electoral divisions, mostly in the North East, but also in the North
West and Wales.[2]

---

[2]   These estimates are based on the analysis to follow, but line up with Tanner's (1990, 197); he
     writes, "In 1911 there were a million miners in England and Wales, spread over seven major

This national integration – a feature of the British political economy which perhaps sets it apart from the American and Canadian political economies considered in earlier chapters – is generally reflected in elections to the House of Commons. In elections held between 1885 and 1910, for example, national levels of support for Britain's two major parties were fairly balanced, on the whole and within most districts. Support for the Conservatives in the six elections between 1886 and 1910, for example, ranged from about 45 percent in the median district in North Eastern England (Yorkshire), to about 56 percent in the median district in South East England. (Note, however, that because of the disproportionality in the mapping of votes to seats, this general balance did not contribute to national competitiveness: the Tories form the government for most of this period, at least until the 1900 election of the Liberal Party.)

In fact, the electoral coalitions that sustained this balance were quite stable, for reasons that are important to understanding the strategic incentives of the newly formed Labour party: First, party allegiances largely coincided with religious identity. "The vast majority" of Conservative party supporters, Bealey and Pelling (1958, 8) claim, "must have been at least nominal adherents of the Church of England"; Protestant dissenters and others (including recent immigrants to England) regularly supported the Liberals. Further,

the spatial distribution of Nonconformist and Anglican religious attendance continued to be closely correlated with the distribution of (respectively) Liberal and Tory support. Middle-class Nonconformist and working-class Anglican attenders seem to have been more likely to deny their "class" position and vote for the party associated with their religious preference. (Tanner 1990, 81)

Some of this allegiance reflected the predominant issues of the period, particularly the role of the Anglican Church in public education and, to some extent, the issue of Irish Home Rule, but as Tanner (1990, 81) suggests, the parties themselves were active in linking religious and partisan identities: "They forged genuinely *political* cultures," or in the framework used here, local partisan networks that reinforced the importance of religious identities to partisan group membership.

One consequence of the relationship between religious identity and partisanship in Britain at the end of the nineteenth century was that many solidly working-class districts in the North West, the Greater London area, the East Midlands, and the Southern port cities were solidly Tory districts. "Tory success," Tanner (1990, 165) suggests, "was built ... on cultural affinities with working-class social activities, on attendance to ethnic tensions, and allied to this, on support for the protection of British values, British jobs, and British international prestige." In the North West, the "combination of casual,

coalfields. They constituted at least 30 per cent of the electorate in thirty-six constituencies, more than 10 per cent in another thirty-eight."

unskilled, and dangerous employment, and squalid social conditions, helped create a conservative and pessimistic culture, based on short-term interest, gambling, violence, fatalism, the pawnbroker, and an acerbic hedonism." Liberal support for social policies that emphasized education, for example, had little traction. Instead, a "xenophobic Protestant Conservatism" that "had powerful roots in a religious/ethnic/economic hostility to the Catholic Irish" took hold (Tanner 1990, 131). By contrast, the miners of the North East, who tended to adhere to Nonconformist faiths, generally supported Liberals, in spite of their similarly dangerous employment and difficult living conditions.

Second, although the beginnings of national party politics are often traced to the late nineteenth century (see Cox 1987), elections in England during this period were largely determined by the strength of local partisan networks. The involvement of national party leaders in local elections was limited to infrequent visits and public lectures. Individual candidates, however, were responsible for bearing the costs of the administration of the election, the mobilization of voters, and importantly, for the maintenance of local partisan networks between elections. As Pelling (1967, 11) notes, "[a] candidate was expected to be generous to all sorts of local causes if he wanted the willing support of the electors." Further, "from the moment a candidate appears in the field, he is fair game, and every man's hand is in his pocket" (Rider Haggard, a candidate for Norfolk East in 1895, quoted in Pelling 1967). Incentives to constantly invest in local partisan networks were enhanced by relatively short campaign periods. Parliaments were often dissolved, and new elections held within fairly short periods of time. Shortly after the Labour Representation Committee was established in 1900, for example, Parliament was dissolved on September 25, and elections were held between September 28 and October 24, 1900. This meant that "constituencies had to be 'nursed' over a long period ... 'It is the visit to the village feasts, the chat in the village schoolroom, the likeness over the chimney corner, and the pleasant friendly musical evenings in the winter, which are the articles of war' " (Pelling 1967, 14). Finally, Pelling (1967) provides evidence that especially small districts were relatively insulated from national swings in support for the two major parties. All of this suggests that, in the absence of dramatic changes in the composition of district electorates, local partisan networks were well established and quite stable. The availability of new voters, who were ripe for mobilization, may have been especially important for Labour entry into politics.

The third feature of the political economy that undoubtedly structured Labour party entry incentives derives from the Redistribution of Seats Act of 1885, which established the electoral district boundaries for contests held between 1885 and 1918. District boundaries were drawn with the explicit goal of constructing districts that coincided with the "pursuits of the people." Pelling (1967, 9) notes that, "In larger towns, divisions representing the business or middle-class residential interest were usually separated out from the working-class quarters; in the counties, the agricultural and industrial areas were given distinct representation, and thus the 'landed interest' was given further lease of life." This strategic construction of district boundaries contributed to the stability of party competition between 1885 and 1900. However, the separation of voters by "pursuit" also exaggerated the effects of migration on distributions of electoral power within districts (more on this below) and, especially where populations increased, created real opportunities for new party entry.

This section of the discussion has briefly highlighted features of the British political economy at the end of the nineteenth century that were especially important to understanding the strategic decision-making of the political entrepreneurs who formed and mobilized the Labour Party. Using methods detailed in Chapter 4, the next section will build on the overview presented here in order to characterize the British electoral geography of income in considerable detail, and will precisely identify where demographic changes created opportunities for new party entry. Then, as in previous chapters, Section 6.3 will develop an account of Labour Party strategic formation and entry into electoral contests, drawing largely on archival and historical analysis. Finally, the relationship between Labour entry decisions and changing electoral geography will be evaluated in a more rigorous empirical analysis. In the end, as we shall see, changing electoral geography was especially important to Labour entry decisions; that these changes were concentrated in primarily industrial areas would have important implications for the type of policy interests that the new party would articulate.

6.2 THE ELECTORAL GEOGRAPHY OF INCOME IN ENGLAND AND WALES, 1881–1900

This section identifies those districts where the electoral power of low-income voters increased in the decades just prior to the formation and entry of British Labour. The strategy for characterizing the changing distribution of British income is somewhat different from that followed in the analyses of other cases. While individual-level census data are available for only one year (1881), the boundaries of electoral districts did not change between 1885 and 1910. This means that although the changing electoral power of low-income voters cannot be estimated directly as the difference in the percentage of low-income voters in 1906 and 1885, dramatic changes in the composition of each district can be evaluated with simple changes in the size of the electorate. We will be especially interested in which districts experience big changes in population, and whether these changes are occurring more frequently in districts with large proportions of low-income voters in 1885.

To evaluate the changing electoral geography of Great Britain between 1885 and 1906, then, this analysis will estimate the distribution of income within each district in 1885, using a similar strategy to the strategy used for the US analysis (described in more detail below), and the change in the size of the electorate, just before the 1906 election. As later analysis will demonstrate, these two variables will provide the key predictors of Labour party entry: Labour candidates are more likely to enter electoral contests in those districts that had large numbers of low-income voters in 1885 *and* which experienced dramatic increases in the size of the electorate just before the 1906 election.

To map the electoral geography of income, British census geography must first be matched to the electoral district boundaries. Census geography in Britain is similarly structured to American census geography, with registration districts and subdistricts nested within counties. For most of England and Wales, civil parishes are nested within registration subdistricts, and can be matched to districts fairly easily; in some boroughs, however, civil parishes may combine several registration subdistricts. The *Report of the Boundary Commissioners for England and Wales* (1885) established new electoral boundaries, with the explicit goal of equalizing the distribution of the electorate across districts – and constructing districts that were "united in purpose" – and was used here to match civil parishes to their electoral divisions. For each county and borough, the *Report* describes the composition of each electoral division, usually with reference to civil parishes, and provides detailed maps delineating the new boundaries.

To generate estimates of income, with the goal of mapping the electoral geography of low-income voters, this analysis follows a strategy similar to the strategy used in the American case. Specifically, this analysis uses official reports of salaries and wages for each industry or occupation (and for some occupations, region), for approximately the same year (1881), to estimate the earnings of each voting-aged man. This analysis relies heavily on the British Board of Trade's *General Report of the Manual Labour Classes in the United Kingdom*, for example, which surveyed firms' payroll data to generate estimates of wages and salaries, as well as the number and type of workers (men, women, and lads) in each occupation category. As with the American case, this analysis uses estimates wages and salaries for men in active full-time employment. When possible (i.e., for agricultural workers), regional estimates of wages are used in place of national averages. For those occupations that were not included in the *Report*, *Estimates for Civil Service and Revenue*, which documents all government expenditures, and other government reports provide estimates for many professional and public sector positions including, for example, civil engineers and architects. This strategy yields 153 distinct annual wage or salary estimates in 37 industry categories. Figure 6.1 and Table 6.1 report general summaries of the national income distribution; further technical details are reported in Appendix 6.A.

Note that British suffrage rights were complicated during this period: Tanner (1990), for example, identifies seven major categories of parliamentary franchise. The *Representation of the People Act, 1884* extended voting rights to most men aged twenty-one and older, living in London, or in the boroughs and counties, to property owners ("freeholders") and long-term leaseholders

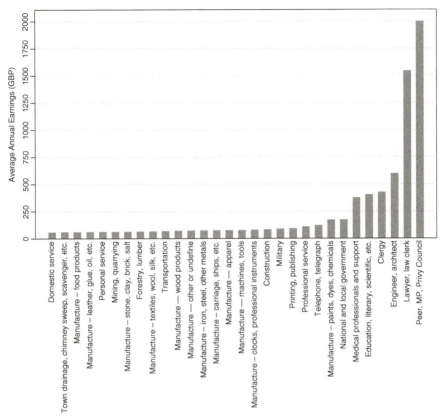

FIGURE 6.1. Average annual earnings, by industry, in Great Britain, 1881.

Note: This figure reports average earnings for each industrial category.

Sources: Please refer to text and Appendix 6.A for details.

of properties whose annual rental value exceeded £10 (by "occupation"). Eligibility, however, was not automatic. Local officials (i.e., the Poor Law Overseers, or the Borough Clerks in London) were responsible for compiling the electoral registers, but the parties often played an important role in registering voters and supplementing these lists. As Tanner (1990) notes, the national party organizations encouraged local parties to begin annual registration drives simultaneously with the Overseers' and Clerks' compilations.

These two features of the electoral rolls – incomplete suffrage and the party's role in registration – have implications for the analysis that follows: First, estimates of income and labor force characteristics are based on an approximation of the electorate, and include all men over the age of twenty-one who have estimated annual earnings of at least £40.[3] Second, to estimate the

---

3 This relatively high threshold is used with the assumption that an individual could contribute no than a quarter – a fairly low, but reasonable, share – of their earnings to rent, and excludes approximately 14 percent of voting-aged men for whom wages could be estimated. This

TABLE 6.1. *Characteristics of the British
national income distributions, 1881 and 2010.*

	1881	2010
Gini index	0.356	0.327
Income ratios of selected percentiles		
90/10	2.36	4.95
95/50	1.58	3.21
50/10	1.68	2.09
Shares of household income quintiles		
Q1	9%	3%
Q2	14%	7%
Q3	15%	14%
Q4	18%	24%
Q5	44%	51%

Notes: This table reports characteristics of the national income distribution for Great Britain (1881), using the wage estimates described in the main discussion. For comparison, the same statistics are reported for the current British income distribution.

Sources: Great Britain (2011): Office of National Statistics. "The effects of taxes and benefits on household income, 2011/12 – Reference Tables" and "Percentile points from 1 to 99 for total income before and after tax, 1999–00 to 2010–11."

impact of changing electoral geography, this analysis uses estimates of changes in the total population of each district, rather than changes in the size of the electorate. This is because changes in the size of the electorate likely reflect parties' mobilization efforts and would be related to Labour entry decisions.

In the end, Table 6.2 reports the distributions of low-income voters and local population change, as well as characteristics of the labor force, for different regions of Britain. For each region, districts in rural counties are distinguished from the more densely populated districts in provincial boroughs. Table 6.2 reports the distribution of labor force characteristics, as well as the distributions of the key independent variables, the electoral power of low-income voters

corresponds with Brand's (1974) estimate that, with the 1885 reforms, 17 percent of voting-aged men were excluded. McKibbin (1990, Table 3.4) offers considerably lower estimates of rates of enfranchisement – about 63 percent in 1901 – suggesting that registries, probably because registration was not automatic, were incomplete. A contemporary observer, Buxton (1892), directly attributes the relatively low rates of franchisement to a registration system "so replete with technicalities, complications and anomalies that every obstacle is put in the way of getting on, and every facility exists for getting struck off, the register" (quoted in Blewett 1972, 359–60).

TABLE 6.2. *The electoral geography of Great Britain, 1885–1906.*

	% Low-income (1881)	Change in population (1891–1901)	Change in electorate (1885–1900)	% Agriculture (1881)	% Mining (1881)	% Manufacturing (1881)
Greater London	31	2,136	1,311	3	1	57
South Eastern England						
Counties	43	7,008	882	16	1	56
Provincial boroughs	35	4,754	1,678	6	1	59
South Western England						
Counties	42	337	509	10	2	58
Provincial boroughs	34	4,645	2,637	5	2	61
Midlands						
Counties	36	4,957	1,590	10	8	60
Provincial boroughs	21	6,112	1,338	2	2	73
North Eastern England						
Counties	31	3,523	3,523	15	11	39
Provincial boroughs	26	8,114	2,482	4	2	72
North Western England						
Counties	29	9,192	2,655	8	6	55
Provincial boroughs	27	5,878	1,848	2	2	67
Wales						
Counties	31	2,931	726	2	14	64
Provincial boroughs	32	5,032	1,298	4	24	53
Total (England & Wales)	33	4,431	1,153	6	2	60

Notes: This table reports estimated median percentages of low-income voters, the median change in the size of each district's electorate, and the composition of the labor force. Appendix 6.A provides technical details of estimates of income, occupation/industry categories, and definitions of regions.

Sources: Population: "Table V. Parliamentary Counties and Boroughs and their Several Divisions," *Census of England and Wales, 1901: Summary Tables.* Electorate: Caramani (2000) and Craig (1974).

(here, those eligible voters earning less than £59), and the change in the population, between 1891 and 1901.

Where were low-income voters most concentrated during the late nineteenth century? And, how did electoral geography change over the last few decades of the late nineteenth century? In fact, as Table 6.3 shows, while the concentration of low-income voters tended to be higher in the counties of the South East, high-growth districts were more common in the largely industrial areas of the North. Of course, low-income voters had significant electoral power in northern districts too. They were pivotal (i.e., formed the numerical majority) in twenty-seven of the eighty-three districts in the North East, and eighteen of the seventy-one districts of the North West. Particularly because of the large numbers of newly arrived eligible voters in these regions, we might expect that the districts in these regions would represent especially attractive electoral opportunities for a newly formed party. Similarly, we might also expect that the relatively high-growth but low-income districts in South Eastern England offered Labour access to a population that was especially ripe for mobilization.

While this section has focused on the measurement of key independent variables for this analysis, the next section of this discussion will provide the context for the dependent variable – that is, the Labour Party's strategic entry decisions. Using historical research and drawing on some archival materials, the next section will show that the formation and entry of the Labour Party fits well with the account of party formation offered in Chapter 2. That is, a core group of political entrepreneurs were instrumental in establishing and mobilizing the party and also played key decision-making roles in deciding where Labour Party candidates would (and *would not*) contest elections. As in previous chapters, the following section will evaluate these entry decisions more rigorously, using the measures of key variables developed here.

6.3   THE ORIGINS OF BRITISH LABOUR

Existing accounts of Labour Party formation tend to emphasize its "emergence" (e.g., Moore 1978) – in Stokes's (1999b) framework, they are bottom-up political sociological accounts – rather than the role of strategic decisions made by political entrepreneurs. Some analysts, for example, suggest that the Taff Vale decision, which imposed restrictions on the ability of workers to organize, played a catalyzing role and mobilized the working class as a partisan constituency (e.g., Boix 2011).[4] Other labor and social historians have frequently treated the replacement of politics structured by religion with that class-based political conflict reflected in Labour's ascension as an inevitable

---

4   Even with the increase in union membership following the Taff Vale decision, Boix (2011) suggests that limited franchise rights, and incentives to vote strategically for the Liberals, undermined Labour's mobilization efforts. Blewett (1972) and others suggest (McKibbin 1990) that Taff Vale actually mobilized support for the established *Liberal* Party.

development (for a discussion of this point, see Tanner 1990, 6). "Industrial unrest," they argue, "was regarded as the motor force of Labour expansion" (e.g., Pelling 1967, Pelling 1965, Bealey & Pelling 1958, Reid 1955). But as Tanner (1990, 12) argues, "the nature of a party's electoral base, and the nature of its aims, are powerfully related." This section will suggest that the Labour Party, like the other parties considered here, reflects not a social force, but the careful strategic decision-making of a small group of political entrepreneurs who bore the costs of mobilizing an initially unstable coalition of groups, recruited candidates, and mobilized voters.

Two organizations preceded the formation of the Labour Representation Committee (which would quickly become the Labour Party): the Independent Labour Party and the smaller Social-Democratic Federation were organizations established with the goal of representing working-class interests. In founding the ILP, however, Keir Hardie sought the explicit creation of a political party that would undermine sectional partisan loyalties and articulate working-class demands. Neither of these parties, however, were successful in recruiting many candidates in the few elections they contested, nor were the party leaders consistent in their relationship to the established parties. Bealey and Pelling (1958, 10) write that "willing as he always was to embrace the whole of the Liberal programme, [Hardie] yet proclaimed his aim was the complete elimination of the Liberal Party – a remark that indicated his hope of winning support, above all, from the Liberal rank and file."

The formation of the Labour Party marked an important turning point. The party was founded at a convention organized by the leadership of the ILP, the SDF, and the Trades Union Congress (TUC) Parliamentary Committee, with the explicit purpose of establishing a new and independent party. In recounting the events of this founding convention, Bealey and Pelling (1958) are astonished by the extent to which the ILP leadership, especially Hardie, but also Ramsay MacDonald, were successful in gaining support for their rather pragmatic, office-seeking agenda – at the expense, for example, of SDF commitments to socialist policy. Hardie put forward an amendment that called for

a distinct Labour Group in Parliament, who shall have their own Whips, and agree upon their policy, which must embrace a readiness to co-operate with any party which for the time being may be engaged in promoting legislation in the direct interest of labour, and be equally ready to associate themselves with any party in opposing measures having an opposite tendency. (quoted in Bealey & Pelling 1958, 28)

At this early convention, the leadership of the new Labour Party were also successful in establishing a highly centralized party organization in which the executive committee would regulate membership, administer dues, and identify official Labour Party candidates. Indeed, later minutes of the Committee would often include lists of "candidatures approved" and discussions of candidate recruitment processes (see, e.g., The Labour Party 1967, 92).

There are two features of Labour Party strategy, vis-à-vis the established Liberals, that may be especially helpful in identifying the structure of their strategic entry decisions.

One feature lies in an accident of timing. As suggested above, the campaign period between the dissolution of Parliament and elections was remarkably short. This must have seemed to be especially the case for the newly formed Labour Party in 1900. The founding convention, held in February, preceded the election at the end of September by only seven short months. As a consequence, while Labour could not recruit or mobilize a full slate of candidates for the 1900 election (fifteen candidates would contest elections on the Labour ticket), candidates in nineteen districts identified themselves as Liberal–Labour candidates. These candidates were nevertheless endorsed by the Labour Representation Committee (see Bealey & Pelling 1958, 43), and a comparison of the districts contested by Lib–Lab candidates to those districts contested by Liberal candidates can provide helpful insights into where the changing electoral geography created opportunities for new parties.

The second helpful insight into early Labour party strategic decision-making results from their entry into a "progressive alliance" with the Liberal Party in 1903. Importantly, the coordination in competition was initiated by the Labour Party. MacDonald, with apparently only Hardie's knowledge, approached the Liberal Party whip, Jesse Herbert, with several lists of districts, proposing (1) "that the Liberal party shall not nominate a candidate in fourteen named constituencies which are single-member constituencies, and shall not nominate more than one candidate in eleven double-member constituencies," (2) identifying "a possible desire on the part of the L.R.C. to fight sixteen single-member seats, and in one double-member constituency," and (3) also including a list of districts that were "merely under consideration" for Labour Party entry. Herbert, in his correspondence with Liberal Party leader William Henry Gladstone, suggests that Labour "can be permitted to run candidates without Liberal competition, and without any considerable local difficulties in 36 seats out of the 52 mentioned by them in the 3 lists." In at least sixteen of the remaining districts, "some discussion is necessary." In response to this initial proposal, Gladstone agreed that the Liberal Council could "use its influence with local associations to abstain from nominating a Liberal candidate, and to unite in support of any recognized and competent Labour candidate."

Many districts included in the Gladstone–MacDonald agreement were places where working-class support for the Conservative party was especially strong, and thus it might be tempting to conclude that the Liberals "permitted" Labour challengers precisely where they had nothing to lose. However, Labour would also contest several districts that were Liberal strongholds: Bernstein (1983) draws particular attention to Norwich (in the South East), Leeds (North East), and Leicester (Midlands) as districts where Labour recruited candidates, and where support for the Liberal party was well established. Note that each of these districts, in fact, experienced tremendous growth at the end of the nineteenth century: Leeds, in particular, was one of the fastest growing cities in the United Kingdom. Further, Bernstein (1983, 626) describes Leeds' Eastern division – Labour would recruit candidates here, and in Leeds South – as the "poorest" part of the city. Bernstein describes Leicester in a way that is similar to Leeds, noting that its rate of population increase, as measured by the decennial census, exceeded 40 percent twice between 1861 and 1901. Although Leicester was a fairly prosperous city for much of this period – the percentage of low-income voters is estimated to be about 20 percent in 1885 – unemployment increased dramatically beginning in 1901, and as Bernstein (1983, 630) suggests, rates of poverty are likely underestimated.

In addition to selecting districts in which to recruit candidates, MacDonald worked to limit the recruitment activities of local Labour organizations, where they were unlikely to be succesful: Herbert, in his correspondence with Gladstone, identified several districts in which MacDonald overrode local organizations to ensure that Labour candidates did *not* enter the electoral contests. For example, Herbert reports that:

MacDonald is opposed to a Labour Candidate standing in W. Salford. He says there has been some mistake. That when his Committee considered the Salfords he (MacDonald) was under the impression that they were fixing a man for the South, and not for West Salford. He is mortified at the mistake. He will see the Salford leaders within the next day or two ... and will try to remove the man from there to S. Salford. (Bealey 1956, 271)

Herbert reports that MacDonald was similarly involved in the "retirement" of the "Labour man" standing in West Bristol, for example.

In the end, the historical evidence suggests that the LRC decision to enter each electoral contest was carefully and deliberately made, on a district-by-district basis, by the political entrepreneurs who founded and mobilized the early Labour Party. In fact, as seen in Table 6.3,

[t]hree-fifths of the Labour candidates stood in Lancashire, Yorkshire and the North East. As well as the five in Scotland, there were only four candidates in the whole London area, five in the Midlands, and two in Wales. This shows clearly the north-eastern bias of LRC strength. It was clearly a party rooted in the most heavily unionized areas, the heartland of the Industrial Revolution. (Thorpe 2008, 21–2)

Importantly, as Table 6.2 shows, the North East (which includes Yorkshire) and the North West (i.e., Lancashire) are precisely those regions that experienced profound migration at the end of the nineteenth century, and likely offered especially attractive opportunities for the newly formed Labour Party. Of course, the next section of this discussion will test the relationship between new party entry and changes in the local distribution of electoral power more

TABLE 6.3. *Entry of Labour and Lib–Lab candidates,*
by region.

	Labour entry (1906)	Lib–Lab entry (1900)
Greater London (55)	2	4
South Eastern England		
Counties (21)	0	1
Provincial boroughs (58)	5	0
South Western England		
Counties (18)	0	0
Provincial boroughs (48)	1	0
Midlands		
Counties (32)	0	1
Provincial boroughs (44)	4	4
North Eastern England		
Counties (38)	3	3
Provincial boroughs (45)	13	3
North Western England		
Counties (35)	7	1
Provincial boroughs (36)	8	0
Wales		
Counties (11)	0	1
Provincial boroughs (22)	2	0

Notes: This table reports the numbers of districts contested by
Labour and Liberal–Labour candidates in 1906 and 1900, respec-
tively. Definitions of regions are provided in Appendix 6.A.
Sources: Caramani (2000) and Craig (1974).

rigorously. Nevertheless, the suggestion here that the political entrepreneurs
who formed and mobilized the Labour Party were strategic in the recruitment
and endorsement of candidates provides some early support for the account of
party formation offered in Chapter 2.

6.4   THE STRATEGIC ENTRY OF LABOUR PARTY CANDIDATES

This section provides an empirical test of this book's account of the conditions
that favor new party formation and facilitate new party entry, drawing on evidence from late-nineteenth century Britain, and the strategic entry decisions of
the Labour Party. As suggested above, this section will examine the relationship
between local changes in the composition of district electorates and the decision
of Labour party candidates to enter electoral contests in those districts.

Because individual-level census data for Britain are only available for 1881,
tying the strategic decisions of parties and candidates to changes in electoral

geography is a less straightforward task than in the other country cases. This analysis uses (1) estimates of the percentage of low-income voters in 1885, in combination with (2) changes in the size of the total population between 1891 and 1901, to evaluate the effects of changing electoral geography on new party entry decisions. Table 6.4 reports the coefficients from a series of increasingly complex probit regression models in which the dependent variable indicates whether or not a Labour party candidate entered the electoral contest in each district. As in the previous analytic case studies, we are especially interested in whether Labour party candidates entered elections in high-growth districts, where large numbers of new voters were ripe for mobilization.

In fact, the results of this analysis are quite clear: Labour party candidates were especially likely to enter electoral contests in those districts that experienced dramatic growth. Of the forty-five districts contested by Labour candidates, all but two experienced some population growth, and almost half were districts that grew by more than eleven thousand people (i.e., they are districts in the highest growth quartile). Note that the importance of changes in the composition of local populations in creating opportunities for new party entry holds even when other characteristics of those districts, including the composition of the labor force, are taken into account (Column 3). The results also hold where there were relatively large proportions of Irish immigrants (who, on average, comprised only about 3 percent of district electorates, and generally less than 10 percent), and where we might worry that local partisan networks were reinforced by ethnic identity. Finally, we also observe Labour entering contests where the barriers to entry might have been lower, including two-member districts and districts uncontested by one or the other of the two established parties. (More on explicit coordination with the Liberal Party below.)

Because of limited suffrage rights, one might reasonably worry that population growth does not correspond to increases in the number of eligible voters, and that something else, related to population growth (i.e., demands driven by increased density), is structuring Labour entry decisions. Estimating change in the number of eligible voters, however, is complicated by the limited availability of British census data, on the one hand, and the role of parties in registering voters, on the other.

Nevertheless, Table 6.5 reports a replication of the analysis reported in Column (3) of Table 6.4, but using estimates of the change in the size of the (registered) electorate between 1900 (when Labour was formed) and 1906, rather than the change in the population. In fact, Labour candidates were most likely to enter contests in those districts where changes in the size of the electorate were most dramatic. Even within the smaller set of districts (a large number of seats were uncontested in 1900, and so the change in the size of the electorate cannot be calculated), Table 6.5 reports that Labour was most likely to contest those districts that experienced dramatic increases in the sizes of their electorates. Of the twenty-nine districts contested by Labour in the set of districts for which changes in the size of electorates can be calculated,

TABLE 6.4. *Strategic entry of Labour Party candidates, 1906 (population change).*

	DV: Labour Party candidate entry		
	(1)	(2)	(3)
Proportion low-income eligible voters (1885)	-3.777^a (0.938)	-3.133^a (0.938)	-2.463 (1.704)
Population change (1891–1901, in 1,000s) Quartile 1 [−11,436, 246]	0.016 (0.006)		
Quartile 2 [288, 4,463]		0.387 (0.369)	0.747 (0.427)
Quartile 3 [4,543, 11,300]		0.905^a (0.335)	0.936^b (0.393)
Quartile 4 [11,320, 113,539]		1.131^a (0.330)	1.309^a (0.386)
Proportion in agriculture (1885)			2.031 (2.250)
Proportion in manufacturing (1885)			1.621 (1.389)
Proportion in mining (1885)			−0.554 (1.363)
Proportion Irish (1885)			6.715^a (1.826)
Two seats (1906)			1.526^a (0.337)
Uncontested (1906)			0.799^a (0.221)
Intercept	−0.250 (0.296)	−1.052 (0.420)	−3.273 (1.296)
N	462	462	462
Pseudo R^2	0.094	0.141	0.321

Notes: This table reports probit coefficients for an analysis in which the dependent variable is a binary indicator of whether or not a Labour candidate contested the election. Standard errors are reported in parentheses.
[a] $p < 0.01$.
[b] $p < 0.05$.
Sources: Election data: Caramani (2000) and Craig (1974). Population data: Census of England and Wales, 1901, *Summary Tables: Area, Houses, and Population.*

TABLE 6.5. *Strategic entry of Labour Party candidates, 1906 (change in electorate).*

	DV: Labour Party candidate entry
	(1)
Proportion low-income eligible voters (1885)	−3.106 (2.329)
Change in electorate (1900–1906) Quartile 1 [−1,517, 230]	
Quartile 2 [230, 713]	0.400 (0.448)
Quartile 3 [725, 1,633]	0.646 (0.423)
Quartile 4 [1,633, 16,263]	0.828[b] (0.412)
Proportion in agriculture (1885)	0.830 (3.335)
Proportion in manufacturing (1885)	1.551 (1.793)
Proportion in mining (1885)	−0.031 (1.772)
Proportion Irish (1885)	5.396[b] (2.181)
Two seats (1906)	1.285[a] (0.361)
Uncontested (1906)	0.739[a] (0.271)
Intercept	−2.507 (1.642)
N	288
Pseudo R^2	0.264

Notes: This table reports probit coefficients for an analysis in which the dependent variable is a binary indicator of whether or not a Labour candidate contested the election. Standard errors are reported in parentheses.
[a] $p < 0.01$.
[b] $p < 0.05$.
Sources: Election data: Caramani (2000) and Craig (1974). Population data: Census of England and Wales, 1901, *Summary Tables: Area, Houses, and Population.*

nearly 70 percent saw increases of at least 700 registered voters (Quartiles 3 and 4) between 1900 and 1906. In fact, the high-*population*-growth districts (Quartile 4 in Table 6.4) that were contested by Labour saw their *electorates* increase by at least 1,399 and an average of almost 3,000 voters; the electorates of other districts (i.e., relatively low-growth districts, not contested by Labour) increased by only about 500 voters. Some proportion of these increases in the sizes of the electorate likely reflects Labour's mobilization efforts (i.e., they are endogenous to Labour entry decisions). In any case, these increases provide evidence that there were large numbers of voters who were ripe for mobilization. Their presence provided an important opportunity for Labour's entry.

As an earlier section suggested, the election held in the fall of 1900 provides an interesting test of the strategic entry argument. Although the Labour party was established at the end of February, it was not well-prepared for the surprise election called at the end of September. As a consequence, the Labour party leadership recruited and endorsed candidates contesting the election on a "Lib–Lab" ticket, as well as straight Labour candidates. Table 6.6 reports the results of a comparative analysis in which the key independent variables, reporting changes in electoral geography and the initial electoral power of low-income voters, predict the entry of Liberal candidates in the first column (who contested about 60 percent of electoral contests in England and Wales in 1900), and either Lib–Lab or Labour candidates in the second column.

Notice that while the analysis reported in Column (2) of Table 6.6 replicates the earlier analysis reported in the second column of Table 6.4, the electoral power of low-income voters and changes in the composition of electoral districts account for very little of the variance in Liberal party entry decisions. That is, the districts where the Liberal party endorsed candidates are quite different from those districts in which new party candidates stood for election. Specifically, while twenty-six out of thirty-three Lib–Lab or Labour candidates (79 percent) contested districts that grew by more than 4,543 people (Quartiles 3 and 4), Liberal candidates were about equally likely to contest districts at each level of population growth. This suggests that even in an election for which Labour was generally unprepared, the party saw important opportunities for entry in those high-growth districts of the North East and North West.

This section has offered evidence that the Labour Party, and the political entrepreneurs who organized and mobilized its constituency, recognized important opportunities in those districts where there were especially dramatic changes in the local distribution of electoral power, and recruited candidates to enter contests in those districts.

6.5 SUMMARY AND CONCLUSIONS

This chapter has provided evidence of the importance of electoral geography, especially changes in local distributions of electoral power, for the strategic

TABLE 6.6. *Liberal Party and Lib–Lab entry, 1900.*

	Liberal (1900)	Liberal–Labour or Labour (1900)
Proportion low-income (1885)	-1.088^b	-4.663^a
	(0.488)	(1.199)
Population change (1891–1901)		
Quartile 1 [−11,436, 246]		
Quartile 2 [288, 4,463]	0.004	0.405^b
	(0.168)	(0.377)
Quartile 3 [4,543, 11,300]	−0.142	0.758^b
	(0.170)	(0.348)
Quartile 4 [11,320, 113,539]	−0.124	0.695^b
	(0.170)	(0.350)
Intercept	0.707^a	−0.683
	(0.224)	(0.459)
N	462	462
Pseudo R^2	0.009	0.138

Notes: This table reports probit coefficients for an analysis in which the dependent variable is a binary indicator of whether or not a Liberal, or Liberal–Labour/Labour candidate contested the election. Standard errors are reported in parentheses.
[a] $p < 0.01$.
[b] $p < 0.05$.
Sources: Election data: Caramani (2000) and Craig (1974).

entry decisions of the British Labour Party. Like the American People's Party, and the Canadian CCF and Social Credit, the newly formed Labour Party recruited candidates and mobilized voters in those districts that had experienced profound changes in the composition of their electorates. Specifically, Labour was especially likely to recruit candidates in districts where large numbers of newly arrived voters were ripe for mobilization. That these districts were largely industrial, rather than agricultural, had important implications for the nature of the appeals Labour would make. Unlike the Populists and the CCF, the Labour Party elite were largely unconcerned about the mobilization of agricultural workers and the representation of their interests. As suggested above, MacDonald and others were nevertheless flexible and pragmatic in their commitment to socialism and made clear "the parliamentary character" of their political aims (Bealey & Pelling 1958, 180). Labour, like the other parties considered here, was formed by office-seeking political entrepreneurs who recognized in Britain's changing electoral geography opportunities for entry and the mobilization of a new constituency.

Of course, the British context is distinguished by other features of its political system, as well. Unlike the federal systems of North America, there were no opportunities for political entrepreneurs in subnational governments. Nevertheless, we observe the Labour Party leaders responding to quite local changes in the distribution of electoral power, particularly in northern England.

There are two further attributes that distinguish the case of British Labour, and have important implications for this book's general argument about party entry: First, unlike in the US and Canada, immigration was not an important source of the changes in Britain's electoral geography.[5] This means that the migrants who represented Labour's electoral opportunities may have belonged to other local partisan networks in their home counties, but had (or at least appeared to have) shed ties to these networks when they relocated. Partisanship, then, at least as it appeared to political entrepreneurs in Britain at the beginning of the twentieth century, is a function of local context.

Second, franchise rights were restricted when the Labour Party entered electoral competition. While we will observe similar suffrage restrictions at the turn of the twentieth century in Sweden, the limited franchise sets the British case apart from the US in the 1890s, where male suffrage was formally universal, and Canada in the 1930s, where all citizens were entitled to vote. What this means is that many of the people who would benefit from Labour's policies – "Adequate Maintenance from National Funds for the Aged Poor, Public Provision of Better Houses for the People, Useful Work for the Unemployed, Adequate Maintenance for Children, ..." – could not have advocated for them, and it is unlikely that the party resulted from the "emergence" of new demands. Rather, Labour's platform was crafted by strategic, forward-looking office-seekers who worked to mobilize newly pivotal voters with generally vague efforts on behalf of the working class.[6]

The next chapter, the last of the analytic case studies, examines the strategic entry decisions of the Swedish Democrats. Again, this is a case in which suffrage rights were limited, but changes in electoral geography result from the new eligibility of large numbers of working-class voters. Although the Social Democratic Party was formed in 1889, it would not enter electoral contests until the 1905 election, following dramatic changes in Sweden's electoral geography. In the Swedish case, like in Britain, changes in local distributions of electoral power favored an industrial working class, and we observe strategic political entrepreneurs mobilizing these low-income voters as a partisan constituency.

---

[5] In 1881, less than 2 percent of voting-aged men were born outside of the United Kingdom; less than 4 percent were born in Ireland. There were seven districts (out of 464) in which more than 20 percent of voting-aged men were born in Ireland, and only two of these were high-growth districts.

[6] The platform concludes, though, with an affirmation of its commitment to socialism: "The object of these measures is to enable the people ultimately to obtain the Socialisation of the Means of Production, Distribution, and Exchange, to be controlled by a Democratic State in the interests of the entire Community, and the Complete Emancipation of labour from the Domination of Capitalism and Landlordism, with the Establishment of Social and Economic Equality between the Sexes."

6.A APPENDIX: SUPPORTING MATERIALS

Matching Census and Electoral Geography

The North Atlantic Population Project (NAPP), described in Chapter 3, provides the individual-level census data used in the analysis of British electoral geography. To characterize the electoral geography of income, this analysis followed a strategy similar to that used in the American case:

First, using descriptions provided in the *Report of the Boundary Commissioners for England and Wales* (1885), most parishes were allocated to their proper electoral divisions.

Then, for parishes that were not listed in the *Report*, this analysis drew on two additional resources to ensure their proper allocation: First, this analysis relied on data provided through www.VisionofBritain.org.uk, and uses historical material which is copyright-protected by the Great Britain Historical GIS Project and the University of Portsmouth. High-quality, searchable versions of these maps are published on the *Vision of Britain* website, and provided an extremely useful resource for the allocation of parishes to their proper electoral districts.

Second, Youngs's (1980) *Guide to Local Administrative Units of England* lists all parishes within each county, and identifies the appropriate electoral division for each period. The *Gazetteer of the British Isles* also proved a useful resource for tracing changes in parish names and boundaries. For London, especially, it was sometimes helpful to refer to the descriptions of registration districts and subdistricts that are provided by the enumerators to match households to their proper electoral division.

Because the available geographic information was more limited in the British case, the allocation for the urban areas in England to electoral divisions is less precise than, for example, the allocation of American urban areas to

TABLE 6.A.1. *British census and electoral geography.*

	1881
Census geography (England & Wales)	
Counties	53
Registration districts	630
Subdistricts	2,075
Parishes	13,530
Electoral divisions	462
Average voters per division	12,969

congressional districts. Nevertheless, almost 99 percent of British households were allocated to electoral divisions; all but three electoral divisions (each in the Greater London area, where divisions are very small) are accounted for in the working data files.

Estimating Wages and Earnings

As suggested in the main text of this chapter, this analysis uses official reports of salaries and wages for each industry or occupation (and for some occupations, region) for approximately the same year (1881) to estimate the earnings of each voting-aged man. The British Board of Trade's *General Report of the Manual Labour Classes in the United Kingdom* uses surveyed firms' payroll data to generate estimates of wages and salaries, as well as the number and type of workers (men, women, and lads) in each occupation category. This analysis uses estimates wages and salaries for men in active full-time employment. Regional estimates of wages for agricultural workers are used in place of national averages.

For those occupations that were not included in the *Report*, *Estimates for Civil Service and Revenue*, which documents all government expenditures, and other government reports (*Navy Estimates for the Year 1880–1*) provide estimates for many professional and public sector positions, including, for example, civil engineers and architects. This strategy yields 153 distinct annual wage or salary estimates in 37 industry categories, for all but about 78,000 of the almost six million adult men over the age of 18 who report an occupation. The two largest occupation categories without wage estimates are gardeners (not domestic) and grocers who specialize in tea, coffee, or chocolate. (Each of these categories represents about 11 percent of those reporting occupations, but missing wages.) Like in the US case, those with missing wages generally account for small proportions of any electoral division. There are, however, eight districts where reasonable wage estimates are missing for about one third of voting-aged men who report occupations. Fishermen comprise the largest group, accounting for about half of these men in Great Grimsby and the St. Ives district of Cornwall. Calculations of the proportion of low-income voters exclude those for whom wage estimates are missing.

7

The Swedish Social Democratic Party, and the Long-Term Implications of Electoral Reform

The strategic entry of Sweden's Social Democrats offers a unique analytic perspective on how changing electoral geography creates new opportunities for political parties. While migration accounts for some of the changes in electoral geography that we observe in Sweden at the end of the nineteenth century, most of the changes in local distributions of electoral power resulted from the incorporation of newly eligible voters. As we shall see, although many of these new voters were long-term residents of their district, they were not part of local partisan or electoral networks until rapid economic growth increased their incomes above 800 kronor, the income level required for voter eligibility. The dramatic increase in newly available voters in some districts, especially in urban areas, created an important opportunity for the Swedish Social Democratic Party that is similar to the opportunities created by migration in the US, Canada, and the UK. Although the Social Democrats were formed in 1889, it was only after the dramatic changes in electoral geography that preceded the 1902 and especially the 1905 elections that the Social Democratic Party began to recruit candidates to compete in elections on its own label.

This chapter, like those that precede it, provides an overview of the political economy of Sweden during the late nineteenth and early twentieth centuries. Then, using historical census data and reports on typical wages during this period, this chapter maps the electoral geography of income and generates estimates of the changing size of the electorate for each electoral district. These estimates, along with official reports of the numbers of eligible voters, are used to identify electoral opportunities for the Social Democrats – and, indeed, the evidence suggests that Social Democrats were especially likely to enter electoral contests in those districts in which the number of newly available voters was comparatively large. Finally, this chapter will use the income profiles generated for each district to consider how the electoral reforms that followed shortly after the Social Democrats' entry protected the quality of representation for low-income citizens in the long term. This last section sets the stage for the next chapter, which considers the implications of historical and contemporary electoral geography, in the US and abroad, for the political representation of low-income voters.

7.1 THE POLITICAL ECONOMY AND ELECTORAL GEOGRAPHY OF SWEDEN, 1890–1906

When the Swedish Social Democratic Party was established in 1889, its leaders confronted a highly regionalized political and economic context. The harsh climate of Sweden's northern counties – roughly, north of Lake Vänern, Sweden's largest lake – generally limited agricultural production to grains, and industry to mining and forestry (Bagge, Lundberg, & Svennilson 1933). More general agricultural production was concentrated in Sweden's southern region, the area roughly below Lake Vänern and the more narrow Lake Vättern. By 1900, about 33 percent of workers in Sweden's manufacturing sector lived in one of the three major cities: Stockholm in the east, Göteborg in the west, and Malmö in the south. Of course, Stockholm was (and remains) Sweden's largest city, and in 1900 industrial workers outnumbered the professional and agricultural workers living there by large proportions.[1]

During this period, as in the other countries considered here, wages were generally higher in industrial sectors than in agricultural sectors, with a few important regional deviations: earnings for agricultural workers generally increased from south to north. According to Bagge, Lundberg, and Svennilson's (1933) estimated day rates, agricultural workers in Norrbotten, Sweden's northernmost county, earned almost twice what was earned in Kronoberg, a county in Sweden's south. While differences in lengths of growing seasons undoubtedly complicate this comparison of earnings (in fact, dense forests present a real challenge to farming in Kronoberg), these lower wages are reflected in the relatively high rates of income poverty in the south seen in Figure 7.1.

To generate Figure 7.1, which reports the proportion of low-income voters living in each electoral district, like in the analyses of the US, Canada, and the UK, Swedish census geography (i.e., counties and parishes) was matched to electoral district boundaries. Then, using analysis of wages earned during the late nineteenth century (Bagge, Lundberg, & Svennilson 1933) and individual-level census data, profiles of each district were constructed from the distributions of occupations and industries. As in the earlier analyses, when possible, wage estimates reflect regional variation in earnings. "Low income," as in earlier chapters, refers to those with earnings in the bottom third of the national voting-aged male distribution. Appendix 7.A provides a

---

[1] Industrial workers, including those in manufacturing, transportation, construction, and mining, comprised about 58 percent of men over the age of twenty-one.

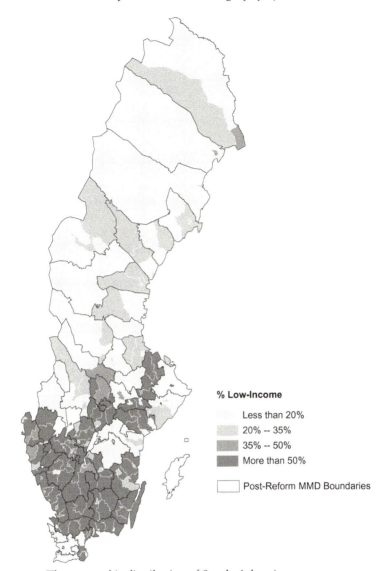

FIGURE 7.1. The geographic distribution of Sweden's low-income voters, 1900.

Notes: This figure reports the proportion of men over the age of twenty-one with earnings in first third of the national income distribution, as a percentage of each electoral district. SMDs are delineated with white lines; black lines denote the boundaries of the MMDs established in the 1909 electoral reforms.

Sources: Data are based on individual-level census data, available through NAPP. Wage data are based on estimates reported in Bagge, Lundberg, and Svennilson (1933). This map is based on a revision of the Geografiska Sverigedata Lantmäteriet (2015) digital map of (contemporary) administrative boundaries. See Appendix 7.A for technical details.

full description of the data used here, and later in this chapter. For now, the map in Figure 7.1 can provide a helpful guide to Sweden's political economic context at the end of the nineteenth century. (The map also includes the boundaries adopted in the 1909 electoral reform, for future reference.)

One feature of Sweden's political economy that becomes obvious in Figure 7.1 is that although differences between the north and the south are apparent, in fact, because most of the population resides south of Lake Vänern, there are also important differences in urban and rural concentrations of poverty. As Rustow (1955) notes, until the end of the nineteenth century, rural–urban differences would provide the main basis of political conflict. And, as we shall see, this conflict was only exacerbated by Sweden's electoral rules. (Part of the Social Democrats' success would result from their work to bridge this cleavage, and their mobilization of rural voters as well as urban workers.)

The rules that governed Sweden's elections at the beginning of the twentieth century were the result of major electoral reforms, adopted in 1866, which replaced government by Four Estates with a bicameral legislature. While the Första Kammaren ("First Chamber") was composed of members who were indirectly elected by local governments, members of the Andra Kammaren ("Second Chamber") were indirectly or directly elected in mostly single-member districts. By 1902, elections to the lower house were indirect in only ten districts; this number was reduced to five rural districts for the 1905 election. (These districts will be excluded from later analyses.) Several multi-member districts remained at the turn of the century, exclusively in urban areas, where eligible voters cast as many votes as there were seats contested.

Importantly, the suffrage restrictions established by the 1866 reforms required voters to have significant landholdings or an annual income of 800 kronor. "This made the size and composition of the electorate dependent on economic growth and the value of the currency. 'A sudden change in the value of money or in the wage level,' as Professor Andrén has noted, 'would have produced something that would have pretty much resembled a political revolution'" (Rustow 1971, 19). In fact, the size of the electorate increased only modestly between 1866 and 1890, from about 22 percent of men over the age of twenty-one in 1872 to 23 percent in 1890.

Over the course of the 1890s, however, the number of workers earning more than 800 kronor increased dramatically. By 1905, an estimated 30.6 percent of men over the age of twenty-one met the income and property criteria for voter eligibility (see also Velander in Sundbärg 1904; Lewin 1988, 329). With this economic growth, the composition of the electorate began to change. Tingsten (1973, 5) writes,

During the decades immediately following [the 1866] parliamentary reform this category [of eligible voters] comprised most of the independent and a few of the unpropertied farmers, and well-to-do urban dwellers, including a great many independent craftsmen. With increasing prosperity, other groups – primarily industrial workers in the highest paid occupations – joined this category.

In the analysis of historical wages presented below, changes in wages and eligibility status were largest among boot and shoe makers, general factory workers, stone workers, and men who worked in sawmills.[2]

The malapportionment of Sweden's electoral districts amplified the changes in electoral geography resulting from changes in the size of the eligible electorate. As Rustow (1955, 24) notes, when the 1866 reforms assigned "one representative to the towns and cities for every 10,000 and to the rural areas for every 40,000 inhabitants, it gave to the townspeople an influence in the lower chamber out of all proportion to their numbers within either the population or the electorate." After one further reform in 1892, and through internal migration, this imbalance was somewhat corrected by 1905, but each rural member still represented about twice as many inhabitants as urban representatives (i.e., about 27,166 for each member elected in rural districts, and 14,823 for members elected in urban districts; calculated from data reported in Table 4, Sveriges Officiella Statistik 1906, 35).[3] Because the dramatic increases in wages were especially concentrated among workers in manufacturing sectors, industrial districts represented the most promising opportunities for new parties. In fact, as we shall see, the Social Democrats were especially likely to recruit candidates in Stockholm and Malmö.

Figure 7.2 provides a summary of the changing nature of Sweden's electoral geography, and in particular identifies the location of electoral opportunities for new party entry. Figure 7.2(a) reports categories of the change in the percentage of eligible voters between December 1895 and December 1904, based on official reports (Sveriges Officiella Statistik 1897, Sveriges Officiella Statistik 1906). The quartiles reported in Figure 7.2(b) similarly correspond to changes in the percentage of men who were eligible to vote, but are based on estimated changes in earnings. The analysis that follows will use both the official reports and estimates based on earnings to identify potential opportunities for new parties, especially for the Social Democrats. (Differences between Figure 7.2(a) and (b) likely reflect the coarseness of the wage data; more complete analysis of the wage data is reported in Appendix 7.A.)

7.2 THE FORMATION AND ENTRY OF THE SOCIAL DEMOCRATS

Like the other parties considered in this book, the Swedish Social Democratic Party resulted from the efforts of a small group of political entrepreneurs, who devoted great energy to organizing conventions and recruiting party members

---

[2] Wage increases were largest, in absolute terms, among metal workers, but averaged above 800 kronor in 1890, and so did not change their voter eligibility status. The wages of miners and quarrymen similarly increased during this period, but remained, on average, less than 800 kronor.

[3] When only eligible voters are considered, the malapportionment remains but is lessened further: Each urban representative was the delegate of 1,483 eligible voters, on average; rural districts included an average of 2,089 eligible voters.

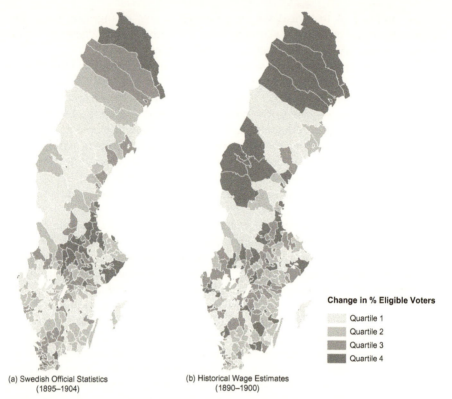

Change in % Eligible Voters

Quartile 1
Quartile 2
Quartile 3
Quartile 4

(a) Swedish Official Statistics   (b) Historical Wage Estimates
        (1895–1904)   (1890–1900)

FIGURE 7.2. The changing electoral geography of Sweden.

Notes: This figure reports absolute changes in the percentage of men aged twenty-one and older who were eligible to vote, based on official reports (a) and estimates of earnings (b). Darker shading corresponds to larger changes. The quartiles are defined as follows: (a) <1%, 1%–1.6%, 1.6%–3.5%, and >3.5%; (b) <6.8%, 6.8%–10%, 10%–15%, and >15%.

Sources: (a) Sveriges Officiella Statistik (1897), (1906). (b) Please refer to the text, and to Appendix 7.A.

and candidates. For the Swedish Social Democrats, it was Hjalmar Branting, especially, who invested – and was invested in – the future of the party. As Gidlund (1992, 100) writes, "the initiative to call a conference for the purpose of forming a cohesive political party came from the tailor and agitator" – that is, political outsider – August Palm. In 1889, Palm chose Branting to become the editor of *Social Demokraten*, the Stockholm newspaper Palm had established in 1888. At the time, Branting was an ambitious young man who had only recently left his career as a scientist to become a journalist. As a key figure in the Stockholm Social Democratic Association, Branting took on an important role in organizing the founding convention, which included delegates from sixty-nine different trade union and social organizations, and all major geographic regions of the country.

Initially, the anti-authoritarian Social Democrats were hesitant to adopt an explicitly hierarchical structure, preferring instead a leadership structure that gave equal status to the geographic diversity of interests, and delegates that were elected from northern/central, western, and southern districts. Over the next ten years, however, the party organization became increasingly centralized with consolidated authority. By 1894, for example, the conference had established a leadership council with clear decision-making responsibilities, and the Stockholm members of this council formed a "true, active executive" who would direct the party's mobilization efforts (Gidlund 1992, 101). Branting, one of the original party leaders, was part of this group, and would eventually be elected the "chief" of this executive. And, by 1900, the original district structure for the party's organization was replaced with local Social Democratic branches, who were "directly subordinate to the party executive, the sole central leadership" (quoted in Gidlund 1992, 102).

The focus of the party shifted over the 1890s as well. During the party's early years, it was divided on the "tactical question" of whether to pursue universal suffrage as a primary goal through non-violent agitation, and especially participation in elections, or to pursue full political and social equality through potentially violent extra-parliamentary participation. By the mid-1890s, largely because of Branting's efforts, "a more moderate course on all questions – the evaluation of the franchise, participation in elections, collaboration with other groups – was now accepted without controversy. At the same time, the revolutionary line, which had probably claimed a majority within the party at earlier congresses, was no longer of any consequence" (Tingsten 1973, 376). In spite of this commitment to electoral participation, however, the Social Democratic party would not recruit candidates – nor would its leaders enter electoral contests on the party's own label – until the 1902 election.[4]

What changed between the mid-1890s and the early 1900s, that made entry into electoral competition viable in the party's strategic calculus? As suggested above, at their founding convention held in 1889, would-be Social Democrats faced a country in which the major political division was essentially regional. At least as a partial consequence, party organizations, and especially ties between organizations across districts, were weak. As Rustow (1955, 34) suggests, "the strict separation of urban and rural districts therefore further reduced the need for political organization: the real antagonists did not meet on the hustings." Instead, party organization was confined to the legislature and existed only in the Second Chamber. "The early parties thus had no call for elaborate constituency organizations or systematic election campaigns: the few hundred active voters in the average district could easily be reached by more informal means"(Rustow 1955, 33).

---

4   Branting would enter the 1896 election, but as a liberal and with liberal support.

In his long-term analysis of the campaigns and campaign strategies of Swedish parties, Esaiasson (1991) finds that the 1890s marked the beginning of a period of increasingly "national politicization" and a new era of party competition in which central party organizations began to play a prominent role. This was especially true of the Social Democrats, for whom the need to build an electoral coalition that included low-income agricultural workers, along with those working in urban industrial settings, was especially important. Unlike the Social Democratic Party in Germany, for example, as Tingsten (1973, 177–8) writes, the development of Swedish Social Democratic ideas proceeded in a way that was "independent of Marxism," particularly on the question of the role of agricultural workers. As Branting saw it, agricultural workers in Sweden at the turn of the century would play a different role in Swedish society, than they might elsewhere: " 'The new class of small farmers will be important not as possessors of land, but as workers on the land …' " Furthermore, "the class of small farmers should therefore feel solidarity with the workers, and work with workers to reorganize society so that it no longer serves the interests of those few who possess the capital, but rather that it is becomes an organized planned system of producing and consuming groups, cooperating with each other" (Tingsten 1973, 178–9). But this view was likely bolstered by strategic concerns: Tingsten (1973, 177–8; see also Verney 1957, 195) notes further that "the arguments for [the recruitment and mobilization of farmers] put forward in debates were the question of immediate advantages to the poor farmers, and the need to win political support from this class. It appeared impossible that the party could gain the majority, without the cooperation of a large proportion of farmers."

There is further evidence of the Party Congress's strategic calculus, and in particular the strategic allocation of campaign resources, in Hadenius, Sveveborg, and Weibull's (1968, 59–60) account of the social democratic press and newspapers between 1899 and 1909. They write that "the Party was the only central organization which concerned itself with newspaper questions. Central trade unions (for example, the Swedish Typographers' Union) supported individual newspapers, but there was no endeavor to influence or to contribute financially to the press as a whole …" From the very beginning, the Party Congress adopted stipulations about regulating how local presses should be approved as Party organs, and the Party dramatically increased its influence over finances and content over the next two decades (Hadenius, Sveveborg, & Weibull 1968, 60). Evidence of a national party strategy lies in those districts where there "were both local Party branches and a need for Party propaganda (manifested by newspaper associations, among other things) but … newspapers of a Social Democratic complexion never appeared there or that they were compelled to close down." In these cases – notably, Falun, Halmstad, Östersund, Nyköping, Landskrona, Motala, Västerås, and Linköping (with a few exceptions, cities in the south) – "the Party Executive intervened. They either prevented the founding of newspapers or refused to help a newspaper already started. Similarly there were cases in which they intervened actively to initiate the starting of a newspaper or to keep alive newspapers already started" (Hadenius, Sveveborg, & Weibull 1968, 66). Further, "[i]n *local* quarters there was much enthusiasm and goodwill. The *central* headquarters was compelled to make a realistic assessment of the resources and possibilities ... The main thing was that [a newspaper's] existence corresponded to a need of the local and central Party authorities" (Hadenius, Sveveborg, & Weibull 1968, 68; emphasis added).[5]

If the Party Executive was keenly active in print mobilization efforts, surely it was also strategic in mobilization efforts more generally, including the recruitment and selection of candidates. In fact, Gidlund (1992, 103) writes that the local party branches, the "labor communes" that replaced the original districts, were "created by agitators who, on behalf of the party executive, traveled extensively around the country." Indeed, the party's resources during the late nineteenth and early twentieth centuries were "dominated" by the costs of mobilization and the strategic creation of local Social Democratic associations. Although many workers continued to be ineligible to vote, the "organizational work in the labor communes and SAP districts provided training and practical experience for future representational duties" (Gidlund 1992, 104).

Thus, although direct evidence of recruitment of candidates is more limited in the Swedish case, there is some evidence that the party leadership carefully directed the development of local party organizations. In fact, a careful empirical examination of the districts where Social Democrats contested seats reveals a clear pattern of strategic entry. The rest of this section will present some descriptive analysis of Social Democratic entry; the next section presents a more rigorous evaluation of their response to new electoral opportunities.

There are real challenges in identifying candidates' party labels during the period in which elections were contested under SMD rules: official reports only included the vote totals and attributes of winning candidates (e.g., Sveriges Officiella Statistik 1906). To facilitate their analysis of long-term trends in Swedish voting behavior, Lewin, Jansson, and Sörbom (1972) successfully sorted through detailed newspaper reports of elections in each district to identify the party affiliation of each candidate. However, in their analysis and accompanying datasets, election returns were aggregated and reported only at the county level, and unfortunately, the original materials have been lost in the fifty years since their original study. To a large extent, using Lewin, Jansson, and Sörbom's (1972) analysis as a guide and reference, I have replicated their archival work, and this analysis similarly draws on newspapers to identify those districts in which the Social Democrats recruited candidates. Whether or not a candidate contested the election on a Social Democratic ticket was confirmed in 145 of the 195 districts where legislators were directly elected in 1905.

---

5 In four of these districts in which the central Party limited press mobilization efforts, and for which Social Democrat entry could be confirmed (more on this below), the Party did not recruit candidates to compete on its ticket in the 1905 election, despite local enthusiasm. (The other four towns are in counties, although not necessarily districts, in which Social Democrats competed.)

Because of these challenges in identifying the partisanship of candidates, the analysis that follows will proceed in several steps: First, this analysis will use Lewin, Jansson, and Sörbom's (1972) data to identify all those districts within counties in which there were Social Democratic challenges for both the 1902 and 1905 elections. This will exaggerate the number of Social Democratic entries and introduce some measurement error, and potentially some bias, into the analysis. If, for example, Social Democrats are recruited only in those districts within counties in which the size of the electorate has most dramatically increased, (mis)reporting Social Democratic entry in even low-growth districts will lead to an underestimation of the main relationship. Alternatively, if changes in the composition of the electorate did not contribute to Social Democratic entry decisions, the miscoding of the key dependent variable will generate the appearance of a relationship only if some feature of the miscoded districts is correlated with increases in the number of eligible voters.

To address this concern, the analysis will be replicated for the smaller number of districts in which Social Democratic entry in the 1905 election can be confirmed.[6] To the extent that district exclusion is unrelated to Social Democratic entry decisions, restriction to this limited sample will provide an unbiased representation of the extent to which changes in electoral geography structured Social Democratic entry decisions.

Figure 7.3 identifies districts in those counties in which Lewin, Jansson, and Sörbom (1972) report the entry of Social Democratic candidates (a), and those districts in which I could confirm the entry (or absence) of Social Democratic candidates using local newspaper reports (b). The Social Democrats also entered races in more rural areas too, including Norunda and Örbyhus härad in Uppsala, where agricultural workers accounted for nearly half of the male workforce. While, on average, their low earnings precluded the suffrage eligibility of these agricultural workers, their landholdings may have been sufficient to attract the mobilization efforts of the Social Democrats. Importantly, and as the next section will demonstrate more rigorously, a comparison of Figures 7.2 and 7.3 suggests that the Social Democrats were in fact more likely to enter those districts in which there were relatively large numbers of newly eligible voters.

7.3 SUFFRAGE EXPANSION AND NEW OPPORTUNITIES FOR ENTRY

This section provides a more rigorous test of the argument presented in the previous section. Clearly, the formation and strategic entry decisions of the Swedish Social Democrats fit well with the framework presented in Chapter 2,

---

[6] This smaller sample omits at least some of the districts in Uppsala, Södermanlands, Jönköpings, Kalmar, Malmöhus, Västmanlands, Kopparbergs, Gäfleborgs, and Norbottens läns, in which Social Democratic candidate entry is not confirmed.

(a) Entry coded for county   (b) Verified District Entry
(Lewin, Jansson, & Sorbom 1972)

FIGURE 7.3. The strategic entry of Social Democratic Candidates, (1905).
Notes: This figure identifies districts in those counties in which Social Democratic candidates contested the 1905 election (a), and those districts in which the entry of Social Democratic candidates is confirmed (b). See the text, and Appendix 7.A for more details.

in that a core group of political entrepreneurs invested in the organization and structure of the party, and carefully allocated mobilization efforts and resources. Further, the Social Democrats crafted their ideological appeals – to both urban and rural voters – in a way that responded to the unique electoral context of Sweden. Is there evidence that the party was also strategic in its entry decisions? That the Social Democrats declined to enter electoral competition on their own label until dramatic economic growth increased the size of the electorate in some districts, creating new constituencies that were ripe for mobilization, suggests a strategic calculus at work. Does the pattern of entry similarly reflect this calculus?

As suggested above, the Swedish case offers a unique analytic perspective: new voters created new electoral opportunities for party entry through their increased earnings and new eligibility. One might worry, as a consequence, that these newly eligible voters were already incorporated into the established local party networks through other social ties, and they were not available for mobilization by new parties in quite the same way as migrants. Of course, as already mentioned, because of the nature of political competition, local party organizations were generally weak in Sweden before the establishment of the Social Democrats. But in fact, migration provides an important source of electoral opportunity in Sweden, too: many newly eligible (and indeed already eligible) voters were migrants.

Figure 7.4 provides some evidence of the nature of the Social Democrats' strategic entry calculus. In each panel, the horizontal axis reports rates of population growth between 1895 and 1904 – that is, over rates of population change. The vertical axis reports changes in the percentage of the population that were eligible to vote. Obviously, these variables are closely related, and

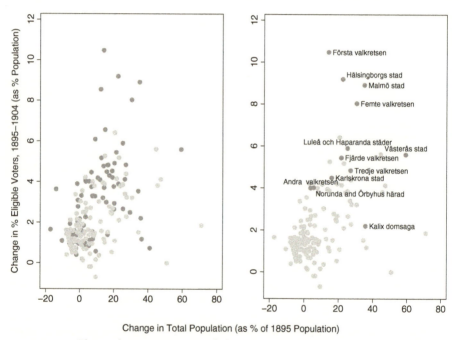

Change in Total Population (as % of 1895 Population)

FIGURE 7.4. Electoral opportunities and the entry of Social Democratic Candidates, 1905.

Notes: This figure reports district-level population growth (horizontal axis) and district-level increases in the percentage of eligible voters (vertical axis). Darker points indicate those districts in those counties in which Lewin, Jansson, and Sörbom (1972) report Social Democratic candidate entry (left panel) and confirmed Social Democratic candidate entry (right panel).

Sources: Calculations based on Sveriges Officiella Statistik (1897, 1906).

TABLE 7.1. *Voters ripe for mobilization, Sweden, 1900.*

	Ineligible	Always eligible	Newly eligible	Total
Permanent resident	84%	61%	65%	75%
Migrant	16%	39%	35%	25%
N	601,329	82,688	352,346	1,036,363

Notes: This table reports estimates of the percentage of migrants – those men, aged twenty-five and older, residing in a county other than that in which they were born – in each category of would-be voters. Eligibility is determined by estimates of earnings in 1890 and 1900. "Ineligible" voters worked in occupations that earned, on average, less than 800 kronor in both 1890 and 1900. "Always eligible" voters worked in occupations that earned more than 800 kronor in both 1890 and 1900. "Newly eligible" voters are those working in occupations that earned less than 800 kronors in 1890 and more than 800 kronor in 1900.
Sources: NAPP Sweden (1890, 1900).

indeed, Table 7.1 suggests that large proportions of those who are identified as newly eligible were born outside of the county in which they resided in 1900. The solid points indicate those districts in counties in which Social Democrats enter elections (left panel) and those districts in which Social Democratic candidate entry was confirmed (right panel). Clearly, the Social Democrats were especially likely to enter in those districts with the largest proportion of newly available voters.

Table 7.2 presents a more rigorous test of Social Democratic candidate entry decisions in 1905, using the two measures of change in the size of the electorate (based on income estimates, and on the official reports), and incorporates other variables that might have guided strategic entry decisions (composition of the labor force, and multi-member districts).[7] In the most complete, conservative specification (Model 6), Social Democratic entry is predicted to occur almost never in districts with less than a five percentage point increase in the size of the electorate (Quartiles 1–3) and with a probability of 27 percent in districts with more dramatic increases in the size of the electorate.[8] This estimated effect is substantial, particularly because the model includes other features thought

---

[7] Results for 1902, when the Social Democrats entered considerably fewer electoral contests in eight counties, are reported in Appendix 7.A.

[8] The estimate from Model 6, which uses verified entry as the dependent variable, and estimates the relationship using a reduced sample, is slightly less than the difference in predicted probability of Social Democratic entry from Model 5, which uses the Lewin, Jansson, and Sörbom data: Social Democrats are expected to enter about one third of those districts in the first quartile, and two-thirds of the districts in the fourth quartile.

TABLE 7.2. *Strategic entry of Social Democratic Candidates, 1905.*

	DV: Social Democrat candidate entry					
	(1) Estimated wages	(2) Estimated wages	(3) Official reports	(4) Official reports	(5) Official reports	(6) Verified entry[b]
Change in eligible voters[a]	1.081 (0.738)		24.320[c] (5.813)			69.045[c] (22.728)
Quartile 1						
Quartile 2		0.451 (0.261)		-0.021 (0.264)	0.002 (0.265)	
Quartile 3		0.197 (0.263)		0.138 (0.261)	0.197 (0.261)	
Quartile 4		0.528[d] (0.262)		0.841[c] (0.266)	1.012[c] (0.363)	
Proportion in manufacturing, construction, transportation (1890)					2.754 (2.085)	-3.534 (4.332)
Proportion in agricultural, fishing (1890)					2.967 (1.601)	-1.107 (3.007)
Median annual income (1890, in thousands kronor)					1.732 (1.028)	1.709 (2.244)
Multi-member district					0.412 (0.529)	0.647 (0.709)
Intercept	-0.299[d] (0.137)	-0.451[d] (0.192)	-0.728[c] (0.164)	-0.391[d] (0.190)	-3.706 (1.717)	-2.586 (3.448)
N	195	195	195	195	195	138
Pseudo R^2	0.008	0.019	0.075	0.055	0.080	0.578

Notes: This table reports probit coefficients in analyses in which the dependent variable is an indicator of whether or not a Social Democratic candidate entered the 1905 electoral contest.

[a] Columns (1) and (2) use estimates of the size of the voting-eligible population (as a proportion of men, aged twenty-five and older), based on estimated earnings and wages. Columns (3)–(6) use estimates of the voting-eligible population based on official reports.

[b] The analyses in columns (1)–(5) use Lewin, Jansson, and Sörbom's (1972) county-level coding of Social Democratic entry as the dependent variable. Column (6) instead includes only those districts in which Social Democratic entry is confirmed. See the text for more details.

[c] $p < 0.01$.   [d] $p < 0.05$.

to have made particular districts especially attractive to the Social Democrats, including an industrial labor force.

Certainly, the Swedish Social Democrats were especially likely to enter electoral districts where newly eligible voters were ripe for mobilization. An examination of the high-growth (fourth quartile) districts that the Social Democrats did *not* enter is also helpful. The Social Democrats, for example, did not enter electoral competition in the nine-member district that included the city of Göteborg, despite the fact that the size of the voting-eligible population increased from about 9 percent to 15 percent between 1895 and 1904. Göteborg stands out among the urban districts in that it is by far the largest, with more than twenty thousand citizens who were eligible to vote. The five districts of Stockholm had, on average and by contrast, about fourteen thousand eligible voters, and elected four or five seats each. Seats in Stockholm, in 1905, were typically won with between two and three thousand votes; in Göteborg, seven of the winning candidates had secured more than four thousand votes. All of this suggests that although Göteborg may have represented a significant opportunity in terms of large numbers of new voters who were ripe for mobilization, the effort required to mobilize a sufficient number of these voters to be effective would have been costly. These costs would have been especially apparent if Göteborg was compared to other districts, like Västerås stad, where fewer than one thousand votes were needed to secure the seat.

In the end, the empirical evidence and historical record suggests that the description of party entry presented in Chapter 2 fits the Swedish Social Democrats quite well. The party was established by a core group of office-seekers who recognized, in changing electoral geography, a group of voters who were ripe for mobilization, and tailored the ideological appeals of the party to reflect its interests. The party's resources, especially investment in the party press, were strategically allocated, and candidates were recruited to compete in those districts in which the size of the electorate had changed most dramatically and where the electoral opportunity was most appealing.

As suggested above, what sets the Swedish case apart from the other cases considered in this analysis is that the opportunity for party entry comes from the entrance of newly eligible voters, and that it was their unintended entry that changed Sweden's electoral geography. In fact, a commitment to universal male suffrage was a core tenet of the Swedish Social Democrats from their founding convention, and the Social Democrats would continue to advocate for electoral reform following the 1905 election. In 1908, the Riksdag would adopt universal suffrage provisions for the Second Chamber (conditional on the fulfillment of tax liabilities and military service), but would compensate established parties for this suffrage expansion with the adoption of proportional representation rules. The next section takes full advantage of this chapter's analysis of Swedish electoral geography to examine the implications of electoral reform for the long-term representation of low-income and working-class citizens.

7.4   THE IMPLICATIONS OF ELECTORAL REFORM FOR THE POLITICAL REPRESENTATION OF THE POOR

Suffrage reform, as suggested above, featured prominently in the early commitments of the Swedish Social Democrats. The need for permanent reform, however, was intensified by the dramatic entry of large numbers of new voters in the 1905 election. Without reform, those earning just slightly more than 800 kronor would lose their eligibility to vote if an economic decline reduced their wages. Shortly following the 1905 election, general support for (near) universal male suffrage was expressed by all of the major political parties, including even the Conservatives, who became convinced of the "futility of stubborn resistance" to all reform (Rustow 1955). But from the perspective of the Conservatives, the adoption of universal suffrage was especially troubling. "In the rapid wave of industrialization that was ... sweeping the country, the political map was being repainted red ... Could anything be done to change this trend? Could a skillful Conservative politician take any step that would prevent the party from becoming the victim of what appeared to be a long-term disaster?" (Lewin 1988, 70). Political attention shifted to which additional reforms should be adopted, along with male suffrage, to provide "guarantees" of Conservative longevity.

Conservative Premier Arvid Lindman's "Great Compromise" was set apart from earlier Liberal universal male suffrage proposals by its commitment to proportional representation in both houses of the legislature. Rustow (1955, 62) reports that

[the reform bill's] conservative advocates reasoned, quite realistically, that universal suffrage, if combined with the existing plurality system of elections, would give the Liberal-Socialist forces an overwhelming majority in the popular house as well as a deciding voice in joint votes on financial questions. If the conservatives, on the other hand, succeeded in preserving the plutocratic basis of the senate and in forcing the adoption of proportionalism for the lower house, the left wing majority in the latter would be substantially reduced and the conservatives could hope to maintain their traditional control of the purse.

While the Liberals wavered in their support of proportional representation, their initial opposition to MMD rules was consistent with the incentives of a majority party (although Liberal Party leader Karl Staaff led the government for only a short time), and was reflected in the parliamentary record (see, e.g., Verney 1957, Rustow 1955).[9] An earlier bill, introduced by the Liberal Premier Karl Staaff, incorporated universal male suffrage in single-member districts and majority thresholds. Staaff, in particular, was conscious of the costs MMD rules

---

[9] Boix (2010, 409) anticipates Conservative support and Liberal opposition to PR electoral rules, because of the distribution of their partisan constituencies in Sweden, especially the overlapping electorates, "at least in some towns and among some agrarian strata." Simply, the Liberals could assume that suffrage expansion would work to their benefit, especially in SMDs.

would impose on the Liberal party (see, e.g., Lewin 1988, 84). The debate on Lindman's proposed reforms was complicated by questions about the relative standing of the First and Second Chambers, the independent implications of the proposed reforms, and the age of enfranchisement, and initially the Liberals were surprised by the scope of the proposed reforms.[10] Nevertheless, in the end, Branting would "argue categorically that the bill was unacceptable and that it was a device for keeping power in the hands of the rich" (Verney 1957, 165), and only the Social Democrats would oppose Lindman's proposal.

What could have been the basis of Branting's concern? While Branting initially conceded the "inherent justice" of PR electoral rules, this section will legitimate the Social Democrats' opposition to the adoption of PR (see also Calvo 2009).[11] This section will also suggest that the Social Democrats may not have fully recognized the long-term benefits electoral reform would provide for their low-income constituency. Using an analysis of the electoral geography of income, this section will examine how the simultaneous expansion of suffrage rights to all men over the age of twenty-four (who had paid their taxes, and fulfilled military service obligations) and the adoption of proportional representation affected the electoral power of Sweden's low-income citizens. This analysis will show that although these reforms may have limited the electoral power of low-income voters at the time of their adoption, in fact, they would provide for the long-term representation of low-income citizens' interests. As we saw in Chapter 3, MMD rules, on the one hand, limited opportunities for party entry, but also (more on this in Chapter 8) reduced variability in electoral power. In effect, PR rules provide a ceiling, but also a relatively high floor, in the mapping of votes to seats. Later reforms, including the adoption of a compensatory tier that undermines any advantage of geographical concentration, would similarly provide "guarantees" to low-income citizens.

Earlier in this chapter, I suggested that at the turn of the century the Swedish political economy was highly regionalized, with profound urban–rural differences in the composition of the labor force. When SMD elections are imposed on top of an uneven geographic distribution of, for example, income groups or labor force characteristics, there can be advantages for geographically concentrated groups. Figure 7.5 explores the implications of electoral reform for the representation of industrial workers (a) and low-income voters (b). In each panel, the horizontal axis reports the proportion of seats an industrial

---

10 The Liberals' failure to win support for Staaff's bill in the Senate, which had rallied around "double-proportionality" – MMD rules and proportionality in both legislative houses, and implied equality of the chambers – led to the dissolution of Staaff's cabinet, and the Riksdag. And, part of the eventual "compromise," for example, derived from a right-leaning Liberal's insistence (upon threat of resignation) that the reforms also reduce income qualifications and incorporate salaries for members of the upper house.
11 Lewin (1988) offers an extended discussion of each party's position on Lindman's proposal, but groups the Liberals and Social Democrats together as "the Left."

or low-income voting bloc could elect under SMD rules, but with full male suffrage, for each county, if all members turned out to vote, and all voted as a bloc. The vertical axis reports the proportion of seats each bloc could elect in each county if seats are allocated according to the 1908 PR MMD reforms. Counties that are above the dashed diagonal line are those places where the electoral reform favors each group, typically those counties where the group is more dispersed throughout the county. However, counties that are below the diagonal line are those places where each voting bloc stands to lose seats: each group is geographically concentrated such that they are pivotal in a number of SMDs (under universal male suffrage). The post-reform proportionality penalizes geographically concentrated groups and redistributes some of each group's electoral power to others.

Figure 7.5 focuses attention on voters who were industrial workers, or otherwise low-income earners (mainly agricultural workers), rather than the newly enfranchised voters that were the focus of the previous section. This, of course, reflects the anticipated adoption of universal male suffrage, but also the way in which the Social Democrats saw their constituency. As suggested above, Branting and other Social Democratic leaders recognized the strategic importance of a broad-based coalition that bridged both urban and rural constituents. By the time the electoral reforms were implemented, the Social Democrats had become "a mass movement including not only industrial workers but also farm hands, tenants, and smallholders" (Rustow 1955, 76).

The strategic basis of Social Democrats' opposition to the adoption of MMD rules becomes clear in Figure 7.5. The electoral geography of several of the counties where the Social Democrats entered electoral competition in 1905, under SMD, offered a real advantage. Specifically, if the Social Democrats could mobilize industrial workers as a voting bloc under universal male suffrage and SMD rules, they would have been able to win large proportions of the seats in urban counties – that is, counties with large numbers of seats, where the Social Democrats had already effectively begun to build local constituencies (denoted with gray points). The adoption of MMD rules undermined the electoral power of the industrial workers in these districts, seen below the diagonal line in Figure 7.5(a), and redistributed their electoral power to other groups. Advantages that the Social Democrats may have had with low-income voters, Figure 7.5(b), were similarly undermined in early-entry districts in Kalmar and Sodermanland. As the electoral reforms became imminent, however, the Social Democrats began to enter electoral competition in several of those districts where electoral geography was to their advantage. This includes, for example, Göteborg and Bohus, and Örebro, and those other counties seen above the diagonal line and denoted with black points.

The post-1909 electoral reforms would have profound implications for the nature of Swedish party competition. As Rustow (1955, 70) writes, following the electoral reform,

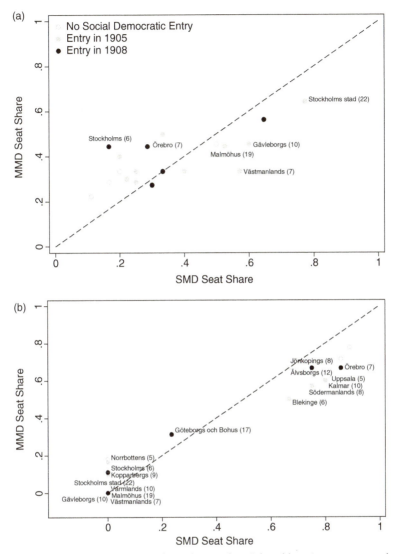

FIGURE 7.5. The electoral power of Sweden's industrial and low-income voters, before and after electoral reform, and by county.

Notes: This figure reports the share of seats won by an industrial voting bloc (a) and low-income voters (b), by county, before and after Sweden's electoral reform. Solid points indicate Social Democratic entry in either 1905 or 1909. The total number of seats elected in the county are reported in parentheses.

TABLE 7.3. *The electoral power of*
Sweden's industrial and low-income
voters, before and after electoral reform.

	SMD	MMD
Industrial workers	40%	39%
Low-income voters	31%	30%

Note: This table reports the total share of seats won
by an industrial voting bloc and low-income voters,
before and after Sweden's electoral reform.

[t]he days were past when a politician could announce his candidacy to an informal gathering at a country-town tavern, win his election with little or no outside support, and proceed to join the parliamentary group of his choice or, if he preferred, remain an independent. In order to win the votes of the new inclusive electorate the candidate had to appear at mass meetings in the towns, make extensive trips by rail or road to the outlying rural areas, and have his name put on a party list. In short he required the financial and political backing of a large-scale party organization.

By replacing SMDs with MMDs that included an average of eight times as many eligible voters, but also by keeping district magnitudes relatively small (most of the fifty-six districts elected between three and five members), the electoral reforms encouraged the development of relatively large, broad-based parties (Hermansson 2016, 108). Although not majorities, large proportions of each district were needed to win seats. In fact, the Social Democrats' early groundwork in bridging the rural–urban cleavage – made necessary by Sweden's turn-of-the-century electoral geography – and the mobilization of low-income citizens as a bloc (rather than urban or rural constituents) provided an important organizational advantage, and the Social Democrats would dominate Swedish politics for most of the twentieth century.

A different way to think about the longer-term implications of Sweden's electoral reform is independent of partisan constituencies, and instead focuses on the distribution of electoral power across groups in society. Table 7.3 reports estimates of the total shares of seats low-income and industrial voters could elect, if all members turned out to vote, as a voting bloc. Of course, the size of the industrial constituency would change over the course of the twentieth century, as the structure of the economy changed and suffrage rights were expanded to women: Based on the 1900 census data, about 42 percent of voting-aged men worked in manufacturing, construction, and transportation industries; Lewin, Jansson, and Sörbom (1972) estimate that "workers" comprised slightly more than 30 percent of those over the age of fifteen in 1900, and eventually, 55 percent of the population by 1960.[12] To the extent that the Social Democrats saw industrial workers as part of their core constituency, and anticipated that industry would continue to be concentrated in urban settings, they quite reasonably anticipated the costs associated with the proposed electoral reforms, as seen in Figure 7.5.

By the definition used here, the low-income constituency is fixed at one third of the national voting-eligible (male) population. It turns out that, using a conservative strategy to estimate the total electoral power of low-income voters, if all low-income voters turned out to vote, and all voted for the same party, they would fare only very slightly worse under MMD rules than under SMD rules, at least in the early 1900s. Specifically, a low-income voting bloc could elect about 72 and 69 seats out of 230, under SMD and MMD seats, respectively. (One might also wonder how the much larger MMDs would affect the ability to mobilize low-income voters as a bloc.) If legislators are incentivized to be responsive to their electoral constituency, from the current political economic perspective, which often emphasizes important differences between SMD and MMD electoral rules (see, e.g., Iversen & Soskice 2006), that SMD and MMD rules can generate similar outcomes may be surprising. In fact, as the next chapter will show, under some conditions, SMD electoral rules can provide low-income voters with levels of electoral power that are similar to the fully proportional (i.e., equitable) result.

Is it likely that this equivalence between SMD and MMD rules, in terms of the electoral power of low-income voters, would have been sustained in Sweden? That is, if the electoral reforms had failed, and elections were contested under SMD electoral rules, would we expect low-income voters to be pivotal in the election of about 31 percent of the Riksdag, throughout the twentieth century? For this to be the case, low-income voters must remain geographically concentrated in a substantial number of districts. At the turn of the century, for example, as we have seen in Figure 7.1, low-income voters were, in fact, highly concentrated. (This is also reflected in Figure 7.5(b), where low-income voters win large proportions of the seats in some counties, and few in other places.) Under SMD electoral rules, however, when a concentrated group becomes more dispersed, it loses its representational advantage. How did the geographic distribution of income change over the course of the twentieth century?

While income data for the full twentieth century are not available, when the current geographic distribution of income (2013, Table 7.4) is compared to the historical distribution in Figure 7.1, there is evidence that low-income voters in fact became more evenly distributed throughout the country (whether

---

[12] Przeworski and Sprague (1986) estimate that workers comprise a much smaller percentage of the total adult population, suggesting that by 1960, all manual wage earners in mining, manufacturing, construction, transportation, and agriculture, and the inactive members of their households, account for only about 34 percent of the population.

TABLE 7.4. *The distribution of low-income voters in Sweden, 2013.*

District	Percent low-income
Stockholm	29
Stockholms län	26
Uppsala	33
Södermanlands	38
Östergötlands	38
Jönköpings	35
Kronobergs	37
Kalmar	38
Gotlands	41
Blekinge	39
Skåne läns södra	31
Skåne läns nörra och östra	39
Skäne läns västra	38
Hallands	30
Malmö	48
Göteborgs	37
Västra Götalands läns västra	29
Västra Götalands läns norra	36
Västra Götalands läns södra	37
Västra Götalands läns östra	38
Värmlands	41
Örebro	39
Västmanlands	36
Dalarnas	40
Gävleborgs	40
Västernorrlands	37
Jämtlands	41
Västerbottens	37
Norrbottens	34

Notes: This table reports the contemporary distribution of low-income voters according to contemporary electoral district boundaries.

Source: Based on calculations made from Statistiska centralbyrån (2013), published online as "Disponibel inkomst per konsumtionsenhet i deciler. Medelvärde, tkr efter region, inkomstslag, år och Statistiska mått."

through migration or the equalization of wages). There is no contemporary electoral district, for example, in which low-income voters comprise less than 20 percent of the population (which we observe in many of the northern districts in 1900), or in which they form the numerical majority, although they are close to a numerical majority in Malmö. (Notice that the percentages of low-income voters exceeded fifty in most of the southern districts in 1900). While the contemporary MMD boundaries are different from those adopted in 1908, both sets of boundaries generally correspond to historical county and province boundaries (although the contemporary districts often combine historical districts). It is unlikely, therefore, that boundary differences account for differences we observe in the contemporary and historical concentration of low-income voters.

Importantly, because MMD electoral rules, in contrast to SMD electoral rules, moderate representational advantages of geographic concentration (see also Monroe & Rose 2002), and indeed, the effects of local changes in the distribution of electoral power, the more even contemporary geographic distribution of income means that the electoral power of low-income voters would likely be reduced under SMD rules. As a consequence, what Table 7.4 suggests is that while the electoral reform may have effectively provided a ceiling to short-term electoral gains the Social Democrats might have accumulated under SMD electoral rules, elections under MMD rules also provided a potential platform of support that was substantial, which further changes in the distribution of income groups would be unable to undermine.[13]

7.5 SUMMARY AND CONCLUSIONS

This chapter has focused on the electoral geography of income in Sweden at the beginning of the twentieth century and builds on the previous analytic case studies in two important respects: First, the Swedish case provides further evidence of the general way in which changes in electoral geography created electoral opportunities for a new party's entry into electoral competition. In Sweden, unlike the other cases considered here, changes in local distributions of electoral power resulted from (unintentional) suffrage expansions, as well as migration. Nevertheless, we observed the new Social Democratic party responding to these changes in electoral geography in the same way as British Labour, the Canadian CCF and Social Credit, and the American Populists. Specifically, the Social Democrats recruited candidates in those districts where there were large numbers of new voters – whether they entered the electorate through their new eligibility or through migration – who were ripe for mobilization. And, like the other cases, the Social Democrats were pragmatic in the development of their platforms, adopting policies that reflected the interests of their new – urban and rural – low-income constituency.

---

[13] It is certainly plausible that the adoption of MMD electoral rules contributed to incentives to equalize income (see, e.g., Iversen & Soskice 2006), and that the comparison of Figure 7.1 and Table 7.4 reflects more the equalization of earnings, rather than the dispersion of low-income earners.

The Swedish case also provides an opportunity to explore the implications of the electoral reforms that followed so quickly after the entry of the Social Democrats. Party positions on the adoption of MMDs and PR rules, at least in the Swedish case, fit well with Boix's (1999) and others' (see, e.g., Rodden 2010, Calvo 2009) expectations. Specifically, the Social Democrats recognized that, under universal suffrage, the adoption of MMD electoral rules would provide a ceiling on their electoral gains, and possibly stifle their early momentum. However, as suggested in the previous section, because MMD rules also moderate the effects of demographic change on the distribution of electoral power, the "guarantees" sought by the Conservatives in fact provided long-term guarantees for the representation of low-income citizens.

In the final chapter, this book will investigate cross-national, and in the US, cross-state, variation in the contemporary electoral power of low-income citizens, and implications for policy and public spending. Chapter 8 will also build on this chapter's analysis of electoral reform, and the long-term implications of early electoral geography for the political representation of low-income citizens. In the end, this book will suggest how American electoral geography has undermined opportunities for new party entry in the US, and in particular the quality of the political representation of low-income Americans.

7.A APPENDIX: SUPPORTING MATERIALS

Matching Census and Electoral Geography

The individual-level census data that provide the empirical foundation for this chapter are from the NAPP Swedish census datasets. Unlike the American, British, and Canadian censuses, local church leaders (i.e., not census enumerators) prepared Swedish census enumeration reports, based on their civil registries. Swedish census geography is therefore organized by parishes within counties, and these were used to allocate would-be voters to their appropriate electoral district.

Norberg, Tjerneld, and Asker (1985–1992) provide the details for the allocation of most parishes. An online resource based on Norberg, Tjerneld, and Asker (1985–1992) lists parishes and districts by counties, and was also extremely helpful.[14] Statistics Sweden (Statistika centralbyrån, SCB) provided further information about the location of parishes, including maps with historic county and parish boundary delineations. Finally, the maps presented in this chapter are based on revisions of contemporary parish boundary maps provided by Lantmäteriet.[15] Historical parishes were matched to contemporary parishes by name, with the Statistics Sweden (SCB) six-digit code provided in the NAPP and Lantmäteriet datafiles, and in a few cases by location.

[14] http://sv.wikipedia.org/wiki/Kategori:Historiska_valkretsar_i_Sverige
[15] www.lantmateriet.se/en/Maps-and-geographic-information/Maps/oppna-data/hamta-oppna-geodata/

TABLE 7.A.1. *Swedish census and electoral geography, 1890 and 1900.*

	1890 & 1900
Census geography	
Counties	25
Parishes	2,525
Electoral districts	
SMDs	200
Average population (1895)	24,548
Average population (1904)	26,303
MMDs	56

Note: Estimates of average population size are based on Sveriges Officiella Statistik (1897) and Sveriges Officiella Statistik (1906).

TABLE 7.A.2. *Verified entry of Social Democratic Candidates, 1905.*

	Lewin, Jansson, and Sörbom (1972)		
	No Social Democrat entry	*Social* Democrat entry	Total
Verified – No entry	112	24	136
Verified – Entry	0	12	12
Not Verified (Missing data)	0	52	52
Total	112	88	200

Note: This table provides a comparison of the two dependent variables used in the analysis presented in this chapter.

Table 7.A.1 provides the summary details of this match for 1890 and 1900.

Estimating Wages and Earnings

As suggested in the main text of this discussion, most wage data are based on estimates of annual earnings reported in Bagge, Lundberg, and Svennilson (1933), and are based on occupation categories (coded according to HISCO standards). County-level estimates are reported for most agricultural workers. Estimates of annual wages for municipal workers (including skilled artisans and unskilled construction workers) vary by city, for four categories of major cities.

TABLE 7.A.3. *Strategic entry of the Social Democratic Candidates, 1902.*

	(1) Estimated wages	(2) Estimated wages	DV: Social Democrat candidate entry (3) Official reports	(4) Official reports	(5) Official reports
Change in eligible voters[a]					
Quartile 1	0.342 (0.767)		25.981^b (6.126)		
Quartile 2		0.975^b (0.307)		0.386 (0.301)	0.377 (0.301)
Quartile 3		1.131^b (0.306)		0.817^b (0.290)	0.864^b (0.303)
Quartile 4		0.889^b (0.309)		1.128^b (0.287)	1.006^b (0.371)
Percentage in manufacturing, construction, transportation (1890)					0.619 (2.301)
Percentage agricultural, fishing (1890)					0.596 (1.666)
Median annual income (1890, in thousands kronor)					−0.587 (1.027)
Multi-member district					1.456^c (0.611)
Intercept	−0.441^b (0.143)	−1.207^b (0.248)	−0.833^b (0.141)	−1.027^b (0.225)	−1.331 (1.796)
N	190	190	190	190	190
Pseudo R^2	0.001	0.068	0.084	0.078	0.106

Notes: This table reports probit coefficients in analyses in which the dependent variable is an indicator of whether or not a Social Democratic candidate entered the 1902 electoral contest (Lewin, Jansson, & Sörbom 1972).
[a] Columns (1) and (2) use estimates of the change in the size of the voting-eligible population (as a proportion of men aged twenty-five and older),
based on estimated earnings and wages, 1890–1900. Columns (3)–(5) use estimates of the voting eligible population based on official reports,
1894–1901 (Sveriges Officiella Statistik 1897, 1903; as proportion of total population).
^{b} $p < 0.01$. ^{c} $p < 0.05$.

Estimates of wages and earnings for several occupations (e.g., dock hands and seamen) were reported in Wright (1905).

Note that reasonable estimates of wages and earnings were unavailable for almost 17 percent of the voting-aged men who reported occupations in 1890 (19 percent in 1900). Because most of these occupations are professional or near-professional occupations, this analysis includes these likely high-income earners in all calculations, and likely overestimates the proportion of those who meet voting-eligible income criteria.

Identifying Social Democratic Candidates

To verify the entry of Social Democratic candidates in the 1905 election, this analysis used the following newspaper reports of district-level election results:

- "Riksdagsmannavalen." *Östergötlands Veckoblad Östgöta Posten* N:37. September 15, 1905. Page 5.
- "Riksdagsmannavalen." *Östergötlands Veckoblad Östgöta Posten* N:40. October 6, 1905. Page 3.
- "De nya Andra-kammarvalen." *Dalpilen. Kopparbergs Läns Nyhets-och Annons-Tidning.* N:69. September 5, 1905. Page 2.

Any candidate that was identified as a "socialdemokrat" or a "socialist" was identified as a Social Democratic candidate for this analysis. Together, these reports include the results of contests held in 123 districts.

As noted in the main text of this chapter, Lewin, Jansson, and Sörbom (1972) report whether or not a Social Democratic candidate contested an election in each county. Any district in a county for which Lewin, Jansson, and Sörbom report no Social Democratic candidates is coded as a district in which no Social Democratic candidates entered in the "verified" version of this variable. Table 7.A.2 provides a summary of the verified measure.

Strategic Entry in 1902

The Social Democrats first recruited candidates to contest the election on their own label in 1902. The analysis presented in Table 7.A.3 replicates the analysis presented in the main text of this chapter, but instead uses the 1902 election. The dependent variable – entry of a Social Democratic candidate – is based on Lewin, Jansson, and Sörbom's (1972) reports of Social Democratic entry, and all districts in counties in which Lewin, Jansson, and Sörbom identify Social Democratic candidates are coded here as if a Social Democratic candidate did in fact enter the electoral contest. As a consequence, the rate of Social Democratic entry is likely exaggerated.

8

"It Didn't Happen Here": The General Implications of Electoral Geography for the Political Representation of the Poor

The previous four chapters have presented analytic case studies of the strategic entry decisions of low-income peoples' parties. In the US, Canada, Great Britain, and Sweden – very different political economic contexts – we have observed political entrepreneurs responding to changes in local distributions of electoral power, entering electoral contests in those districts where these changes are most profound, and tailoring their political appeals to those groups who experienced important increases in their influence over electoral outcomes. The nature of these early appeals, however, and especially the structure of these early electoral coalitions (i.e., which groups were mobilized), had long-term implications for the development of social policy in each country.

What might distinguish the democracies of North America, then, from those in Europe, is the location of historical electoral opportunities. In the US, and in Canada, changes in the local distributions of electoral power, at least across income groups, were predominantly in the less-populated, agricultural regions of each country. New parties responded to these opportunities for entry with platforms that tempered social democratic impulses, and with proposals that reflected the interests of an agricultural working class. At least in Great Britain and Sweden, changes in local distributions of electoral power favored those in industrial and manufacturing sectors, and the mobilizing efforts of the new parties incorporated their interests with more explicit socialist or social democratic appeals.

Notice that this analysis is premised on the idea that opportunities for new party entry are limited. If populations and district boundaries are generally stable, then so too are local partisan networks. Established parties will be able to take positions that are optimal, given the electoral geography of their countries, and effectively limit opportunities for new party entry. What this means is that, because changes in local distributions of electoral power have generally, and on average, decreased in many countries, especially the US, opportunities for new party entry have become increasingly rare. Party systems, therefore, likely reflect the interests of those groups who have benefited from historical changes in the electoral geography of each country.

That the presence of social democratic or labor parties contributes to the generosity of social spending, and the effectiveness of social policy, is well established (see, e.g., Moller *et al.* 2003, Huber & Stephens 2001). One might wonder, however, if contemporary distributions of electoral power can overcome the historical distributions of electoral power in each country. Are there incentives for legislators to represent the interests of low-income citizens, even where the success of low-income peoples' parties is limited?

Chapter 8 extends the political economic logic of electoral geography to consider whether contemporary geographic distributions of low-income voters might create (or undermine) incentives for responsive social policy, even in the absence (presence) of historical opportunities for partisan representation. Further, this chapter considers whether cross-national (and cross-state) differences in the electoral power of low-income voters can, in fact, account for differences in the overall generosity of social programs. Simply, if legislators pursue policies that represent the interests of those whose support they require to maintain their seats, social policy ought to be more generous in those places where low-income voters are more frequently pivotal.

This chapter begins by examining the relationship between the electoral power of low-income voters and social policy in the US states – fifty systems with nearly equivalent electoral institutions – and then for a subset of developed democracies that includes both majoritarian and PR electoral systems. This analysis shows that the electoral power of low-income voters can vary substantially across states or systems, even when the electoral rules governing these states and systems are quite similar.

This chapter will then show that cross-state and cross-national differences in the electoral power of low-income voters are associated with current levels of social spending. Because changes in the amounts of welfare benefits or earned-income tax credits can be easily perceived and attributed to incumbent legislators, following Franzese (2002), social policies and minimum income provisions may be especially well suited for manipulation by re-election-motivated legislators. If levels of social spending, for example, reflect differences in the electoral power of low-income voters, this might provide evidence of real differences in the quality of political representation.

It turns out, as suggested in the introduction to this book, that low-income Americans are rarely pivotal in elections to the House of Representatives – they have comparatively limited electoral power. If all low-income citizens turn out to vote, and all cast ballots for the same party, the poorest 33 percent of the population would elect only about 5 percent of the seats in the House. The penultimate section of this chapter returns to a motivating question of this book, and argues that the key to understanding the limited responsiveness of American legislators to low-income voters, and indeed, the absence of

low-income partisan representation, lies in the consequences of the current
and historical geographic distribution of income within our country. The final
section offers a summary statement of this book's contributions.

8.1 ELECTORAL POWER AND SOCIAL POLICY

Do differences in electoral geography matter for the political representation
of low-income voters? This section suggests that when legislators owe their
seats to the decisive support of low-income voters, they will have strong
incentives to craft responsive social policy and provide more extensive income
support, even when low-income voters are not part of their (national) partisan
constituency. (Low-income voters may, nevertheless, be part of local partisan
networks.) As a consequence, we ought to observe the most generous social
policy in those states or countries in which a low-income voting bloc is most
powerful (i.e., where large numbers of legislators share these incentives to be
responsive to low-income voters). This section provides some justification for
these expectations, and then evaluates the relationship between the electoral
power of low-income voters in each state or country and several measures
of the effectiveness of social policy, in the US states and in some developed
democracies.

While providing evidence in favor of a causal relationship is difficult, there
are two reasons why we might expect social policy to be more generous in those
systems in which low-income voters are especially powerful:

First, as suggested above, it may be helpful to think about safety net
programs as a distributive benefit (i.e., subject to "pork-barrel" politics).
In the context of the theoretical arguments developed in Chapter 2, and
to the extent that income groups are geographically segregated, safety net
policies provided benefits to geographically well-defined groups (like high-
ways, bridges, and football stadiums). Further, as suggested above, because
changes in, for example, the amount of welfare benefits or earned-income
tax credits can be easily perceived and attributed to incumbent legislators
and governments, social policies are especially well suited for manipulation
by re-election-motivated legislators (see Franzese 2002). Simply, when their
electoral success is dependent upon the support of low-income citizens,
legislators have strong incentives to ensure that social programs are generous
and effective.

A second reason why we might expect electoral power to influence spending
on social programs and safety net benefit amounts has to do with the implications of historical electoral geographies for the development of party systems,
and ultimately for electoral reform: When changes in electoral geography
created incentives for newly formed parties to mobilize a low-income industrial
constituency, the adoption of MMD rules often quickly followed (perhaps
to provide "guarantees" against universal suffrage, as in the Swedish case;
see Rodden 2011, Boix 1999). While the MMD electoral rules may have

established an upper threshold on the success of the new parties, particularly when their basis of support was geographically concentrated, they also provided a platform that ensured a relatively stable and equitable distribution of electoral power. It seems likely, therefore, that the contemporary electoral power of a low-income voting bloc, in the MMD systems, closely corresponds to their electoral power in the relatively long term (i.e., under current district structure and distributions of seats). To the extent, then, that low-income voters are represented by parties of the left in these countries, we might expect their contemporary levels of electoral power to be closely related to the long-term success of left parties – a strong correlate of expansive social programs.[1]

Therefore, we may expect contemporary distributions of electoral power to explain current levels of social spending, both because of the current incentive structures they create, and because of their relationship to historical electoral geographies.[2]

As in earlier analysis, the "electoral power" of a low-income voting bloc is an estimate of the share of seats in a legislature that low-income citizens could elect, if all low-income citizens turned out to vote, and all low-income citizens cast ballots for the same party. Because not everyone votes, and low-income citizens support different parties, this estimate will provide an upper bound of the potential electoral power of low-income citizens. (In fact, to the extent that low-income citizens are powerful, parties and candidates face strong incentives to mobilize turnout and partisan coherence; see Jusko 2015b). Again, "low income" refers to all eligible voters whose (usually, household) incomes fall in the first third of the state or national income distribution. In a fully equitable electoral system, in which all votes are equally weighted, low-income voters should be pivotal in one third of electoral contests. Appendix 8.A provides the technical details of this analysis.

Because the measurement challenges in the cross-national analysis are somewhat more complex – simply, each country contributes a different data source, in which income measures and geographic information vary – this analysis begins with the more straightforward examination of electoral power in the US state legislatures, in which all estimates derive from the same data source. The set of US states, too, provides an extremely good illustration of

---

[1] In fact, estimates of electoral power are highly correlated with the average seat share held by left parties in these countries and the cumulative number of left cabinets, between 1960 and 2010 ($R = 0.64$ and $R = 0.69$, respectively). In the US, the correlation between the post-1996 state legislative strength of the Democrats, who others might consider a party that represents the interests of low-income voters, and the electoral power of low-income voters, is relatively low, about $R = 0.18$.

[2] A related point: Where local party networks are especially strong, members of low-income peoples' parties may represent districts that are now relatively wealthy, and vice versa. By thinking about safety net policies as benefits provided to geographically well-defined and pivotal constituents, we can make sense of incumbents who seem out of step with their parties on issues related to social programs.

how different geographic distributions of income interact with (more or less) the same electoral rules to create important differences in the numbers of legislators who have incentives to be responsive to the poor. This cross-state variation provides a helpful context for understanding the implications of the other electoral rules that we later observe in the broadly comparative analysis.

Figure 8.1 reports the shares of low-income voters in each state (lower house) legislative district.[3] Notice that, if low-income voters were evenly distributed

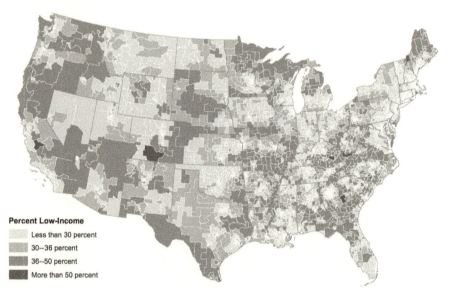

Percent Low-Income
- Less than 30 percent
- 30--36 percent
- 36--50 percent
- More than 50 percent

FIGURE 8.1. Electoral geography of state House districts.

Notes: This figure reports the percentage of low-income households in each state legislative district.
Source: Electoral power: US Census Bureau, 2008–2012 American Community Survey.

---

[3] State House of Representative districts are used everywhere but Nebraska, where the state legislature is unicameral.

These data are based on five-year (2008–2012) estimates from the American Community Survey, an extremely high-quality survey especially designed to facilitate analysis of small geographic areas. The comparative analysis to follow will use market income (wages and salaries) whenever possible; for the state legislative district level of geographic aggregation, the best available measure of household income includes income from all sources. Because low-income households are identified relative to the state distribution (i.e., they comprise the first third of the state's income distribution), the inclusion of social transfers is less problematic: so long as the distribution of social transfers does not change the ranking of households in the state distribution, estimates of the share of low-income households in each district are reliable. Details of how estimation errors are accommodated are presented in Appendix 8.A.

Figure 8.1, state legislative districts are distinguished according to the share of low-income across electoral districts, most districts would be shaded the second shade of gray (indicating that a low-income voting bloc comprises between 30 and 36 percent of the district; this range allows for reasonable sampling error), and low-income voters would never be pivotal in electoral contests.[4]

In fact, this is not far from the truth: When the total numbers of seats in each state's House are taken into account, low-income voters are pivotal in up to 13 percent of state legislative contests. There is, however, sufficient variation across states to evaluate the implications of differences in the electoral power of low-income voters for their representation. For example, in Alabama and Mississippi (which, as we shall see, have notoriously limited safety net programs), there are no districts in which low-income citizens necessarily contribute to winning coalitions. Similarly, in Texas, another state in which safety programs are known to be limited, the electoral support of low-income citizens is necessary for only one (of 150) legislators. (Texas's District 37 includes the city of Brownsville, and the southernmost tip of the state.) In Connecticut, where low-income voters are most frequently pivotal, they contribute to the winning coalitions in 14 (out of 151) House races.

One might raise the following concerns about this analysis. First, as suggested above, the estimates of electoral power rely on the assumptions that everyone turns out to vote, and everyone votes by type (i.e., all low-income voters cast ballots for the same candidates, within each district). Of course,

households, with the darkest shaded areas representing those districts in which a low-income voting bloc is pivotal (i.e., exceeds 50 percent of the population).

4 Elections under SMD rules are about the formation of winning coalitions. One way to estimate the electoral power of different groups is to estimate the proportion of winning coalitions in which each particular group is crucial to the success of the coalition. Specifically, what proportion of winning coalitions are dependent upon the support of a particular group? (This proportion is often referred to as the Shapley–Shubik Index; Shapley and Shubik 1954). If coalitions can be formed without restriction (e.g., coalitions of low- and high-income voters are not excluded), and there are three potential coalition partners, there are six potential winning coalitions and, typically, each partner's membership is decisive in one third of them: Simply, coalitions of low- and middle-income voters, and coalitions of low- and high-income voters, are dependent upon the support of low-income voters. With three income groups, then, if each group turns out to vote in equal proportions, each group will exert an equal influence over the elections in their district. It is only when one group's share of the electorate exceeds 50 percent that the group's share of winning coalitions exceeds one third. When a group's share of the electorate exceeds 50 percent, therefore, it is truly *pivotal* in the outcome of the election. Therefore, intuitively, of course, but also with these coalition dynamics in mind, I use a threshold of 50 percent to allocate seats when elections are contested in SMD systems, including in the US state legislatures. Others, including Lijphart (1994) and Boix (1999), instead use a threshold of 35 percent for all SMD systems, and allocate a district's seat to the low-income voting bloc if the proportion of low-income voters exceeds 35 percent. Earlier versions of this manuscript and Jusko (2008) followed this practice because this relatively low "effective threshold of representation" – recall that low-income citizens comprise the bottom third, or 33 percent of the national income distribution – diminishes differences between SMD and MMD proportional representation systems in the representation of low-income citizens. Here, the more intuitive threshold is used instead.

neither of these assumptions hold. The estimates of electoral power, therefore, as suggested above, represent upper bounds on the shares of state Houses that owe their seats to the electoral support of low-income citizens. (And still they are quite low!) Second, these estimates of electoral power rely on knife-edge thresholds. That is, seats are counted as contributing to a low-income voting bloc's electoral power if low-income voters exceed 50 percent of the district's population. On the one hand, this threshold replicates elections held under majoritarian rules. On the other hand, because of the structure of the data – e.g., the population of each district likely includes some who are not eligible voters – these estimates of electoral power are imprecise. However, to the extent that ineligible voters are over-represented among low-income households, estimates of low-income electoral power are likely *exaggerated*.

Figure 8.2 plots estimates of a low-income voting bloc's electoral power in each state against two standard measures of the generosity of social policy, the maximum Temporary Assistance for Needy Families (TANF) benefits for a family of three with no income, and average monthly unemployment insurance benefits. Eligibility criteria and benefit amounts for both programs are largely determined by state governments, and benefit amounts have remained relatively stable, particularly for TANF. Maximum TANF benefits in Mississippi, for example, have been set at $170 per month since 1998.

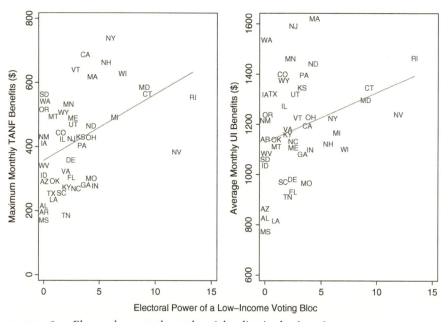

FIGURE 8.2. Electoral geography and social policy in the American states.
Sources: Maximum Monthly TANF Payments: Urban Institute (2008–2011). Average Monthly Unemployment Benefits: US Department of Labor (2013).

TABLE 8.1. *Electoral geography and social policy in the US.*

	Maximum monthly TANF payments		Average monthly unemployment benefits	
	(1)	(2)	(1)	(2)
Electoral power	20.72[a]	10.61[b]	23.83[a]	11.77
	(6.32)	(5.13)	(8.58)	(7.86)
Partisan control		51.99		82.24[b]
		(26.20)		(40.18)
South		−194.29[a]		−193.974
		(33.24)		(50.92)
Partisan control × South		−37.57		−126.52
		(46.15)		(70.70)
Intercept	356.61[a]	453.62[a]	1097.14[a]	1205.63[a]
	(26.90)	(25.83)	(36.53)	(39.57)
N	47	47	47	47
Adjusted R^2	0.18	0.53	0.13	0.37

Notes: This table reports coefficients estimated in an ordinary least squares regression model; standard errors are reported in parentheses.
[a] $p < 0.01$. [b] $p < 0.05$.
Sources: Maximum monthly TANF payments: Urban Institute (2008–2011). Average monthly unemployment benefits: US Department of Labor (2013).

In each panel of Figure 8.2 we observe a positive relationship between social transfer amounts and the electoral power of a low-income voting bloc. That is, larger benefits are provided in those states where a low-income voting bloc is relatively powerful. In bivariate linear models, an increase of an additional seat (1 percent of the median state legislature, or one point on the measure of electoral power) is associated with an additional $21 in monthly TANF support, and $24 in monthly UI benefits (about 5 and 2 percent of average amounts, respectively; the bivariate correlations are $R = 0.44$ and $R = 0.38$). As Table 8.1 reports, the positive relationship is maintained even when potentially confounding partisan and regional effects are taken into account (although the relationship between electoral power and unemployment benefits is then estimated with considerable variance).[5]

To the extent that the US states provide a common political economic context, with similar electoral rules and a shared party system, they provide a good opportunity to evaluate how differences in electoral power are related to differences in policy outcomes. In fact, this analysis suggests that legislators

---

5 Here, the measure of partisan control is the percentage of legislative sessions since the 1996 welfare reform, when the states assumed legislative control over the main American safety net program, TANF, in which the Democrats controlled both houses of the state legislatures.

are responsive to local distributions in electoral power, and implement policies that favor those whose support they require to maintain their seats.

A broadly comparative analysis of the implications of differences in the national electoral power of low-income voters for social policy is complicated by differences in government structures (e.g., policy jurisdictions), and therefore is necessarily more suggestive than conclusive. Nevertheless, using the best available income data for each country to calculate the proportion in each electoral district, and then allocating seats to a low-income voting bloc according to each system's electoral rules, the electoral power of low-income voters can be calculated for each country.[6]

Table 8.2 reports estimates of the electoral power of a low-income voting bloc, for each country, and organized by district structure. Note, first, that as we saw in the US state legislatures, the success of a low-income voting bloc varies across systems even with the same type of electoral system, and particularly across countries with SMD electoral rules. The electoral power of low-income voters also varies, however, among the MMD PR systems. While, in these systems, low-income voters are generally assured of at least equitable representation (33 percent of the seats in the lower house), in the MMD systems, in a few cases, their concentration in districts that elect few members (i.e., that have low district magnitudes), leads to their over-representation in the legislature. More importantly, however, at least in the case of contemporary France, low-income voters can be equitably represented even under SMD electoral rules. That is, PR rules are not necessary to achieve at least a proportional result.[7]

What is it that generates differences in low-income citizens' electoral power, even when the electoral rules are the same? A comparison of the distribution of income in France and the US can be helpful here. Notice, as reported in Table 8.2, that low-income voters in France are pivotal in nearly a third

---

[6] In all SMD systems, including systems with run-off elections, seats are allocated to any income group that comprises more than 50 percent of the electorate in the district (more technically, when the income of the median voter is equal to or less than the thirty-third percentile of the national income distribution). To simplify the allocation of seats in systems with proportional representation rules, Droop quotas are used everywhere, even in systems with Highest Average allocations. In SMD and MMD systems with compensatory tiers, in which disproportionality in the vote-to-seat mappings are corrected with secondary national or regional seat allocations, electoral power is estimated based on the first tier allocations: it is the first tier allocations that have the potential to structure electoral competition within each district, and create incentives to be responsive to locally relevant interests. Of course, to the extent that upper tiers are truly compensatory, incentives to respond to locally powerful income groups are diminished, and we might expect differences in local electoral power to account for less cross-national variance in social policy.

[7] In fact, in the historical cases, low-income voters formed the numerical majority in nearly 40 percent of seats in the US in 1892, 35 percent of seats in Canada in 1935, and 36 percent of seats in Sweden in 1905. (They were pivotal in only 11 percent of seats in England and Wales in 1906.)

TABLE 8.2. *Seats elected by a low-income voting bloc.*

Country	(1) # districts	(2) Electoral power
A. Single-member district systems		
United States (2013)	23	5.3
Australia (2011)	11	7.3
Canada (2006)	42	13.6
Great Britain (2013)	147	23.2
France (2011)	174	31.3
B. National district systems		
Netherlands		33
C. Varying-district-magnitude systems		
Austria		34.8
Denmark		34.1
Finland		39.5
Norway		36.6
Sweden		36.7

Notes: This table reports estimates of the number of seats that a low-income voting bloc could secure if all low-income citizens cast ballots, and cast ballots for the same party. Refer to Appendix 8.A for details of how these estimates were calculated.

of French circonscriptions, but only in about 5 percent of US congressional districts. Why might the same proportion of the population be pivotal in such dramatically different numbers of electoral contests?

The answer, of course, lies in the extent to which income groups are segregated and district boundaries coincide with de facto boundaries between groups. When SMD boundaries frequently coincide with boundaries that distinguish areas where low-income voters live, for example from wealthier areas, low-income voters may be more frequently pivotal in the election of legislators. Alternatively, if electoral districts are generally heterogeneous with regards to the composition of income groups (as is the case in most US state legislative districts), low-income voters will rarely form the numerical majority of their districts.

Figure 8.3 provides some insight into the comparison between France and the US: In each subfigure, the left-hand panel reports median incomes for subdistrict units (communes and census tracts), and the right panel reports each district's median incomes. The vertical lines note the levels of income that correspond, approximately, to the thirty-third percentile of the national household income distribution. In both France and the US, we find some subdistrict units (about 25 percent of subdistrict units in France, and 14 percent in the US) with median household incomes that fall below the "low income"

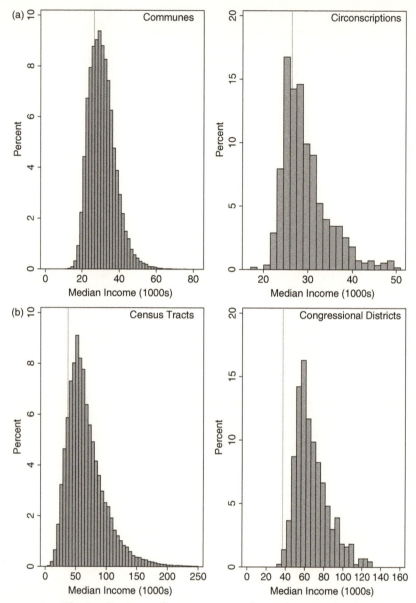

FIGURE 8.3. The implications of contemporary electoral geography in France and the US.

Note: This figure reports the distributions of median income levels for subdistrict units and electoral districts for France (2011) and the US (2011).

Source: See notes for Table 8.2.

threshold. When we look at the district-level distribution, however, important cross-national differences (anticipated by Table 8.2) emerge: While there are a significant number of French circonscriptions in which the median voter is a low-income voter, there are almost no US congressional districts in which a low-income voter is pivotal.

Another way to look at the differences in American and French electoral geography is to compare the within-district income variation to variation in median income across districts. To the extent that income is segregated, and low-income voters are more frequently pivotal, we would expect larger across-district variation compared to within-district variation. However, when electoral districts are heterogeneous with regards to income, then we might expect larger within-district variation in income. Table 8.3 provides this comparison using the subdistrict median income data, and reports estimates of the standard deviation of median income *between* and *within* electoral districts. Quite clearly, in the US, within-district variation in income exceeds cross-district variation. The opposite patterns – between-district variation exceeds within-district variation – characterize the electoral geography of income in France. This implies that low-income voters are segregated into French circonscriptions in ways that enhance their electoral power, and in contrast to the geographic distribution of low-income Americans.[8]

Finally, notice in Table 8.3 that the size of a US congressional district is much larger – by a factor of almost seven – than the average French district. This undoubtedly contributes to the heterogeneity of American congressional districts, and dilutes the electoral power of low-income voters. In fact, Appendix 8.A provides some evidence that the electoral power of low-income voters may be *enhanced* by the political districting process: Of the twenty-three congressional districts in which low-income voters form the numerical majority, fifteen are more "gerrymandered" than the average district in their state,[9] and

---

[8] In its emphasis on electoral power, this acknowledges the tension between the geographic concentration of a particular group and the potential for "wasted votes." That is, to maximize the legislative representation of low-income voters, one would need to construct districts so as to maximize the number of districts in which low-income voters comprise one voter more than half of the electorate. Recall that under SMD electoral rules, a party needs (at most) the support of half of the voters, in half of the seats – only 25 percent of the votes cast – in order to form the majority in the legislature. (Parties can win with a smaller proportion of votes cast, when elections are contests by more than two parties.) It is possible, therefore, that a low-income voting bloc, efficiently distributed -w ith maximum electoral power, given its proportion – could elect the majority of seats in the legislature.

[9] Ingraham's (2014) index is based on district compactness. Specifically, imagine imposing a circle on top of each district, such that it was entirely covered. This measure of gerrymandering calculates the ratio of the area covered by the district to the full area covered by the circle, and subtracts this index from one, so that districts that are less compact – more gerrymandered – take higher values. Table 8.A.1 reports the ratio of each district's gerrymander index score to the state average, to allow for the general compactness of districts to vary across states. (Districts in states that are not compact themselves, may be generally less compact).

TABLE 8.3. *Between- and within-district variation in income, in France and the US.*

	France (*Communes*)	US (Census tracts)
Between-district standard deviation in median income	5,719	17,590
Average *within-district* standard deviation in median income	5,056	25,264
Ratio	1.13	0.69
Average size of district	108,000	710,767
Median size of subdistrict units (households)	1,008	1,601
Average number of subdistrict units	57	175

Notes: This table summarizes important differences in the distribution of income in the US and in France.

Sources: US: 2011 American Community Survey five-year estimates, reported in Data Profiles (Series HC01–VC74 reports the number of households, and HC01–VC112 reports median income). 2010 Census tracts are allocated to 113th Congressional District boundaries using the Missouri Census Data Center MABLE/Geocorr12: Geographic Correspondence Engine. Metropolitan France: Insee-DGFiP "Revenus fiscaux localisés des ménages – Année 2011." Allocations of *communes* and municipal *arrondissements* are based on my own allocation of *cantons* to districts, as described in the "Tableau des circonscriptions électorales des départements (élection des députés; version en vigueur du 25 novembre 1986 au 1 août 2009)."

all but seven are majority-minority districts. (In the 113th Congress, Democrats represented eighteen of these districts in which low-income voters were pivotal.) One might reasonably conclude, therefore, that because of the heterogeneous distribution of income (even in very small geographic areas), without the intentional manipulation of electoral boundaries, low-income Americans would be pivotal in even fewer electoral contests than they are currently.

What might these cross-national differences in the electoral power of low-income voters mean, then, for social policy, and the quality of their political representation? While MMD electoral rules tend to moderate differences in the geographic concentrations of low-income voters, low-income voters may benefit from the disproportionality of districts that elect few legislators (see also Monroe & Rose 2002). Under SMD rules, by contrast, differences in the geographic concentration of low-income voters become especially stark: In the US, where districts are large and especially heterogeneous, low-income voters are rarely pivotal in the election of national legislators. (Even in state legislatures, low-income voters are rarely pivotal in more than 10 percent of electoral contests.) In France, by contrast, low-income voters are frequently pivotal and are approximately proportionately represented in their national legislature.

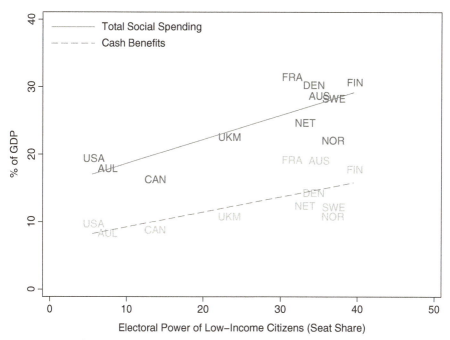

FIGURE 8.4. Electoral geography and social policy in contemporary democracies. *Sources:* Electoral power of low-income voters: see note for Table 8.2 and Appendix 8.A. Social spending and cash transfers: Organisation For Economic Co-operation and Development (OECD) (2014).

While the cross-national relationship between electoral power and social policy, as suggested above, is likely complicated by innumerable features of each political system, we might reasonably ask whether those systems in which electoral geography favors low-income voters are also those systems in which levels of social spending are relatively more generous. In fact, as Figure 8.4 demonstrates, there is a strong, positive relationship between the electoral power of low-income voters and two measures of social policy, specifically, general social spending and per capita spending on cash transfers. While the small number of cases limits more rigorous analysis, this relationship seems to be especially strong in SMD systems, but is also present in MMD systems. (The correlations between social spending and electoral power in MMD and SMD systems are $R = 0.26$ and $R = 0.89$, respectively.)[10] This broadly comparative analysis, therefore, provides some evidence that legislators, generally, are responsive to national distributions of electoral power.

---

[10] This analysis replicates a result established by Jusko (2008), which estimated low-income electoral power for a more inclusive set of developed democracies, using different strategies for estimating electoral power, and for the year 2000.

Summary

This section has investigated contemporary distributions of electoral power across US state legislatures and in a broadly comparative, cross-national analysis, and makes three contributions. First, this analysis has demonstrated that the ways votes map into seats varies substantially, even among electoral systems with similar electoral rules. To be sure, MMD rules contribute to an equitable mapping of votes to seats, but depending on the distribution of groups across districts, SMD rules can generate similarly equitable distributions of electoral power.

Second, those systems in which low-income voters have comparatively high levels of electoral power are also those systems in which social spending and benefit amounts tend to be relatively generous.

Finally, this section has focused attention on the limited electoral power of low-income Americans.[11] In national legislative contests, low-income Americans are pivotal in about 5 percent of elections. In most states, low-income Americans are pivotal in fewer than 10 percent of state legislative contests. In sum, this implies that very few elected representatives face strong incentives to mobilize, or to be responsive to, low-income voters, or to incorporate low-income communities into local partisan networks. As this analysis suggests, the limited electoral power of low-income voters may account for the comparatively limited effectiveness of American social policies, and perhaps the lack of responsiveness, observed by Bartels (2008), Gilens (2012), and others (e.g., Gilens & Page 2014). One might wonder if the limited incentives to mobilize low-income Americans contributes to their apparent lack of political efficacy and general alienation (for an analysis of the implications of contemporary electoral geography for voter turnout, see Jusko 2015b). More importantly, one might worry that the inequitable representation of low-income Americans leaves some ripe for mobilization by anti-establishment, or even anti-democratic, candidates.

The effects of the limited electoral power of low-income Americans is likely compounded by the singular absence, at least among developed democracies, of a low-income people's party. Indeed, who represents the interests of the poor in American policy-making? The next section points to features of American contemporary and historical electoral geography that have undermined opportunities for a third party, and provides a fresh perspective on the absence of a major social democratic or labor party in the US.

8.2 "IT DIDN'T HAPPEN HERE"

Previous accounts of the absence (actually, the very limited success) of a social democratic or labor party in the US have typically emphasized limited demand for working class protections. For example, in the classic analysis,

---

[11] The similarly limited electoral power of low-income Australians was not apparent in the earlier version of this analysis, and warrants further explanation (see Jusko 2008).

Sombart (1976[1906]) focused attention on the relative affluence of American workers compared to European workers. Although, in the introduction to a later edition, Lipset (1968, xi) focused on American electoral institutions, and particularly primary competitions, his initial analysis (and his later collaborative work, Lipset & Marks 2000) similarly draws attention to the economic and sociohistorical structures that undermined the potential for a third party – that is, the *demand* for working-class representation. More recently, Archer (2010) draws attention to local, state, and national repression of organized labor, as well as the reluctance of national labor leaders, notably Samuel Gompers, to participate in electoral politics. Archer (2010) attributes this reluctance to form a labor party, in part, to the already intense partisan loyalties of working-class voters that were reinforced by religious identities. These accounts, like other comparative sociological accounts of party formation, place little emphasis on the work of established party candidates in maintaining these loyalties.

Political economic accounts of two-party competition in the US typically emphasize incentives created by plurality rules, and incorporate Duverger's Law – that "the simple-majority single-ballot system favors the two-party system" (Duverger 1954). Riker (1982), for example, suggests that because of what Duverger identified as "mechanical effects" and "psychological factors" associated with first-past-the-post electoral rules, office-seekers may be unwilling to invest their mobilization efforts in parties with only small chances of holding office. Similarly, Rosenstone, Behr, and Lazarus (1984, 18) find that "the single member-district plurality system not only explains two-party dominance, it also ensures short lives for third parties that do appear." This is because, Rosenstone, Behr, and Lazarus (18) write,

Third-party voters must be willing to support candidates who they know have no chance of winning. Moreover, because third parties wither so quickly, there is little opportunity for voters to grow accustomed to backing them, or for the cycle of discouragement to be broken.

Of course, the voters' unwillingness to waste votes, and support parties and candidates that are unlikely to be successful, reflects Duverger's (1954) psychological factors. The mechanical effect concerns the way votes map into seats, and in particular, that SMD electoral rules under-represent small parties: they often win less than a proportionate share of seats. As a consequence, the incentives of voters and candidates ought to sustain two-party competition.

Hirano and Snyder (2007) point out, however, that prior to 1935, third-party candidates often contested US House, Governor, and Senate contests, with some success. Indeed, the relatively stable two-party competition of the post-war period is notable, in American history, as well as among other systems with SMD electoral rules. Cox (1997) and others (e.g., Clark & Golder 2006) draw attention to the interaction between social structures and electoral institutions in their revisions or "rehabilitations" of Duverger's

Law, suggesting that parties reflect the underlying shared interests of "spiritual families," and that when societies are especially heterogeneous, multi-party competition may become the norm, even when elections are contested in SMDs.

An emphasis on electoral geography, and opportunities for new party entry, similarly draws attention to the role of social heterogeneity, but in particular, the way groups are distributed in space. Specifically, it seems likely that both the influence of Duverger's mechanical effects and psychological factors are moderated by local distributions of electoral power. For example, when groups are concentrated in some number of districts such that they are pivotal, the parties and candidates that can mobilize their support are assured of some number of seats (and possibly opportunities to serve in governing coalitions). That is, the mechanical effect of SMD electoral rules may work to benefit some groups, and undermine psychological resistance to voting for third parties.

Importantly, by focusing on electoral geography, the account of new party entry offered here provides a fresh perspective on this classic question of comparative political science: why is there no social democratic or labor party in the US?

In fact, there are three features of American electoral geography that may have undermined opportunities for a major third party, and especially for a social democratic or labor party. First, notice in Figure 3.2 that local population change decreased over the course of the twentieth century, and especially after about 1940. If the argument presented in Chapter 2 is correct, the limited population movement implies that there were fewer opportunities for new party entry in the post-war period because local partisan networks were stable, and few voters were ripe for mobilization. In fact, in Figure 3.3, we observe fewer new parties *of any type* entering electoral competition in the US after the 1930s; Hirano and Snyder also notice a "clear decline in third-party electoral support" in House and state-wide contests, beginning in the 1930s.[12]

Second, the negative implications of relative population stability for new party entry were enhanced by dramatic increases in the size of congressional districts. Over the last century, the size of American House of Representative districts has increased dramatically, from about 184,000 in 1890 to over 710,000 in 2010. On the one hand, this likely contributed to more heterogeneous districts, at least with respect to income. In 1892, for example, low-income voters were pivotal in almost *40 percent* of congressional districts; as noted above, in 2010, low-income voters formed the numerical majority in less than 10 percent of districts. On the other hand, the barriers to new party entry likely increase with the size of the district. Simply, bigger changes in local populations are needed to alter local distributions of electoral power. (One might naturally wonder about the implications of the strategic manipulation of electoral district boundaries, or gerrymandering. To the extent that these efforts

---

[12] Hirano and Snyder (2007) attribute the decline in third-party voting to the Democratic co-optation of the left.

are successful, it seems likely that they bolster local partisan networks, and protect incumbent legislators from changes in local distributions of electoral power that favor groups excluded of these networks.)

Finally, local population change in the US has typically been more profound outside of the manufacturing and industrial regions of the Northeast, at least since 1870. Notice that, in Figure 3.2, average rates of local population change are always less than rates of population change observed in other regions. At least in part, the population density of the Northeast provided an upper bound on the extent to which migration or immigration could alter local distributions in electoral power. Put slightly differently, in agricultural areas where populations were relatively small, the rapid growth observed at the end of the nineteenth century had the capacity to dramatically alter local distributions of electoral power. This means that, even when there were opportunities to mobilize new constituencies, in districts where there had been important changes in the distributions of electoral power, appeals to farmers would have likely been more effective than social democratic appeals.

From the perspective of electoral geography of groups and the strategic entry of new parties developed here, therefore, these three features of American electoral geography – decreasing rates of local population change, increasing congressional district size, and the concentration of changes in the local distribution of electoral power outside of industrial/manufacturing regions – likely undermined opportunities for a major third party, and especially for a social democratic or labor party, in the US. This is not to suggest that factors identified by other scholars, including the effects of electoral competition for the presidency, are unimportant. Rather, this brief analysis implies that even without the other factors that set the US apart, long-term changes in American electoral geography provide an explanation for the absence of a major third party. More importantly, a focus on historical electoral geography can offer an explanation both for the entry of (at least) the last major third party, the People's Party, as well as an account of the general stability of America's two-party system.

8.3 ELECTORAL GEOGRAPHY, PARTY ENTRY, AND POLITICAL REPRESENTATION: SUMMARY AND CONCLUSIONS

This book has offered a general explanation for why some groups, and not others, are mobilized as partisan constituencies.

To the extent that established parties are limited in their abilities to respond to changes in electoral geography, changes in local distributions of electoral power create opportunities for new parties to enter electoral competition. Political entrepreneurs will craft appeals to mobilize those groups who have benefited from these changes in electoral geography, and enter contests in those districts where the changes in local distributions of power are most profound. Party systems, therefore, represent the interests of those groups who were favored by historical changes in the electoral geography of each country.

Although Chapter 3 offers some general support for the importance of changing electoral geographies, and provides a general analysis of when any and all new parties enter electoral competition, most of this book involves the application of this argument to one group – low-income voters. By focusing on a hypothetical group, defined in an arbitrary but not unreasonable way, this analysis is insulated from concerns about the endogenous bubbling-up of partisan identities. Instead, this book evaluates the implications of political entrepreneurs' incentives to mobilize a low-income voting bloc *as a bloc*, thereby creating and/or manipulating the very group identities that structure contemporary party systems.

Critical to the account of party system development offered here is the idea that established parties cultivate local partisan networks that sustain their electoral coalitions. It is not sufficient, for example, for a new party to set out with the intention of representing a particular group or its grievances. Rather, the members of this group must be ripe for mobilization – newly arrived, newly eligible, or otherwise free to take up a new partisan identity. Further, this group must be large enough and pivotal in enough electoral contests that mobilizing its support furthers the political entrepreneurs' office-seeking goals.

This book has focused on the changing electoral geography of low-income citizens in the US, Canada, Great Britain, and Sweden in critical periods just before the entry of major low-income peoples' parties. In each case, the new parties' candidates entered contests in those districts where changes in electoral geography especially favored low-income voters. Specifically, Chapter 4 provided evidence that the American People's Party entered those electoral districts in which the electoral power of low-income voters had increased most substantially. In the Canadian case, in Chapter 5, we observed that the political entrepreneurs who established the CCF and Social Credit responded to the same incentives as the American "third-party men" – changes in the electoral power of low-income voters – but developed very different ideological appeals. The fact that the CCF and Social Credit contested many of the same districts, and sought to mobilize the same constituency, is especially difficult to reconcile with an up-from-the-bottom demand approach to party formation.

The two European cases, Great Britain and Sweden, provide useful comparisons to the US and Canada in that, in Chapters 6 and 7, we also observed political entrepreneurs forming low-income peoples' parties and entering electoral competition in those districts where recent changes in the local distribution of power were most profound. Nevertheless, the locations and interests of the newly pivotal voters were quite different. As a consequence, the British and Swedish political entrepreneurs crafted appeals that reflected their opportunities in predominantly industrial regions. The Swedish case is particularly notable because the changes in local distributions of electoral power resulted from prosperity and growth; any role for economic grievance in the entry of the Social Democrats is necessarily limited. Large numbers of industrial workers saw their wages increase so much that, in 1905, they met long-established suffrage criteria. It was the concentration of these new voters in some urban and industrial areas that created the opportunity for the Social Democratic Party's entry into electoral competition.

Finally, this chapter has considered the implications of contemporary electoral power, with the question of whether current electoral geographies might create incentives for the political representation of low-income voters, even if historical opportunities for their partisan representation were limited. Indeed, low-income Americans are rarely pivotal in the election of legislators, in national or state legislatures. With few incentives to mobilize, or represent the interests of, low-income citizens, it is not surprising that American legislators implement social programs that are limited, at least in comparison to those offered by other post-industrial democracies. From the perspective of electoral geography and electoral power, the limited responsiveness of American legislators to low-income voters, and indeed, the absence of partisan representation for low-income and working class voters, are no longer puzzling features of contemporary American politics. Instead, these are the clear consequences of the political economic incentive structures created by current and historical electoral geographies.

This book, therefore, offers an innovative account of the origins of cross-national differences in the political representation of low-income citizens. It has demonstrated how the changing electoral geographies of the late nineteenth and early twentieth centuries created incentives for political entrepreneurs to form and mobilize low-income constituencies. When migration, immigration, or suffrage expansions enhanced the electoral power of low-income voters, political entrepreneurs recognized a constituency that was ripe for mobilization, and recruited candidates and tailored new party platforms accordingly. Whether these "third-party men" developed populist or social democratic platforms reflects the location and interests of newly pivotal voters. When newly pivotal voters were predominantly agricultural, new parties developed populist platforms; alternatively, social democratic platforms reflected the interests of newly pivotal industrial workers. Importantly, this book shows that elections do not simply aggregate the preferences around which parties and candidates mobilize. Rather, it has provided evidence that the preferences expressed by parties and candidates are direct consequences of which groups are favored by changes in the local distributions of electoral power.

8.A APPENDIX: SUPPORTING MATERIALS

Measuring the Electoral Power of a Low-Income Voting Bloc

This section reports the specific details of the estimation strategy for each country, and lists the electoral districts in which a low-income voting bloc could elect (lower house) members of the national legislature; it is organized according to types of electoral systems, with the main distinction reflecting the number of legislators elected in each district.

Single-Member District Systems

Australia.   Although an SMD system, Australia relies on a method of preferential voting with instant run-off elections: if no candidate receives the majority of votes cast, the votes from ballots favoring the least popular candidates are reallocated based on their stated ranked preferences until a candidate receives the support of more than 50 percent of votes cast. Low-income districts are those in which more than 50 percent of households have weekly incomes less than A$999. Income data are reported in categories, rather than percentiles; this category corresponds to the thirty-seventh percentile, yielding estimates of electoral power that are probably slightly high. (Standard errors of the proportion of low-income households – i.e., those earning less than A$999 – and associated confidence intervals are incorporated into estimates of electoral power measures: a district is a low-income district if the estimated proportion of low-income households, plus 1.96 times the standard error of the estimate, exceeds 50 percent).

Canada.   The 2006 Census "Federal Riding Profile" (corresponding to the 2005 calendar year, and based on the 2003 Representation Order; Statistics Canada 2003), reports the median household income for each riding. Districts are identified as "low-income" districts if the estimated median household income (or the lower bound of the 95 percent confidence interval of the estimate) was less than Can$39,999. Because of the way the data are reported – in income categories, rather than percentiles – this low-income threshold corresponds to the thirty-sixth percentile of the national income distribution, and so this estimate of electoral power is likely slightly exaggerated.

France.   Legislative seats in France are allocated in single-member districts when a candidate secures 50 percent of the votes cast in their district. If, after the first-round election, no candidate has secured this majority, the two candidates who secured the largest vote shares stand in a second-round election. The candidate winning this second-round election will then be allocated the seat.

   Under current rules, seats are allocated in 555 single-member electoral districts (*circonscriptions électorales*, plus fifteen overseas SMDs). Although income data are not reported for districts, they are reported for about 3,700 smaller *cantons*, villages, and urban *arrondissements*. To identify low-income districts, first, the complete set of smaller geographic units were allocated to their electoral districts, and then a weighted average of household median incomes was estimated for each district, based on the population contributed by each smaller unit. Standard errors are estimated for contributing geographic units. Low-income districts are those in which the weighted-average-median (or the lower bound of its confidence interval) for a district is less than €19,467 (the thirtieth percentile of national income distribution in metropolitan France). Alternatively, if a linear distribution between decile thresholds is assumed, and a threshold of €20,941 is used instead, there are as many as 246 districts (44 percent) in which a low-income voting bloc is likely to be pivotal.

Great Britain. To identify those electoral constituencies in which low-income citizens are likely to be pivotal, I used data collected from the most recent *Annual Survey of Hours and Earnings* (ASHE; 2013). For each parliamentary constituency, the ASHE data report the median gross income for all workers. Constituencies are identified as low-income districts if the estimated median income (or, again, the lower bound of the 95 percent confidence interval of the estimate) is less than £15,166. This threshold corresponds to the thirtieth percentile, and as a consequence, the estimate of electoral power is probably slightly underestimated. If a linear distribution of income is assumed, and a threshold of £16,285 is used instead, then 257 (40.6 percent) districts are identified as low-income.

United States. Estimates of the percentage of each congressional district electorate composed of low-income households are generated using the 2013 American Community Survey One-Year Estimates. Table S1901 reports the median total household income for each congressional district. Districts are identified as low-income districts if the estimated median income (or the lower bound of the 95 percent confidence interval) is less than $34,999 (the thirty-fourth percentile of the national household income distribution).

Varying-District-Magnitude Systems: (A) Single-Tier Systems

Finland. Legislative seats in Finland are allocated in fifteen multi-member districts that range in the number of seats allocated from one in Aland to thirty-five in Uusimaa, according to the d'Hondt formula (the modified Droop quota, described above, is used here instead). With a few exceptions, the boundaries of the electoral districts correspond to the boundaries of Finland's twenty administrative districts. The city of Helsinki comprises a district in itself, and several electoral districts combine two or three administrative districts. This analysis uses income distribution data reported at the level of the subregion (Statistics Finland's "Table 9. Dwelling population by income decile and by subregional unit," 2013), which can be allocated in a precise way to electoral districts. Low-income households include those that fall in the first three deciles based on the national income distribution; those in the third decile earned an average of €11,401 (Statistics Finland, "Table 5. Household-dwelling units' average income by type of income and by income decile in 1995–2013").

Norway. Legislative elections in Norway are contested in twenty multi-member districts that range in the number of seats elected from four

TABLE 8.A.1. *Low-income districts in the US.*

District	District-to-state average gerrymander index ratio	Majority-minority district	Party of Representative (113th Congress)
AL-7	1.07	62% Black	D
AZ-7	1.13	56% Hispanic	D
AR-1	1.09		R
AR-4	0.90		R
CA-16	0.97	58% Hispanic	D
CA-34	0.96	67% Hispanic	D
FL-5	1.37	53% Black	D
GA-2	0.93		D
KY-5	0.95		R
LA-2	1.10	63% Black	D
LA-5	1.05		R
MI-13	1.15	57% Black	D
MS-2	1.16	65% Black	D
NY-13	1.06	53% Hispanic	D
NY-15	0.69	66% Hispanic	D
NC-1	1.09		D
NC-12	1.10	49% Black	D
OH-11	1.05	54% Black	D
PA-2	0.73	59% Black	D
SC-6	1.16	57% Black	D
TX-33	1.19	65% Hispanic	D
TX-34	1.09	83% Hispanic	D
WV-3	0.95		R
Average	1.04		

Notes: This table reports the characteristics of those districts in which low-income voters are pivotal (i.e., comprise more than 50 percent of the district).
Sources: Ingraham (2014). Majority-minority districts: Census (2010).

(in Aust-Agder) to seventeen (in Oslo). The electoral districts correspond to the Norwegian counties; the numbers of seats in each district reflect both the distribution of the population and the geographic size of each county. Here, the additional "leveling" seat allocation is ignored.

Estimates of the electoral power of low-income voters are based on levels of total household income reported by Statistics Norway for each county (Table 07184, "Households, by size of total income," for 2013). Here, low-income households are those with total incomes less than NOK 449,999 (about $57,873, at current exchange levels; 35 percent of the national income distribution).

(B) Multi-Tier Systems

Austria. Legislative seats in Austria's lower house, the National Council, are allocated in multi-member districts in three rounds of allocation: Seats in districts are allocated according to a Hare quota that is calculated for each state. Then, votes are cast to parties within each state, and at the national level, with seats won in the districts and states subtracted from national allocations. Here, the potential number of seats that can be allocated within each district is estimated using state-level Hare quotas (i.e., quotas equal to the number of valid votes cast in 2008, divided by the number of seats allocated within the state): districts elect between one and seven members. Estimates of electoral power are based on first-round (within-district) allocations only.

Although income data are not reported for electoral districts, Statistik Austria (2012) reports the composition of the labor force, for full-time men and women, by sector (twenty-two sectors), for each district, as well as national median earnings for men and women, for each of seventeen sectors. Using national medians for each district–sector–sex category (and national sex-median estimates, for those sectors with missing data), I've estimated the proportion of low-income people within each district. In Austria (2010), the low-income threshold (corresponding to the thirty-third percentile in these data) is about €30,076.

Denmark. Legislative seats in Denmark's *Folketing* are allocated in two tiers, first according to the Sainte-Läque highest average allocation rule in ten multi-member districts, each electing between two and twenty seats, and second, in a compensatory allocation, according to the Danish highest average formula.[13]

To estimate the electoral power of a low-income voting bloc, I used estimates of the income distribution from Table "INDKF32: Disposable family income by municipality, unit, family type and income interval (2012)" published by Statistics Denmark. Here, "low-income families" are those earning less than 200 DKK (post-tax) per week (about 35 percent of the national population). Municipalities were matched to ten multi-member districts, and seats were allocated based on the share of low-income families in each district. (Quotas were calculated on the basis of the number of direct mandates allocated to each district in 2011.)

Sweden. Elections to the *Riksdag* are contested in twenty-nine MMDs, with thirty-nine seats allocated in a second nationwide tier to ensure the proportionality of the result, for those parties securing at least 4 percent of votes cast, or 12 percent of the votes cast in any constituency. A modified

---

[13] This formula is similar to the d'Hondt formula, but like the Sainte-Läque formula, uses a different series of divisors. The compensatory tier is ignored in this analysis.

Sainte-Lägue highest average allocation rule is used for the allocation of seats in both tiers. Following the convention established above, a Droop quota is used in the allocation of first-tier seats in this analysis.

Although LIS data do not report the electoral districts in which each Swedish respondent lives, LIS does report each respondent's county. With two exceptions, the boundaries of the twenty-two counties largely coincide with the boundaries of Sweden's electoral districts: The Skåne county contains four electoral districts, and Västra Götalands county is comprised of five electoral districts. Here, the county proportions of low-income citizens are used for each of the composite districts.

References

Abramitzky, Ran, Leah Platt Boustan, and Katherine Eriksson. 2014. "A Nation of Immigrants: Assimilation and Economic Outcomes in the Age of Mass Migration." *Journal of Political Economy* 122(3):467–506.

Achen, Christopher H. and Larry Bartels. 2016. *Democracy for Realists: Why elections do not produce responsive government*. Princeton University Press.

Adams, James, Michael Clark, Lawrence Ezrow, and Garrett Glasgow. 2004. "Understanding Change and Stability in Party Ideology: Do Parties Respond to Public Opinion or to Past Elections?" *British Journal of Political Science* 34(4):589–610.

Ahmed, Amel. 2013. *Democracy and the Politics of Electoral System Choice: Engineering Electoral Dominance*. Cambridge University Press.

Aldrich, John. 2011. *Why Parties? A Second Look*. University Of Chicago Press.

Alesina, Alberto and Edward L. Glaeser. 2004. *Fighting Poverty in the US and Europe: A world of difference*. Oxford University Press.

Anderson, Christopher J. and Pablo Beramendi. 2012. "Left Parties, Poor Voters, and Electoral Participation in Advanced Industrial Societies." *Comparative Political Studies* 45(6):714–46.

Archer, Robin. 2010. *Why is There No Labor Party in the United States?* Princeton University Press.

Austen-Smith, David. 2000. "Redistributing Income under Proportional Representation." *Journal of Political Economics* 108:1235–69.

Bagge, Gösta, Erik Lundberg, and Ingvar Svennilson. 1933. *Wages in Sweden, 1860–1930*. PS King.

Bartels, Larry. 2008. *Unequal Democracy*. Princeton University Press and the Russell Sage Foundation.

Bartels, Larry. 2015. "The Social Welfare Deficit: Public Opinion, Policy Responsiveness, and Political Inequality in Affluent Democracies." Paper prepared for presentation at the 22nd International Conference of Europeanists, Paris, July 8–10, 2015.

Bartolini, Stefano. 2000. *The Political Mobilization of the European Left, 1860–1980*. Cambridge University Press.

Bawn, Kathleen and Frances Rosenbluth. 2006. "Short versus Long Coalitions: Electoral Accountability and the Size of the Public Sector." *American Journal of Political Science* 50(2):251–66.

Bawn, Kathleen, Martin Cohen, David Karol, Seth Masket, Hans Noel, and John Zaller. 2012. "A Theory of Political Parties: Groups, Policy Demands, and Nominations in American Politics." *Perspectives on Politics* 10(3):571–97.

Bealey, Frank. 1956. "Negotiations Between the Liberal Party and the Labour Representation Committee Before the General Election Of 1906." *Bulletin of the Institute of Historical Research* 29:261–74.

Bealey, Frank and Henry Pelling. 1958. *Labour and Politics, 1900–1906*. Macmillan.

Bensel, Richard Franklin. 2000. *The Political Economy of American Industrialization, 1877–1900*. Cambridge University Press.

Bernstein, George L. 1983. "Liberalism and the Progressive Alliance in the Constituencies, 1900–1914: Three Case Studies." *The Historical Journal* 26(3):614–40.

Blewett, Neal. 1972. *Peers, the Parties and the People*. Springer.

Boix, Carles. 1999. "Setting the Rules of the Game. The Choice of Electoral Systems in Advanced Democracies." *American Political Science Review* 93(3):609–24.

——. 2009. The Emergence of Parties and Party Systems. In *The Oxford Handbook of Comparative Politics*, ed. Carles Boix and Susan C. Stokes. Oxford University Press.

——. 2010. "Electoral Markets, Party Strategies, and Proportional Representation." *American Political Science Review* 104(2):404–14.

——. 2011. "The Rise of Social Democracy." Unpublished manuscript.

Brand, Carl. 1974. *The British Labour Party: Short History* (revised edition). Hoover Institution Press.

Brewer, Mark D. and Jeffrey Stonecash. 2009. *Dynamics of American Political Parties*. Cambridge University Press.

Brooks, Clem and Jeff Manza. 2006. "Why Do Welfare States Persist?" *Journal of Politics* 68(4):816–27.

Budge, Ian. 1994. "A New Spatial Theory of Party Competition: Uncertainty, Ideology and Policy Equilibria Viewed Comparatively and Temporally." *British Journal of Political Science* 24(4):443–67.

Buxton, Sydney. 1892. *A Handbook to Political Questions of the Day: And the Arguments on Either Side*, 9th ed. John Murray.

Cairns, Alan C. 1968. "The Electoral System and the Party System in Canada, 1921–1965." *Canadian Journal of Political Science/Revue canadienne de science politique* 1(1):55–80.

Callander, Steven. 2005. "Duverger's Hypothesis, the Run-Off Rule, and Electoral Competition." *Political Analysis* 13(3):209–32.

Calvo, Ernesto. 2009. "The Competitive Road to Proportional Representation." *World Politics* 61(2):254–95.

Canada. Dominion Bureau of Statistics. 1935. *Seventh Census of Canada, 1931, Vol. 2: Population by Areas*. Patenaude.

Caramani, Daniele. 2000. *Elections in Western Europe since 1815: Electoral Results by Constituencies*. Macmillan Reference.

Caramani, Daniele. 2004. *The Nationalization of Politics: The formation of national electorates and party systems in Western Europe*. Cambridge University Press.

Chen, Jowei and Jonathan Rodden. 2013. "Unintentional Gerrymandering: Political Geography and Electoral Bias in Legislatures." *Quarterly Journal of Political Science* 8(3):239–69.

Chhibber, Pradeep and Ken Kollman. 2004. *The Formation of National Party Systems: Federalism and party competition in Canada, Great Britain, India, and the United States.* Princeton University Press.

Clark, William Roberts and Matt Golder. 2006. "Rehabilitating Duverger's Theory: Testing the Mechanical and Strategic Modifying Effects of Electoral Laws." *Comparative Political Studies* 39(6):679–708.

Cohen, Marty, David Karol, Hans Noel, and John Zaller. 2008. *The Party Decides: Presidential Nominations Before and After Reform.* University of Chicago Press.

Courtney, John C. 2007. Lipset, de Tocqueville, Radical Group Formation, and the Fate of Socialism in Saskatchewan. In *Lipset's "Agrarian Socialism": A Re-Examination.* Canadian Plains Research Center, University of Regina, pp. 13–22.

Cox, Gary. 1987. *The Efficient Secret: The cabinet and the development of political parties in Victorian England.* Cambridge University Press.

——. 1997. *Making Votes Count: strategic coordination in the world's electoral systems.* Cambridge University Press.

——. 2004. A Comparative Approach to Democratic Representation. In *The Evolution of Political Knowledge*, ed. E. Mansfield and R. Sisson. Ohio State University Press.

Craig, F.W.S. 1974. *British Parliamentary Results, 1885–1918.* Macmillan Reference.

Cusack, Thomas, Torben Iversen, and Philipp Rhem. 2007. "Risks at Work: The Demand and Supply Sides of Government Redistribution." *Oxford Review of Economic Policy* 22(3):365–89.

Dalton, Russell, Scott C. Flanagan, Paul Allen Beck, and James E. Alt. 1984. *Electoral Change in Advanced Industrial Democracies: Realignment or Dealignment?* Princeton University Press.

Downs, Anthony. 1957. *An Economic Theory of Democracy.* Harper & Row.

Dubin, Michael J. 1998. *United States Congressional Elections, 1788–1997: The Official Results of the Elections of the 1st Through 105th Congresses.* McFarland.

Ducoff, Louis. 1945. *Wages of Agricultural Labor in the United States.* United States Department of Agriculture.

Duverger, Maurice. 1954. *Political Parties.* John Wiley & Sons.

Earle, Michael J. and H. Gamberg. 1989. "The United Mine Workers and the Coming of the CCF to Capte Breton." *Acadiensis* 19(1):3–26.

Eaton, John. 1882. *Report of the Commissioner of Education for the Year 1880.* Government Printing Office.

Engelmann, Frederick Charles. 1954. *The Co-operative Commonwealth Federation of Canada: A Study of Membership Participation in Party Policy-Making.* PhD thesis. Yale University.

Engelmann, Frederick Charles. 1956. "Membership Participation in Policy-Making in the CCF." *Canadian Journal of Economics and Political Science/Revue canadienne de economiques et science politique* 22(2):161–73.

Epstein, Leon D. 1964. "A Comparative Study of Canadian Parties." *American Political Science Review* 58(1):46–59.

Esaiasson, Peter. 1991. "120 Years of Swedish Election Campaigns: A Story of the Rise and Decline of Political Parties and the Emergence of the Mass Media as Power Brokers." *Scandinavian Political Studies* 14(3):261–76.

Esping-Andersen, Gøsta. 1990. *The Three Worlds of Welfare Capitalism*. Princeton University Press.

Franklin, Mark N., Thomas T. Mackie, and Henry Valen. 2009. *Electoral Change: Response to Evolving Social and Attitudinal Structures in Western Countries*. European Consortium for Political Research Press.

Franzese, Robert J. 2002. *Macroeconomic Policies of Developed Democracies*. Cambridge University Press.

Gallego, Aina. 2007. "Unequal Political Participation in Europe." *International Journal of Sociology* 37(4):10–25.

Geografiska Sverigedata Lantmäteriet. 2015. "GSD – General Map, vector format." Published online at www.lantmateriet.se/en/Maps-and-geographic-information/Maps/oversiktskartan1/.

Gidlund, Gullan. 1992. From Popular Movement to Political Party: Development of the Social Democratic Labor Party Organization. In *Creating Social Democracy: A Century of the Social Democratic Labor Party in Sweden*, ed. Klaus Misgeld, Karl Molin, and Klas Amak. Pennsylvania State University Press, pp. 97–130.

Gilens, Martin. 1999. *Why Americans Hate Welfare: Race, Media and the Politics of Anti-Poverty Policy*. University of Chicago Press.

——. 2012. *Affluence and Influence: Economic Inequality and Political Power in America*. Princeton University Press.

Gilens, Martin and Benjamin Page. 2014. "Testing Theories of American Politics: Elites, Interest Groups, and Average Citizens." *Perspectives on Politics* 12(3):564–81.

Gompers, Samuel. 1892. "Organized Labor in the Campaign." *The North American Review* 155(428):91–6.

Gosnell, Harold. 1937. "Review of *Political Behavior; Studies in Election Statistics* by Herbert Tingsten." *American Political Science Review* 31(6):1164–5.

Green, Alan and Mary MacKinnon. 2012. Unemployment and Relief in Canada. In *Interwar Unemployment in International Perpsective*, ed. Barry Eichengreen and T.J. Hatton. Springer Science and Business Media, pp. 353–95.

Hadenius, Stig, Jan-Olof Sveveborg, and Lennart Weibull. 1968. "The Social Democratic Press and Newspaper Policy in Sweden in 1899–1909." *Scandinavian Political Studies* 3(A3):49–69.

Hall, Tom G. 1967. "California Populism at the Grass-Roots: The Case of Tulare County, 1892." *Southern California Quarterly* 49(2):193–204.

Hannant, Larry. 1985. "The Calgary Working Class and the Social Credit Movement in Alberta, 1932–35." *Labour/Le Travail* 16:97–116.

Hermansson, Jörgen. 2016. The Election System. In *The Oxford Handbook of Swedish Politics*, ed. Jon Pierre. Oxford University Press, pp. 103–114.

Hicks, Alexander. 1999. *Social Democracy and Welfare Capitalism: A Century of Income Security Politics*. Cornell University Press.

Hicks, John D. 1928. "The Birth of the Populist Party." *Minnesota History* 9:219–47.

——. 1931. *The Populist Revolt: A History of the Farmers' Alliance and the People's Party*. University of Minnesota Press.

Hirano, Shigeo. 2008. "Third Parties, Elections, and Roll-Call Votes: The Populist Party and the Late Nineteenth-Century U.S. Congress." *Legislative Studies Quarterly* 33(1):131–60.

Hirano, Shigeo and James Snyder. 2007. "The Decline of Third-Party Voting in the United States." *Journal of Politics* 69(1):1–16.

Hofstadter, Richard. 1955. *The Age of Reform: From Bryan to F.D.R.* Vintage Books.

Holmes, George. 1914. *Estimate of Wages of Farm Labor.* United States Department of Agriculture.

Huber, Evelyne and John D. Stephens. 2001. *Development and Crisis of the Welfare State: Parties and Policies in Global Markets.* University of Chicago Press.

Hug, Simon. 2001. *Altering Party Systems.* University of Michigan Press.

Hunter, Robert. 1904. *Poverty.* Macmillan.

Inglehart, Ronald. 1997. *Modernization and Postmoderation: Cultural, Economic, and Political Change in 43 Countries.* Princeton University Press.

Ingraham, Christopher. May 15, 2014. "Gerrymander Index Scores." *Washington Post.*

Irving, John A. 1959. *The Social Credit Movement in Alberta.* University of Toronto Press.

Iversen, Torben. 1994. "The Logics of Electoral Politics: Spatial, Directional, and Mobilization." *Comparative Political Studies* 27(1):155–89.

———. 2005. *Capitalism, Democracy and Welfare.* Cambridge University Press.

Iversen, Torben and David Soskice. 2001. "An Asset Theory of Social Policy Preferences." *American Political Science Review* 95(4):875–93.

———. 2006. "Electoral Institutions and the Politics of Coalitions: Why Some Democracies Redistribute More than Others." *American Political Science Review* 100(2):165–81.

James, Scott. 2006. *Presidents, Parties, and the State: A Party System Perspective on Democratic Regulatory Choice, 1884–1936.* Cambridge University Press.

Jensen, Richard. 1971. *The Winning of the Midwest: Social and Political Conflict, 1888–1896*, vol. 2. University of Chicago Press.

Johnston, Ronald J., Carol Propper, Rebecca Sarker, and Kelvyn Jones. 2005. "Neighbourhood Social Capital and Neighbourhood Effects." *Environment and Planning* 37(8):1443–59.

Johnston, Ronald J. and Charles J. Pattie. 2003. Representative Democracy and Electoral Geography. In *A Companion to Political Geography*, ed. John Agnew, Katharyne Mitchell, and Gerald Toal. Blackwell Publishing Inc.

Johnston, Ronald J., Charles J. Pattie, and John G. Allsopp. 1988. *A Nation Dividing?: The Electoral Map of Great Britain, 1979–1987.* Longman.

Jusko, Karen Long. 2008. "The Political Representation of the Poor." A dissertation submitted in partial fulfillment of the requirements for the degree of Doctor of Philosophy (Political Science) in The University of Michigan.

———. 2015a. "Electoral Geography and Redistributive Politics." *Journal of Theoretical Politics* 27(2):269–87.

———. 2015b. "Electoral Geography, Strategic Mobilization, and Implications for Voter Turnout." Working paper. Department of Political Science, Stanford University.

Kalyvas, Stathis. 1996. *The Rise of Christian Democracy in Europe.* Cornell Univeristy Press.

Katznelson, Ira. 1986. Working-Class Formation: Constructing Cases and Comparisons. In *Working-Class Formation: Nineteenth-Century Patterns in Western Europe and the United States*, ed. Ira Katznelson and Aristide Zolberg. Princeton University Press.

Kipnis, Ira. 2004. *The American Socialist Movement*. Haymarket Books.

Kitschelt, Herbert, Zdenka Mansfeldova, Radoslaw Markowksi, and Gábor Tóka. 1999. *Post-Communist Party Systems: Competition, Representation, and Inter-Party Cooperation*. Cambridge University Press.

Knoles, George Harmon. 1943. "Populism and Socialism, with Special Reference to the Election of 1892." *Pacific Historical Review* 12(3):295–304.

Kollman, Ken, Allen Hicken, Daniele Caramani, and David Lublin. 2014. "Constituency-Level Elections Archive." [Data file and code book]. Center for Political Studies, University of Michigan [producer and distributor].

Krebheil, Edward. 1916. "Geographic Influences in British Elections." *Geographical Review* 2(6):419–32.

Ksleman, Daniel, Eleanor Neff Powell, and Joshua A. Tucker. 2016. "Crowded Space, Fertile Ground: Party Entry and the Effective Number of Parties." *Political Science Research and Methods* 4(2):317–42.

Kuo, Alex and Karen Long Jusko. 2012. "Electoral Opportunity: The SPD and the 'Agricultural Proletariat.'" Working paper. Department of Political Science, Stanford University.

Lebergott, Stanley. 1964. *Manpower in Economic Growth: The American Record since 1800*. McGraw-Hill.

Leighley, Jan E. and Jonathan Nagler. 2014. *Who Votes Now? Demographics, Issues, Inequality, and Turnout in the United States*. Princeton University Press.

Lewin, Leif. 1988. *Ideology and Strategy: A Century of Swedish Politics*. Cambridge University Press.

Lewin, Leif, Bo Jansson, and Dag Sörbom. 1972. *The Swedish Electorate 1887–1968*. Almquist & Wiksell.

Lewis, Jeffrey, Brandon DeVine, Lincoln Pritcher, and Kenneth C. Martis. 2013. "Digital Boundary Definitions of United States Congressional Districts, 1789–2012." [Data file and code book]. Retrieved from http://cdmaps.polisci.ucla.edu on December 4, 2013.

Library of Parliament. N.d. "History of Federal Ridings Since 1867." Online resource, published at www.lop.parl.gc.ca/About/Parliament/FederalRidingsHistory/

Lijphart, Arend. 1994. *Electoral Systems and Party Systems*. Oxford University Press.

Lipset, Seymour Martin. 1968. *Agrarian Socialism*. University of California Press.

——. 1983. *Political Man: The Social Bases of Politics*. Heinemann.

Lipset, Seymour Martin and Gary Marks. 2000. *It Didn't Happen Here*. W.W. Norton.

Lipset, Seymour Martin and Stein Rokkan. 1967. An Introduction. In *Cleavage Structures, Party Systems, and Voter Alignmenments*, ed. Seymour Martin Lipset and Stein Rokkan. The Free Press, pp. 1–64.

Lizzeri, Alessandro and Nicola Persisco. 2001. "The Provision of Public Goods Under Alternative Electoral Incentives." *American Economic Review* 91(1):225–239.

Logan, John, Jason Jindrich, Hyoungjin Shin, and Weiwei Zhang. 2011. "The Urban Transition Historical GIS Project." Published online at www.s4.brown.edu/UTP/

Long, Clarence D. 1960. *Wages and Earnings in the United States, 1860–1890*. Princeton University Press.

Lupu, Noam and Jonas Pontusson. 2011. "The Structure of Inequality and the Politics of Redistribution." *American Political Science Review* 105(2):316–36.

MacPherson, Crawford Brough. 1953. *Democracy in Alberta: Social Credit and the Party System*. University of Toronto Press.

Martis, Kenneth C. 1982. *The Historical Atlas of United States Congressional Districts: 1789–1983*. The Free Press.

McKibbin, Ross. 1990. *The Ideologies of Class: Social Relations in Britain 1880–1950*. Clarendon Press.

Meltzer, Allan H. and Scott F. Richard. 1981. "A Rational Theory of the Size of Government." *Journal of Political Economy* 89(5):914–927.

Miller, Warren L. 1977. *Electoral Dynamics in Britain since 1918*. Macmillan.

Moene, Karl Ove and Michael Wallerstein. 2001. "Inequality, Social Insurance and Redistribution." *American Political Science Review* 95(4):859–74.

Moller, Stephanie, Evelyne Huber, John D. Stephens, David Bradley, and François Nielsen. 2003. "Determinants of Relative Poverty in Advanced Capitalist Democracies." *American Sociological Review* 68(1):22–51.

Monroe, Burt and Amanda G. Rose. 2002. "Electoral Systems and Unimagined Consequences: Partisan Effects of Districted Proportional Representation." *American Journal of Political Science* 46(1):67–89.

Moore, Roger F. 1978. *The Emergence of the Labour Party, 1880–1924*. Hodder and Stoughton.

Morelli, Massimo. 2004. "Party Formation and Policy Outcomes under Different Electoral Systems." *Review of Economic Studies* 71(3):829–53.

Morse, Stephen P. and Joel D. Weintraub. 2007. "Finding ED Definitions (1880–1940 Enumeration District Definitions Form)." Online database, published at http://stevemorse.org

Norberg, Anders, Andreas Tjerneld, and Bjorn Asker. 1985–1992. *Tvakammarriksdagen 1867–1970*, Vol. 1–5. Sveriges riksdag (Distributor, Almqvist & Wiksell International).

Office of the Surveyor General. 1933–1934. *Federal Electoral Districts, Representation Act 1933*. Canada, Department of the Interior.

Olson Jr., Mancur. 1965. *The Logic of Collective Action*. Harvard University Press.

Olssen, Andrée Lévesque. 1973. *The Canadian Left in Quebec During the Great Depression: The Communist Party of Canada and the Co-operative Commonwealth Federation in Quebec, 1921–1939*. PhD thesis. Duke University.

Organisation For Economic Co-operation and Development (OECD). 2014. "Social Expenditure Database (SOCX)." Published online at www.oecd.org/els/social/expenditure

Parsons, Stanley, Michael Dubin, and Karen Toombs Parsons. 1990. *United States Congressional Districts, 1883–1913*. Greenwood.

Pelling, Henry. 1965. *The Origins of the British Labour Party, 1880–1900*, 2nd ed. Clarendon Press.

——. 1967. *Social Geography of British Elections, 1885–1910*. Springer.

Persson, Torsten, Gerard Roland, and Guido Tabellini. 2007. "Electoral Rules and Government Spending in Parliamentary Democracies" *Quarterly Journal of Political Science* 2(2):155–88.

Persson, Torben and Guido Tabellini. 2003. *The Economic Effects of Constitutions.* MIT Press.

——. 2000. *Political Economics: Explaining Economic Policy.* MIT Press.

Pierson, Paul. 1996. "The New Politics of the Welfare State." *World Politics* 48:143–79.

Piketty, Thomas. 2014. *Capital in the Twenty-First Century.* Harvard University Press.

Pollack, Norman. 1962. *The Populist Response to Industrial America.* Harvard University Press.

Pontusson, Jonas and David Rueda. 2010. "The Politics of Inequality: Voter Mobilization and Left Parties in Advanced Industrial States." *Comparative Political Studies* 43(6):675–705.

Przeworski, Adam. 1985. *Capitalism and Social Democracy.* Cambridge University Press.

Przeworski, Adam and John Sprague. 1986. *Paper Stones.* University of Chicago Press.

Reid, J.H. Stewart. 1955. *The Origins of the British Labour Party.* University of Minnesota Press.

Riker, William H. 1982. "The Two-Party System and Duverger's Law: An Essay on the History of Political Science." *The American Political Science Review* 76(4):753–66.

Rodden, Jonathan. 2010. "The Geographic Distribution of Political Preferences." *Annual Review of Political Science* 13:321–40.

——. 2011. "The Long Shadow of the Industrial Revolution: Political Geography and the Representation of the Left." Working paper. Department of Political Science, Stanford University.

Rokkan, Stein. 1970. *Citizens, Elections, Parties: Approaches to the Comparative Study of the Process of Development.* Universitetsforlaget.

Romer, Thomas. 1975. "Individual Welfare, Majority Voting and the Properties of a Linear Income Tax." *Journal of Public Economics* 4(2):163–85.

Rosenstone, Steven J., Roy L. Behr, and Edward H. Lazarus. 1984. *Third Parties in America.* Princeton University Press.

Rothenbacher, Franz. 2002. *The European Population, 1850–1945.* Palgrave Macmillan.

——. 2005. *The European Population since 1945.* Palgrave Macmillan.

Rusk, Jerrold. 2001. *A Statistical History of the American Electorate.* CQ Press.

Rustow, Dankwart. 1955. *The Politics of Compromise: A Study of Parties and Cabinet Government in Sweden.* Princeton University Press.

——. 1971. "Sweden's Transition to Democracy: Some Notes Towards a Genetic Theory." *Scandinavian Political Studies* 6(A6):9–26.

Sanders, Elizabeth. 1999. *Roots of Reform: Farmers, Workers, and the American State, 1877–1917.* University of Chicago Press.

Scarrow, Howard. 1965. "Distinguishing Between Political Parties – The Case of Canada." *Midwest Journal of Political Science* 9(1):61–76.

Scheve, Kenneth and David Stasavage. 2006. "Religion and Preferences for Social Insurance." *Quarterly Journal of Political Science* 1(3):255–86.

Shapley, Lloyd S. and Martin Shubik. 1954. "A Method for Evaluating the Distribution of Power in a Committee System." *American Political Science Review* 48(3):787–92.

Shayo, Moses. 2009. "A Model of Social Identity with an Application to Political Economy: Nation, Class, and Redistribution." *American Political Science Review* 103(2):147–74.

Shefter, Martin. 1986. Trade Unions and Political Machines: The Organization and Disorganization of the American Working Class in the Late Nineteenth Century. In *Working-Class Formation: Nineteenth-Century Patterns in Western Europe and the United States*, ed. Ira Katznelson and Aristide Zolberg. Princeton University Press.

Sombart, Werner. 1976 [1906]. *Why Is There No Socialism in the United States?* Springer.

Soroka, Stuart and Christopher Wlezien. 2005. "Opinion–Policy Dynamics: Public Preferences and Public Expenditure in the United Kingdom." *British Journal of Political Science* 35(4):665–89.

Southall, Humphrey and the Great Britain Historical GIS Project. "Vision of Britain." On-line resource, published at http://www.visionofbritain.org.uk.

Spahr, Charles Barzillai. 1900. *America's Working People*. Longmans, Green, and Company.

Statistics Canada. 2003. "2001 Federal Electoral District Profile (2003 Representation Order)." Statistics Canada Catalogue No. 94F0044XIE.

———. 2014. "Table A2-14. Population Estimates of Canada, by Province, census dates 1851-1976." Published on-line at www.statcan.gc.ca/access_acces/archive.action?l=eng&loc=A2_14-eng.csv.

———. 2014. "Annual Estimates of Population for Canada, Provinces, and Territories, from July 1, 1971 to July 1, 2014." Published on-line at www.stats.gov.nl.ca/statistics/population/PDF/Annual_Pop_Prov.PDF.

Stokes, Susan C. 1999a. What Do Policy Switches Tell Us about Democracy? In *Democracy, Accountability, and Representation*, ed. Adam Przeworski, Susan Stokes, and Bernard Manin. Yale University Press.

———. 1999b. "Political Parties and Democracy." *Annual Review of Political Science* 2(1):243–67.

Stoll, Heather. 2013. *Changing Societies, Changing Party Systems*. Cambridge University Press.

Stonecash, Jeffrey and Everita Silina. 2005. "The 1896 Realignment: A Reassessment." *American Politics Research* 33(1):3–32.

Strikwerda, Eric. 2012. *The Wages of Relief: Cities and the Unemployed in Prairie Canada, 1929-39*. Athabasca University Press.

Sundbärg, Gustav. 1904. *Sweden, Its People and Its Industry: Historical and Statistical Handbook*. Swedish Central Bureau of Statistics.

Sveriges Officiella Statistik. 1897. *Valstatistik, XVI: Underdåniga Berättelse Rörande Riksdagsmannavalen Åren, 1903-1905*. Statistiska Centralbyråns.

———. 1906. *Valstatistik, XVIII: Underdåniga Berättelse Rörande Riksdagsmannavalen Åren, 1903-1905*. Statistiska Centralbyråns.

Swift, Elaine K., Robert G. Brookshire, David T. Canon, Evelyn C. Fink, John R. Hibbing, Brian D. Humes, Michael J. Malbin, and Martis Kenneth C. 2009. "Congressional Historical Statistics, 1789–1989 [computer file]." Inter-University Consortium for Political and Social Research [distributor], 03371-v2.

Tanner, Duncan. 1990. *Political Change and the Labour Party, 1900-1918*. Cambridge University Press.

Tavits, Margit. 2006. "Party System Change." *Party Politics* 12(1):99–119.

The Labour Party. *The Labour Party Foundation Conference and Annual Conference Reports, 1900-1905*. 1967. The Hammersmith Bookskop Ltd.

Thorpe, Andrew. 2008. *A History of the British Labour Party*. Palgrave Macmillan.

Tingsten, Herbert. 1973. *The Swedish Social Democrats: Their Ideological Development*. Bedminster Press.

Tingsten, Herbert. 1975. *Political Behavior: Studies in Election Statistics*. Arno Press.

Urban Institute. *Welfare Rules Database*. 2008–2011. Published online at http://anfdata.urban.org/wrd/Query/query.cfm

US Census Bureau. 1950. "Enumeration District Maps for the Twelfth through Sixteenth Censuses of the United States, 1900–1940 [microform]."

US Department of Labor. 2013. "Monthly Program and Financial Data: Summary Data for State Programs, by State, Report Period For 01/2012." Published online at http://workforcesecurity.doleta.gov/unemploy/5159report.asp

Verba, Sidney, Norman Nie, and Jae-on Kim. 1978. *Participation and Political Equality: A Seven-National Comparison*. University of Chicago Press.

Verney, Douglas V. 1957. *Parliamentary Reform in Sweden, 1866–1921*. Oxford University Press.

Williams, Daniel K. 2010. *God's Own Party: The Making of the Christian Right*. Oxford University Press.

Wright, Carroll D. 1886. *The First Annual Report of the Commissioner of Labor, March 1886. Industrial Depressions*. Government Printing Office.

———. 1900. *Fifteenth Annual Report of the Commissioner of Labor, 1900*, vols. 1 & 2. Government Printing Office.

———. 1905. *Nineteenth Annual Report of the Commissioner of Labor: Wages and Hours of Labor*. Government Printing Office.

Young, Walter D. 1969. *The Anatomy of a Party: The National CCF*. University of Toronto Press.

Youngs, Frederic A. 1980. *Guide to the Administrative Units of England*, vols. 1 & 2. Royal Historical Society.

Zakuta, Leo. 1958. "Membership in a Becalmed Protest Movement." *Canadian Journal of Economics and Political Science/Revue canadienne de economiques et science politique* 24(2):190–202.

Index

Herbert Kitschelt, Zdenka Mansfeldova, Radek Markowski, and Gabor Toka, *Post-Communist Party Systems*

David Knoke, Franz Urban Pappi, Jeffrey Broadbent, and Yutaka Tsujinaka, eds., *Comparing Policy Networks*

Ken Kollman, *Perils of Centralization: Lessons from Church, State, and Corporation*

Allan Kornberg and Harold D. Clarke, *Citizens and Community: Political Support in a Representative Democracy*

Amie Kreppel, *The European Parliament and the Supranational Party System*

David D. Laitin, *Language Repertoires and State Construction in Africa*

Fabrice E. Lehoucq and Ivan Molina, *Stuffing the Ballot Box: Fraud, Electoral Reform, and Democratization in Costa Rica*

Mark Irving Lichbach and Alan S. Zuckerman, eds., *Comparative Politics: Rationality, Culture, and Structure, 2nd edition*

Evan Lieberman, *Race and Regionalism in the Politics of Taxation in Brazil and South Africa*

Richard M. Locke, *The Promise and Limits of Private Power: Promoting Labor Standards in a Global Economy*

Julia Lynch, *Age in the Welfare State: The Origins of Social Spending on Pensioner's Workers and Children*

Pauline Jones Luong, *Institutional Change and Political Continuity in Post-Soviet Central Asia*

Pauline Jones Luong and Erika Weinthal, *Oil is Not a Curse: Ownership Structure and Institutions in Soviet Successor States*

Doug McAdam, John McCarthy, and Mayer Zald, eds., *Comparative Perspectives on Social Movements*

Lauren M. MacLean, *Informal Institutions and Citizenship in Rural Africa: Risk and Reciprocity in Ghana and Côte d'Ivoire*

Beatriz Magaloni, *Voting for Autocracy: Hegemonic Party Survival and its Demise in Mexico*

James Mahoney, *Colonialism and Postcolonial Development: Spanish America in Comparative Perspective*

James Mahoney and Dietrich Rueschemeyer, eds., *Historical Analysis and the Social Sciences*

Scott Mainwaring and Matthew Soberg Shugart, eds., *Presidentialism and Democracy in Latin America*

Melanie Manion, *Information for Autocrats: Representation in Chinese Local Congresses*

Isabela Mares, *From Open Secrets to Secret Voting: Democratic Electoral Reforms and Voter Autonomy*

Isabela Mares, *The Politics of Social Risk: Business and Welfare State Development*

Isabela Mares, *Taxation, Wage Bargaining, and Unemployment*

Lily Lee Tsai, *Accountability without Democracy: How Solidary Groups Provide Public Goods in Rural China*

Joshua Tucker, *Regional Economic Voting: Russia, Poland, Hungary, Slovakia and the Czech Republic, 1990–1999*

Ashutosh Varshney, *Democracy, Development, and the Countryside*

Yuhua Wang, *Tying the Autocrat's Hand: The Rise of The Rule of Law in China*

Jeremy M. Weinstein, *Inside Rebellion: The Politics of Insurgent Violence*

Stephen I. Wilkinson, *Votes and Violence: Electoral Competition and Ethnic Riots in India*

Andreas Wimmer, *Waves of War: Nationalism, State Formation, and Ethnic Exclusion in the Modern World*

Jason Wittenberg, *Crucibles of Political Loyalty: Church Institutions and Electoral Continuity in Hungary*

Elisabeth J. Wood, *Forging Democracy from Below: Insurgent Transitions in South Africa and El Salvador*

Elisabeth J. Wood, *Insurgent Collective Action and Civil War in El Salvador*

Daniel Ziblatt, *Conservative Parties and the Birth of Democracy*

For EU product safety concerns, contact us at Calle de José Abascal, 56–1°,
28003 Madrid, Spain or eugpsr@cambridge.org.

www.ingramcontent.com/pod-product-compliance
Ingram Content Group UK Ltd.
Pitfield, Milton Keynes, MK11 3LW, UK
UKHW010045140625
459647UK00012BB/1610